The Politics
of Everybody

About the author

Holly Lewis is assistant professor of philosophy at Texas State University, where she teaches continental philosophy, economic and political philosophy, and aesthetics.

The Politics of Everybody

Feminism, Queer Theory, and Marxism at the Intersection

Holly Lewis

Zed Books

LONDON

The Politics of Everybody: Feminism, Queer Theory, and Marxism at the Intersection was first published in 2016 by Zed Books Ltd, The Foundry, 17 Oval Way, London SE11 5RR, UK.

www.zedbooks.co.uk

Typeset in Adobe Garamond Pro by seagulls.net
Index: John Barker
Cover designed by Dougal Burgess

A catalogue record for this book is available from the British Library.

ISBN 978-1-78360-288-9 hb
ISBN 978-1-78360-287-2 pb
ISBN 978-1-78360-289-6 pdf
ISBN 978-1-78360-290-2 epub
ISBN 978-1-78360-291-9 mobi

Printed and bound by CPI Group (UK) Ltd, Croydon, CR0 4YY

Contents

Acknowledgements   xi

Introduction   1
I.   The politics of everybody   1
II.   Communitarian ideals and culture wars   8
III.   How is every body sorted?   12

1.   Terms of the debate   17
I.   Debates in Western gender politics   18
   Epistemology and identity politics   18
   Queer (anti-)identity   25
   Sex and social gender: dichotomy or dialectic?   30
   A final word on queer language   33
II.   What is capitalism?   35
   The origins of capitalism   36
   The basics of capitalist exchange   40
   The extraction of surplus value   42
III.   Philosophy and the Marxian roots of queer political
   thought   46
   Marx and philosophy   47
   Epistemology revisited   51
   Changing words or changing worlds?   55
   The separation of politics and economics   60
   From Western Marxism to poststructuralism   64
IV.   Conclusion   88

2.	**Marxism and gender**	93
I.	Don't be vulgar …	93
II.	From the woman question to the gender question	102
III.	Marxism at the center and the periphery	105
IV.	Marx on women	110
V.	Marx on gender and labor	113
VI.	The major works: Marx's *Ethnological Notebooks* and Engels' *The Origin of the Family, Private Property, and the State*	121
VII.	Early Marxist and socialist feminism	125
	Who is the woman in the woman question?	125
	Sex and the utopian socialists	132
	Sex and the Second International	135
	Sex and the Russian Revolution	139
VIII.	Theories of social reproduction	143
IX.	Race and social reproduction	155
X.	Marxism and the second wave	166
3.	**From queer nationalism to queer Marxism**	187
I.	The vector model of oppression	187
II.	Racecraft and ideological repetition	196
III.	Sexcraft and ideological repetition	198
IV.	Class is not a moral category	201
V.	The rise of queer politics	203
VI.	Marxist critiques of queer theory	212
VII.	Beyond homonormativity and homonationalism	222
VIII.	The spinning compass of American queer politics	230
	The problem of marriage and family	230
	The problem of queer imperialism	238
IX.	The world is a very queer place	245
X.	The queer Marxist critique of postcolonialism	247

4. Conclusions 257

I.   Solidarity means taking sides 257

Solidarity and ideologies of sex/gender 264

II. Ten axioms towards a queer Marxist future 270

Notes 283

Bibliography 311

Index 327

In loving memory of Daniel Lewis

Acknowledgements

My thoughts on gender and sexuality began to take real shape when I co-taught the course 'Trans: Dangerous Border Violations' in 2004 with Sandy Stone, whose brilliance, warmth, and openness have been an inspiration to me since. I must thank Wolfgang Schirmacher for encouraging me despite the fact (or maybe because of the fact) that I was a rather unconventional graduate student. My doctoral work has little to do with this book; however, Alain Badiou's comments have stayed with me: his insistence that amorous subjects and political subjects pursue separate truths helped me distinguish the productive tensions from the irrelevant bluster in queer politics.

This book would not have been possible without the support of the Department of Philosophy at Texas State University. I am incredibly fortunate to have worked under two particularly talented chairs, Vincent Luizzi and Craig Hanks. I thank Beverly Pairett, Camrie Pipper, and my graduate teaching assistants in the Applied Philosophy and Ethics Program for their helpfulness over the years.

Kika Sroka-Miller approached me about writing a book in late 2012. I am grateful that she and Zed Books continued to take me seriously after I decided to write something called *The Politics of Everybody*. I must also give thanks to my mystery reviewers for their insightful remarks, and to my patient copyeditor, Judith Forshaw.

Many of the book's key arguments were presented over the years at the Historical Materialism Conference in London. Though they might not know it, comments made by Alan Sears, Abigail Bakan, Kevin Floyd, Paul Reynolds, and Nat Raha were instructive. And thanks to Ahmed Shawki for helping me get there.

This book is a product of many long nights of debate. I have taken so much over the years from discussions with Snehal Shingavi, Karen Dominguez Burke, Katie Feyh, Tithi Bhattacharya, Sarah Wolf, Dana Cloud, Jason Netek, Jamie Saunders, Sharon Smith, Nikeeta Slade, and Sherry Wolf.

People don't get to spend years with their face shoved in a computer without help from family and friends. I thank my mother, Penelope Lewis, for doing all those invisible things – for so many years – that mothers do, and my friends Damian Pring, Hache Buller, Caitlin Lowell, Erik Allesee, and Angela Smith. Also, I want to thank Cindy Beringer for just being, you know, Cindy. It would take an entire separate book to properly thank my beloved partner in crime, Bug Davidson.

My father, Daniel Lewis, passed away soon after I finished the outline for the book. In addition to being a devoted father, he was deeply committed to fighting racism and taught me to never cross a picket line. You really can't ask for more than that. This book is dedicated to him.

Introduction

I. The politics of everybody

The word *everybody* is politically unsettling. It evokes harmony and erasure, connectedness and enchainment; everybody is everywhere but nowhere in particular; the fact of everybody is inconceivable yet certain; everybody is an ever-changing limit. Everybody is both the us and the them. These days, the idea of everybody is most often used to mystify social relations. Phrases such as 'we're all in this together', 'one big happy family' and 'be a team player' reflect this. But the idea can also inspire us to demand 'our' inclusion in 'their' world; it reminds us that 'we' are the ones who make 'their' world possible – which of course means the world was always 'all of ours' all along. (Of course, most of 'them' find this sort of thinking threatening.) This book doesn't claim that there is a political philosophy or practice called 'the politics of everybody', let alone that I am some sort of visionary here to impart the one true version of that politics. The title simply makes the point that the word 'everybody' is politically provocative. It is particularly provocative because we live in an age where the way we produce things – the mode of production called capitalism – requires ideological individualism. One term for trying to think beyond individualism has been, historically speaking, the idea of the totality. But totality has many

1

connotations that the word 'everybody' does not. Totality connotes stasis, structure, permanence, and closure. Totality is difficult to reconcile with movement and historical change. The word 'everybody', on the other hand, is a little less ambitious, a little more material, and it makes a little more room for the interpersonal.

After the Copernican revolution, humans have had to accept that we're not the center of the universe; we're just a contingent collective floating in space, stuck together on the same planet. Economic expansion reduces the experience of distance; technologies developed to facilitate the circulation of commodities bring us closer to one another – whether we like it or not. In the age of global warming and digital satellites, it is no longer reasonable to imagine the world as a collection of territories with distinct boundaries. However, neither is it reasonable to envision the world as an unbounded multitude[1] that has shed all borders, states, and limits: along with the unprecedented movement of bodies and goods, migrant labor, families fleeing war, prisoners, and former felons, perhaps more than ever, are at once adrift and stuck in place.

The cataclysmic ecological threat posed by the capitalist mode of production (the mindless pace it requires, the inevitable waste created in its boom and bust cycles) threatens everyone and requires real solutions. But genuine solutions require the interruption of profit extraction and must be applied at the point of production. For the few who benefit from this system of production – the industrial capitalists, and the financial capitalists who help them spin their profits into wild fictions – protecting the system from criticism is itself a matter of survival. The capitalist mode of production cannot be faulted. When climate change is not denied outright, at least the blame can be shifted. Environmental devastation becomes *everybody's* fault, and the critical eye is turned toward the consumer. Suddenly, the problem is no longer political; now it is ethical. The word 'everybody' here operates as a diversionary tactic so that capitalist processes don't come under scrutiny.

Personal awareness campaigns – the solution to all liberal pluralism's problems – displace calls for system change. Ethics is the final frontier of social change within the liberal pluralist world because the market is, by nature, blameless. The market is imagined to operate principally at the microeconomic level. It is a manifestation of and a servant to our desires. Thus, the desiring consumer subject is the root of the world's problems. For this reason, mindfulness is the key to global harmony – each of us must be made aware of how thoughtless we are toward one another and Mother Earth, but most of all how we harm ourselves. Yet liberal[2] environmental awareness campaigns all hinge on one hidden truth: that social relations are conditioned by the imperatives of capitalist production. Therefore, such awareness campaigns are actually often their opposite: mystifications. This particular mystification, in part, comes via another cornerstone of liberal ideology: the notion that debate and discussion are inherently valuable. Now, this mystification doesn't occur because discussion is *actually* encouraged. It occurs because those who own the means of production under capitalism also own the means of communication as well as the land where ordinary people would gather to discuss and debate. What comes over the airwaves and fills online news feeds masquerades as debate, but in reality it is nothing more than a wall of noise. That wall of noise serves a number of functions. One of those functions is to assure the public that the interests of the market are also their interests, that the market functions perfectly so long as the people it impoverishes don't trouble it, and that capitalist production is way too complex for the average mind to comprehend. In fact, even great minds shouldn't be able to understand it; the only reason to understand it is in order to know how to wring short-term profits from it. So, under capitalism, the term *everybody* is a political euphemism used by capitalists (and those who believe them) to deflect responsibility for systemic processes onto consumers who cannot control them. But beneath the gloss, there is a deep hatred of 'the everybody' (the faceless masses, other people's kids, other people's nations, other people's religions) combined with a sense of collective ownership of other people's achievements (multiculturalism). Everybody exists to sacrifice for the few.

Still, there are other illiberal ways of imagining the problem of everybody. For fascist politics, the word 'everybody' means everybody in their place. Fascist politics demands a well-ordered world where every group is a whole, where every body acts as one body. So long as they keep within their boundaries, fascists may recognize other similarly purified bodies, other homogeneous nations – good fences make good neighbors. Of course, there is always a danger that one purified nation-body may come to see other purified nation-bodies (or all of them) as pollutants and barriers to the unified body of the world. Either way, fascism involves the cleansing of bodies, if not their eradication. But this doesn't necessarily mean that fascist politics acknowledges antagonism. Fascist politics can destroy bodies and claim to be doing so for the good of everybody. All it need do is pronounce that some bodies are nobodies; then it can eradicate the nobodies until everybody is a somebody. In the fascist schema, the nobodies are easy to spot: they're the ones without an identity, the ones without a home, the ones without a specific place to *be* – the internationalists, the immigrants, the 'street' people, the ones whose land has been stolen, the ones stolen from their lands, the ones who never had a land to begin with, the ones who live in the in-between. The fulcrum of the fascist approach to the political question of everybody is the ecstasy of communal harmony made possible only by expelling foreign bodies. The mid-twentieth-century American consensus, still popular, is that the structural core of fascism is the desire to conform, the impulse to give up one's will to orthodoxy.[3] Ascribing causal agency to orthodoxy and uniformity is not without benefit to liberal ideology. If uniformity is the root cause of violent extermination, the solution to such violence is clearly the heterogeneity of the global marketplace, where creative individuals can construct themselves through a mosaic of international products and novelties.

While, to the fascist imaginary, international markets erase the purity of the collective, for colonial and decolonial subjects[4] the international market is a different sort of erasure. This mix of global cultural material is not a pollution of the fatherland, but a final hollowing out of what has not already been erased by imperial conquest. The chaos of the market blurs the lines between cultural imperialism and appreciative sharing, between appropriation and symbolic support. Because the *material* legacy of colonialism and imperialism is conceptually obscured within the academy, the liberal pluralist solution to colonial erasure is a matter of respecting the hurt feelings of the other, whose hurt feelings are an indictment of the liberal pluralist's own political failure to be inclusive. In order to defend against liberal multiculturalism, the decolonial activist is deeply suspect of any use of the word 'everybody'. Her language, culture, and identity have been usurped by this 'everybody'. Western depictions either hollow her out into a nobody, or treat her as a hallowed object, which is, in the end, just another way of being treated as a nobody. But there is a maddening contradiction at work here: capitalist accumulation was the material engine of colonization, and cultural reclamation is not a sufficient condition for ending it; because capitalist expansion is not threatened by anticolonial struggle alone (Fanon 1963),[5] the anticolonial activist must work alongside others who are also struggling against capitalism. And those 'struggling others' could be anybody – and what is an *anybody* if not an emissary from the everybody?

Socialists have a different illiberal relationship to the word 'everybody'. For Marxists, the liberation of all groups depends on the self-emancipation of one group – one *international* group – the proletariat. Unfortunately, under neoliberalism Marx's ideas have fallen prey to the wall of noise. Marxism and the proletariat operate as caricatures; they are treated more as punctuation marks than as words that could have meaning. As labor struggle has been pushed out of the lean[6] workplace and replaced by an all-for-one-and-one-for-all mentality that has absolutely nothing to do with solidarity, Marxist theory has largely been expelled from the lean university. If actual Marxian economic analysis is absent, proletarian revolution is re-imagined as a nostalgic, reactionary identity politics that positions beefy, mallet-wielding male workers as both the most oppressed and the most important creatures on the planet. This imagery obscures the fact that today's proletarian is more likely to be a young woman on an assembly line than a 'Mallet Man' of the nineteenth century. In the university, Marx is imagined as a philosopher who perhaps made some good points about modern alienation, but who was so focused on the factory that he failed to see the anti-hegemonic roles that could be played by women, subalterns, and middle-class intellectuals. But working class does not entail 'maleness'. Nor is 'proletarian' a fixed social identity loaded with predicates; it is the position of value generation within the capitalist circulation of commodities; and, as the source of value in capitalism, it is also the lynchpin for overcoming it. Capitalism is not a code word for a cabal of evildoers tenting their fingers in sadistic pleasure at the thought of ruining the minds and bodies of working people: it is an impersonal system of material social relations.

Because capitalism is a system of social relations, not a person, static group, or moral agreement, it does not respond to moral arguments or moral outrage. The world's Scrooges will not bring a pheasant to the world's Tiny Tims. The Grinch's heart will not grow three sizes larger and he will not return the Christmas gifts to Whoville. Capitalism responds only to what interrupts the generation of profit; and since it is the source of value, labor is both capitalism's greatest asset and its potential downfall. Labor is not the focal point of Marxist politics because Marx felt more outrage over the fate of working folks than other groups of disenfranchised people, nor is Marxism a moral argument that proletarians are an honorable and valiant people, morally superior to the middle and upper classes. The proletarian is the pivotal political subject because productive labor is the strategic point from which capitalism is dismantled. This is not the same as saying that *only* employed people have agency or political value. Workers, the unemployed, their dependents, and allies routinely find creative ways to collude against capital.[7] Anti-capitalist struggle is not a matter of making people aware of how bad life is under capitalism. It is not a matter of guilting the rich into making concessions. The only awareness campaign capable of making a difference in capitalist accumulation is the one that explains to working people what the liberal awareness campaign intentionally ignores: how the capitalist mode of production actually works. But even awareness about the capitalist mode of production will not change it. You actually have to change it to change it. And changing it is a collective action that requires more than awareness. But it is an action that anybody can join.

The Marxist understanding of 'everybody' is the reverse of fascist ideology. Marxism requires a group from everywhere – which is also to say from nowhere in particular – to end a foundational historical injustice. In Marxist terms, everybody is a somebody and everybody belongs everywhere. Marxists do not seek to eradicate a people or even a group of individual persons named capitalists. Marxism seeks to eradicate a *social relationship*: the relation between the forces who create and sustain the world, and those who expropriate that creativity – be it for personal gain, familial gain, the gain of their particular social stratum, or the gain of a culture or nation. State apparatuses are necessary to maintain this social relationship. But the uneven development of states and the inconsistency of legal practices are not barriers to capital; rather, such disparities afford capital a wider playing field. The history of liberal thought likes to use the language of universalism, but the truth is that it thrives on leveraging difference.

Like the fear-inducing term 'totality', universal politics is also generally characterized as more threatening than emancipatory. Instead of evoking the possibility of human connection, universal inclusivity evokes the destruction of the self, the destruction of history, and the spread of cultural dominance: in short, universalism and totalitarianism are twins in the modern political imaginary. Universalism seems to mean its opposite: that sovereign cultures are absorbed into a dominant culture that arrogates itself as the entire universe. In response to the violence of this brand of universal politics, a paranoid individualism has emerged in which family, community, and culture – plurals of the self – are imagined to form the only bulwark against absorption into the everybody that is a cover for nothingness. Such paranoid individualism is a response to real historical turns under the conditions of capitalist development: colonization, consumerist multiculturalism, imperialism, factory discipline, failed revolutions, and the never-ending rhetoric informing us that there are too many people for the world to handle. But a contradiction is at work here as well. Although the current social and economic system seems to destroy the community and the individual through war and mass production, it ironically produces communities (i.e. nations, 'coalitions of the willing', 'our democracies', cultural markets, and so on) and sovereign individuals (by insisting that we are unique, that we must stand out from the crowd, that one has a duty to express oneself through commodities) through mass production.

II. Communitarian ideals and culture wars

Although Western – particularly American – progressives and conservatives are locked in a culture war, both sides are structured by a buried anxiety about the destruction of the self and its plurals. On the progressive side, this concern is expressed through affirmations of diversity. Let's call this form of liberalism *progressive communitarianism*. Liberalism's other face is conservative and marked by a negative freedom: individuality is expressed by the freedom to exclude, to preserve oneself and one's cultural history. The highest law is that individuals should not be forced to interact with those they disdain. We can call this *conservative communitarianism*. Although progressive communitarianism rejects the idea of cultural domination, it is absolutely distinct from anticolonial movements of national liberation. Progressive communitarianism holds a commitment to a vague pacifism predicated on a respect for human difference and cultural diversity; it sees cultural dominance at the root of alienation, often ignoring the material dominance that situates the cultural. Conservative communitarianism is a commitment to one's own distinct community and no other; it is a campaign against intergroup transformation; the progressive communitarian respect for cultural diversity is viewed as a threat to the communitarian conservative's own cultural specialness. These are the basic commitments in what are called *the culture wars*. The two positions clash on issues of national sovereignty but do so on the same common ground. When a nation is colonized by another, progressive communitarians attribute attempts to erase difference as the core motivation of the aggressor nation; conservative communitarians stand on the argument: 'We erase because they threaten to erase us.' Where progressive communitarians see a paranoid fear of those who are different, conservative communitarians see a genuine threat. Still, both arguments are *cultural* explanations for global unrest. As soon as colonized people resist under terms that are anything other than utter pacifism, the progressive communitarians line up behind conservatives because now the fears of the right-wing communitarians are justified – now the difference really *is* a threat. In other words, liberal pluralism is committed to difference so long as difference isn't antagonistic, so long as it has no substance, so long as it stays in the realm of pure theory – so long as it isn't really different.

Neoliberal political thought, whether progressive or conservative, acknowledges two great classes in the world: not capitalists and proletarians, but producers and consumers. In the United States, Americans of all political persuasions bemoan our mindless consumption; the complaint is even heard among those who struggle to make ends meet. Social change is generally imagined in terms of boycotting big box stores, buying from companies that support your cultural values, and voting with your dollar. Work is not a location for politics; it is the place where your sins begin, where you get the money to become a good consumer. But consumerism and commodification are not causes of exploitation but consequences. There is no categorical split between producers and consumers. All producers must consume. The irony of capitalism is that the more energy you give to it, the less you receive from it. The irony of the anti-consumerist response to capitalism is that consumption-based solutions position the poorest workers and the unemployed as the staunchest proponents of the system; the unwashed masses are treated like accomplices of the megacorporations because they can't afford to buy local, organic, sustainable goods. But what never seems to be local are the steel mills, the tin mines, the factories where gadgets are assembled, and the silica-processing plants. The steel beams holding up the natural foods store are not organic. Proponents of consumer politics forget Adam Smith's insight that the commodity is not just one 'thing', traceable to one person or set of people. It is concretized through invisible processes.

Ethical consumption can't touch the core of these invisible processes. Each of us has a network of invisible caretakers scattered across the globe, fulfilling tasks once performed within the community. People we don't know stitch together our underwear, mine the metals used to make the machines that make our bicycles and pots, harvest our grain, grind the sand to make our drinking glasses. Sometimes our invisible caretakers live in town: lifting boxes from pallets, grading our term papers, preparing food in the backs of restaurants, cleaning our shit off public toilets. But this is not merely a parasitic relation of consumers to workers. One of the fundamental conditions of the capitalist epoch is that workers, who have nothing but their labor to sell, are also forced to live off other people working in the system. It's not just the wealthy consuming manufactured goods; we're all subsumed into the capitalist economy. The only way to mount a challenge against a global system – a global *militarized* system – is through a politics that addresses global subjects and asserts that there is commensurability between them. In other words, the only way to confront the system is to develop solidarity between those who must labor – including those who are unable to labor – in this enormous network of mines, mills, factories, schools, stores, and transport centers: solidarity between the visible and the invisible, the waged and the unwaged.

Solidarity among such a large subset of people is bound to be a fluid, internally shifting collective political subject. Anti-capitalist solidarity implies interrupting the expropriation of surplus value with the end goal of system change. That requires a principle of minimal connection between political actors. Minimal connection simply means that grounds for solidarity are possible. I would like to advance the case that *pointless suffering* might be such a point of commonality. We might suffer for lovers, for art, for political or religious truths, or, sadly, because we think we deserve to suffer. But *pointless* suffering is tragic by definition.[8] The statement that experiencing pointless suffering is universally undesired might seem banal, but the assertion that there is even one commonality among people is surprisingly contentious. This contention is based on the position that if you dip your toe into the waters of universality, soon you'll be swimming in European male dominance. But all gestures toward common human feeling are not alike. So let's call the universalism of market forces and the streamlining of human life into a conduit for the enrichment of the few by the name *universalism from above*, and let's call the solidarity necessary to oppose universalism from above by the name *universalism from below*. Or, alternatively, we could think of it as a political commitment to everybody – not a toothless humanism, but a militant commitment to inclusion that doesn't deny antagonisms.

III. How is every body sorted?

The ideology of immutable sexual difference is an enormous barrier in trying to imagine 'everybody'. The world is generally understood to be split into two ontological categories – male and female – and nobody becomes a 'nobody' faster than those who don't fit into one of these two groups. In addition to the fact that there are antagonisms between the two categories, there are also antagonisms between those within the categories and those outside them. But sex categorization changes according to time and place; it is conditioned by a given society's material organization and the divisions resulting from that particular organization.

In the patriarchal mode from settled civilization to feudal relations, sex was understood as a natural relationship based on hierarchy and complementarity. Woman completed man and served to perpetuate his and his son's existence. This patriarchal model, alien to human existence for hundreds of thousands of years before sedentarization, began to fissure as industrialization changed the physical and historical landscape. As women and children moved into factory work, a renewed nervousness about the ontological power of sex difference developed. Delicacy was enforced upon the women of the upper classes. Women of the lower classes were expected to be maternal, to be sexually available to rich men, and to be masculine enough to be able to shovel dung – sometimes all at once. Class divisions and racial divisions troubled the idea that the maleness and femaleness of the body unfolded from a spiritual essence.

In the twentieth century – especially in urban, industrial regions – gender began to appear as something contingent. There was the truth of sex and then there was *gender*, those sets of social norms layered on top of the real body. Body was nature; gender was culture. And culture implied contingency. The women's movement was galvanized: women's bodies and lives should not have to conform to gender expectations. But many people were left out of this political formula: in particular, those whose bodies *didn't* conform to gender expectations, who faced brutal exclusion for their nonconformity. The excluded weren't necessarily genderless – in fact, often quite the opposite – rather, their genders and their bodies didn't match: their *natural* gender didn't seem to fit with the way their *culture* thought their bodies should look or act. An antagonism developed. There were some who felt that their bodies were true, and that gender was a political imposition shaping people within their 'biological' sex category. Others maintained that a given social gender felt right, except it didn't match cultural expectations of how their bodies were sexed. Then, towards the end of the century, it was discovered that many individuals – intersex people – had been and were being surgically altered by doctors to fit into one of the two 'true' biological sexes; what's more, in different cultures they would be put into different 'true' boxes where they would grow up with different expectations of their social gender. On top of all this, there were people who were amorous toward people of the same sex, while others were amorous toward people who didn't fit into any expected sexual category.

People are not merely carved up into nations and cultures within capitalist social relations, they also inhabit complex bodies that are collectively coded into different functions, functions that operate within the context of nation, culture, and class. Scientific research inspired by the critique of sexual dimorphism is increasingly showing that sex exists on a continuum, with a substantial number of people at a distance from the two extremes. Liberal pluralist politics has easily solved this problem by reconciling the various opinions about sex and gender into a permanent dialogue: there is money to be made by those who support queer rights, and there is money to be made by those who oppose them. Of course, illiberal conservative politics has a clear gender policy and this policy is that gender must be clear. Postcolonial work on sexual diversity has revealed that diverse sexuality was yet another casualty of colonial violence. But how does the Marxist paradigm reconcile its understanding of inclusivity together with gender and sexual alterity? What are the material conditions that shape the politics of sex and gender, and how do they relate to capitalism and anti-capitalism? These questions are what this book hopes to begin to resolve.

It is not a question irrelevant to all but those affected by anti-queer and anti-trans violence. There are forces of purification at work – those who see the world not as a profitable unity of producers and consumers, not as an antagonism between capitalists and workers, not even as an antagonism between colonizers and colonized. They see the world as a battle between 'traditional people' and 'homosexuals' – homosexual being a symbol for all sexual and gender diversity and all struggles against sexism. The 'homosexual' is the nobody who needs to become nothing. These forces are quietly conducting their purifying project among the poor and working classes in Africa, Eastern Europe, and Latin America. Solidarity with queer, trans, and intersex people is non-negotiable when it comes to the international solidarity of the working class.

I write this in the hope of bringing four groups into dialogue: Marxist theorists who are trying to understand where gender fits into the schema of Marxist practice; feminist theorists who wish to incorporate Marxist analysis in their work; Marxist practitioners unfamiliar with the politics and origins of third-wave feminist, queer, and trans politics; and, finally, queer and trans feminist activists unfamiliar with Marxist political economy. There are readers who will belong to overlapping sets and, of course, those who find themselves outside these groups altogether.

Because I hope to bring distinct groups into dialogue, the first chapter defines the terms necessary to ground the book's argument and the debates that inform it. The second chapter contains a history of Marxist-feminism, its internal and external critiques, and an inquiry into the materialist roots of queer and trans oppression from a Marxist-feminist perspective. The third chapter discusses the relationship between ideology and queer theory, questions current popular approaches to queer anti-capitalism, and discusses the barriers to a queer Marxist internationalism. The final chapter includes recommendations for action.

CHAPTER 1

Terms of the debate

This book has the difficult task of speaking to multiple audiences: third-wave feminists and queer theorists who have commitments to gender and sexual liberation but who have little familiarity with Marxian economics; Marxists who want to go beyond facile dismissals of 'identity politics' to better understand the relationship between the objective realities of material existence and the experience of that material existence; and those working to clarify their political and philosophical orientation towards gender. Each readership comes with a distinct set of languages, political histories, and conceptual tools.

Chapter 1 serves as an overview of the concepts fundamental to each political approach. This conceptual outline also foreshadows the overall argument of this book: that to live up to its own inclusive values, Marxist politics must understand gender politics; and that any gender politics of merit will contain an anti-capitalist critique that goes beyond moral posturing.

I. Debates in Western gender politics

Epistemology and identity politics

Within Marxists and various third-wave feminist camps, the term 'identity politics' is more slur than genuine political critique. For Marxists, the slur refers to politics that substitute systemic historical and economic analyses with inquiries into intrapersonal aggression. Marxist political activity does not require a proletarian identity politics because Marxist analysis involves impersonal, macropolitical investigations. However, the majority of current Marxist thought[1] takes anti-oppression seriously and is committed to tackling sexism, imperialism, colonialism, racism, homophobia, and transphobia. So Marxists do understand that identities exist and that being stuck with a particular label has political consequences; there is no denial that capitalism sorts human material according to market criteria and that this creates immense suffering within certain groups. Identity politics is irreconcilable with Marxism only if the former is understood to entail a world where communication and solidarity are possible *only* among those who share specific experiences. Such a requirement would necessarily divide the working classes into insurmountable, static antagonisms. Since capitalism already divides workers – giving some carrots and others sticks – further divisions among the stick-beaten and the carrot-rewarded cannot resolve injustice: for Marxists, only ending capitalism will be equal to the task because the conditions of justice are historical and class specific.[2]

Feminist, queer, and trans critiques of identity politics differ from the Marxist critique. Both the second and third waves of feminist thought criticize the concept of objectivity, and instead champion epistemologies based on situated knowledge. Within feminism, 'identity politics' is a political error that occurs when an individual or group overemphasizes the impact of or naturalizes a given standpoint – for example, reducing a person to the assumed experience of the group with which they are identified, or automatically treating any individual within a group as if they are representative of that group. As a poststructuralist enterprise, queer theory has a very different take. Queer theory asserts that identity, as a conceptual category, serves as a disciplinary apparatus that pigeonholes the fluidity of the self into a politically docile *normativity*. This places the queer subject in a privileged epistemological position: those who experience no gender dissonance vis-à-vis the system are ignorant of its force and its contours.[3] Queer subjects are diverse, but share a collective understanding of gender discipline that forms a basis for political cohesion. For queer theory, the term 'identity politics' is derogatory because it assumes that identities – clear-cut groupings with clear definitions – are desirable. When political thinkers dismiss queer theory as mere identity politics, this is fundamentally incorrect. Queer theory is an *anti-identity* identity politics. The Marxist critique of many (non-Marxist) feminisms and queer theory is that if you want to analyze inequality as systemic, it is necessary to transcend the individual mind. If knowledge is *contained within* a standpoint, rather than capable of being *inflected* by a standpoint, then systemic knowledge is not possible and, as a consequence, inequality cannot be fought systematically.

Each of the frameworks above also takes a different object for its epistemology: the feminist meaning of 'system' is patriarchy, while queer theory understands 'systemicity' to be discursive structures willfully kept in place by those who benefit from the system. The object of Marxist epistemology, on the other hand, is the *material* organization of society (Henning 2014). As a consequence of these different understandings of what is meant by the term *system*, Marxists, queer activists, and feminists (particularly second-wave feminists whose feminism is not wedded to queer politics) tend to talk past one another in their critiques of identity politics. This is not to say that political practitioners of these viewpoints are completely consistent in their epistemological commitments. For example, the Marxist legacy of independent journalism rests on the notion that there are no unbiased witnesses to history. The difference, however, between Marxian approaches to journalism (or, if we divorce the concept from institutions and professions, *speaking from the event*) and poststructuralist approaches is that, for Marxists, the positioned witness is considered able to surpass their own personal, phenomenological experience of events. The Marxist witness can deduce general information from their particular position.[4] The Marxist witness, like the socially disciplined queer subject, is also given an epistemological advantage in that their position allows them to witness the appearance of cracks on the surface of capitalist ideology. But the queer political subject experiences the system as an overwhelming and inscrutable alienating spiritual force, while the Marxist subject's political goals require her to translate her standpoint into an outlook that is objectively valuable.

While Marxists do not entirely negate the value of situated knowledge, queer theorists are often ambivalent or unclear about objectivity. In poststructuralist queer thought, to theorize about the system is itself to 'systematize' knowledge of injustice, thereby eliminating the interpersonal; however, at the same time, queer theory is predicated on what it calls 'dismantling discursive disciplinary apparatuses' – that is, pointing out how systems of ideas shape people. It is hard to point out how systems of ideas shape people without first conceptualizing how the system works – so systematic thought makes you think systematically! The queer theoretical solution for dismantling the system is not a new identity politics or even an opposition to identity politics, but rather a conscious demand for ideological change in the abstract. Change is not imagined as a struggle over material social relations; it is a struggle for *discursive* changes, for collective shifts in language. These changes come at the level of individual speech acts and symbolic ruptures. Political change is understood as the outcome of an aggregate of individual acts. Yet, paradoxically, discursive politics leads to, indeed *requires*, significant policing of language. Because systemic violence is entirely ideological, choosing appropriate terminology becomes a political act. The reverse of this is that using the wrong terminology becomes an act of ideological violence. This creates a significant barrier to political agency because discursive politics demands that people be trained in the correct phraseology (in fact, *self-trained* in the correct phraseology, because collective training would subject others to the violence of normativized discourse). It is difficult to image an internationalist model of discursive politics. If 'system' means 'ideology', and if disrupting ideology is a *linguistic* act, then the terrain of political struggle would reside within distinct language groups and cultures, cultures that then have no real reason to communicate with one another beyond multicultural pleasantries. Cultural incommensurability becomes absolute. We find ourselves under the authority of 'the dictatorship of the fragments' (Best 1989: 361).

Nor is third-wave feminism immune from epistemological inconsistency. For example, third-wave feminists maintain that racism, sexism, and homophobia are systemic, not a mere matter of individual micro-aggressions; yet they assert rather than explain how the system produces gender injustice and how gender injustice comes to be a feature of the social system. When the term 'system' is conceived as an interpersonal network in which certain groups are socially empowered, the political solution to systemic injustice becomes the replacing of anti-feminist policymakers with feminist policymakers. Such an approach conceives of system change as a matter of getting the right individuals into the right positions, and social identity cannot help but determine who is the right individual. Even if this conception of politics concedes the limits of identity (Sarah Palin and Imelda Marcos come to mind), the election of the right individuals to the right political posts is highly valued in this model.

In other words, even though feminists and queer activists embrace the idea of fighting at a systemic level, the meaning of the term 'system' is not always clear, and nor is the political role played by individuals operating within the system. Marxists are, in comparison, quite clear on what constitutes the system: the system is the laws and norms brought about by current material social relations born from earlier material social relations, and the system is also the material social relations themselves. The system can be named: feudalist, capitalist, socialist, and so on. Nuances and shifts within systems – monopoly capitalism, neoliberalism, Keynesianism, and state capitalism – are topics that Marxists outline and debate. A materialist conception of politics does not mean that gender relations are reducible to economic conditions (for example, factory occupation is not a panacea for ending sexual assault). Conditions are not reducible to material social relations; however, they are *generated* from the matrix of material social relations.

If system change does not come through challenges to language and imagery (as poststructuralism and queer theory argue) or by dismantling hierarchical relationships within institutions (as feminism argues), the question for Marxists becomes: 'What can be done in the here and now?' Criticizing language and institutional hierarchies seems doable, but transforming the whole of material social relations? What could be done short of revolution? Marxist responses to this question have ranged from defeatism to desperate moral calls for immediate revolution, to revolutionaries indiscriminately throwing themselves onto the machine in the hope of slowing the gears, to the social democratic argument that socialism will evolve on its own through reforms (Bernstein 1961), to a strategy of militant urban occupations that envision capitalism's imminent destruction, one building at a time.[5]

Many Marxists – myself included – have found Rosa Luxemburg's dialectical approach to the problem to be productive (see Luxemburg 2007). For Luxemburg, revolution is not the polar opposite of reform; nor is Luxemburg worried that political subjects will become complacent if reforms are won. When people fight and win reforms, they are not less likely to continue fighting; they are more likely to continue fighting. Fighting for reforms is a way to build political muscle. In the process of struggling for reforms, solidarities are forged and revolutionary forces develop the political clarity to take on more complicated challenges. This approach also requires that subjects develop the capacity to integrate situated and objective knowledge. If one disdains situated knowledge within a field of struggle, one quickly becomes a caricature of the variety of Leninist revolutionary who rushes into battle to bestow her higher wisdom upon the struggling masses.[6] Trust is earned by paying attention to the situation at hand, not by presenting abstract theories. Moreover, pushing abstract, prefabricated revolutionary platforms obscures the concrete historical and material politics that comprise Marxist practice. Reforming immediate conditions is a component of revolutionary activity. Reconciling ongoing situated knowledge with a deeper understanding of objective material conditions, along with a commitment to changing those conditions, is revolutionary praxis.

While queer thinkers are quick to point out that the liberation of labor does not spontaneously solve all homophobia and transphobia, they have been remiss in pointing out that the radical reframing of discourse does not liberate labor. Disrupting linguistic phenomena is not sufficient to remedy systemic injustice because it cannot substantially disrupt material conditions. Likewise, feminists have correctly pointed out that Marx failed to fully consider social reproductive labor outside the factory, but the feminist move away from Marx and towards a concern with hierarchy and hetero-patriarchy merely denounced capitalism and focused on developing strategies for surviving it: denouncing and enduring do not disrupt a system, let alone end it. While feminist opinion about reform is highly dependent on the particular mode of feminist thought (radical, Black feminist, materialist, etc.), for queer theory, reform is almost impossible by definition, because an entire way of thought must be overhauled. The fact that queer political theory is skeptical of reform is a manifestation of its faith that political transformation is another name for conceptual transformation. In other words, it is a classic example of philosophical idealism.

The critique of political economy cannot be sacrificed in favor of intuitive or situated knowledge, but situated knowledge is necessary for concrete strategy. Genuine antiracist and anti-sexist training happens in the streets, not in the safe space of the university classroom. This is because, in the streets, bonds of solidarity are developed at the level of shared political goals, be those goals immediate reform or revolution. In the classroom, training is a matter of comparing theoretical precepts. (The caveat here is that when the classroom is a site of broad struggle, it becomes a part of 'the streets'.) This means that revolutionary political practice involves both considering and transcending experiential knowledge. If third-wave feminist and trans/queer praxis wishes to be politically (not just sentimentally) anti-capitalist, then it has to start talking about capitalist production. Likewise, if Marxists want to go beyond intellectualized solidarity, Marxist political practice requires an exchange of working-class perspectives. Learning about the language and debates inside queer, trans, and feminist political movements is not useless identity politics but the *concrete* practice of solidarity. This goes beyond the truism that revolutionary forces must contain a diverse cross-section of the population. The relationship between the composition of a political movement and identity is complex. Without actors immanent to the situation at hand, interventions in movements will be perceived as intrusive; however, Marxist groups are in a double bind here: if a collective sends its members into political situations where the member's identity allows access, not only is identity politics reinforced (i.e. Caribbean Marxists are the ones who should know about Caribbean politics, queer Marxists are the ones who should know about gender politics, and so on), but the member is still seen as an emissary from a group, not a subject contributing from the heart. The challenge for any Marxist, then, is at once to be knowledgeable about the world, about themself, and about the group they operate within and to be able to articulate political suggestions that embody these areas of knowledge: a challenging ethos if ever there was one.

Queer (anti-)identity

The integration of queer and trans people into 'the everybody' – or the refusal to integrate queer and trans people – is a critical political choice. Queer theory, with its philosophical roots in the Foucauldian search for marginalized shadow populations, is committed to inclusivity; however, it is also indebted to Heideggerian phenomenology, which confines being-in-the-world to local language networks, which, in turn, stymies the possibility of international analysis. To further complicate the matter, contemporary queer *politics* developed within Western political conditions, particularly American political conditions. Internationalizing the queer, if done by Americans in the spirit of liberal pluralism, will undoubtedly be an imperialist queer politics that reduces concrete politics and histories to parallels with American history and culture. Yet gender non-conformity and homosexuality are not an American or European invention (see Drucker 2015).[7] Same-sex activity and gender non-conforming identities exist around the world and have done so throughout history. Examples of challenges to the myth of universal heterosexual gender dimorphism are numerous: from *kathoey* in Thailand to *hijra* in India and Pakistan, *muxes* in Mexico and sworn virgins in Albania.[8] Moreover, international groups politically adopting the word 'queer' do not necessarily think of themselves as having a political essence that connects them to a global community based on gender and sexuality. The group alQaws for Sexual and Gender Diversity in Palestinian society[9] recognizes that queer politics emerged historically in the United States; however, the group maintains that Palestinian queers do not necessarily share the demands of American queers. Moreover, Palestinian queers do not see the struggle for gender diversity as being separable from the larger Palestinian struggle; they do not participate in Israeli Pride or consider themselves allied with Israeli queers. The politics of alQaws does not primarily consist of reforming discourse or even fighting homophobia. Its political practice is rooted in anticolonial struggle.

Language and identity (or, more pointedly, marginalized identity, which plays the role of a sort of anti-identity identity) have been the center of gravity of queer politics in the United States; the result has been a sort of Anglocentric communalism. Debates about American identities – high femme, lesbian, queer, transgendered butch, transsexual, stud, aggressive, marimacha/o, etc. – sit awkwardly within an international context. In fact, even for those with anti-capitalist sympathies, a fascination with Anglophone identity politics creates the conditions for absorption into a cultural consciousness along the lines of what Jasbir Puar has termed *homonationalism*. While Anglophone queer people are not necessarily proponents of imperialism, it is no surprise that a politics grounded in linguistic idealism has largely failed to embrace anti-imperialist solidarity with other queer people in other parts of the world.

But before too much contempt is heaped upon this inward-gazing form of politics, it is important that we do not overestimate the level of social acceptance that has been extended to queer and trans people in the West. Despite recent marriage equality victories and some reduction in homophobia among the general population (however, it is important to remember that, within a liberal pluralist society, a deeply entrenched conservative opposition is awarded *permanent space*), the suicide rates of gays and lesbians, particularly youth, are consistently high, and the rate of suicide attempts among transgendered people in the United States is an astronomical 41 percent (Grant et al. 2011). The murder rate of Black trans women is shockingly high, and anti-LGBT violence has trended upwards in the US during the second decade of the new millennium. It should be no great mystery why people besieged in every direction, in addition to suffering exploitation and denial of employment, would care deeply about developing a language to describe themselves in order to assert their own existence. Learning about such identities is not opposed to materialist politics, and the insistence on identities can be understood not as an expression of capitalist individualism but as a declaration of the right to self-determination.

Nor does queer and trans people's struggle for self-definition fall outside the realm of material phenomena. Queer and trans status has an impact on the meaning of being a woman, and often reflects struggles around gendered labor and class antagonism. In the 1970s, the lesbian-feminist organizations emerging out of American college life treated working-class butch/femme queer women with disdain. Middle-class feminist academics scorned gender in general as a mode of false consciousness, and they considered masculinity in particular to be a form of social violence. While, on the surface, this antagonism was a debate about language and identity, disgust for the working class was palpable. For those who had to sell *gendered* bodies on the labor market as dockworkers, secretaries, waitresses, prostitutes or showgirls, gender was a bodily expression of everyday life that could not be politically debated away as merely false. For those whose lives were structured by working-class lesbian bar culture, masculine women physically defended the safe space of the bar from homophobic attack. Feminine women could support the community financially by working in the heterosexual world; and femme caretaking held the community together when it was recovering from police repression and sexual violence.[10]

27

The language used by queer women in America in the twentieth century differed from descriptions of gender non-conforming people in Victorian culture. At the beginning of the gay movement, before the word homosexual was invented in Victorian England, German writer Karl Heinrich Ulrichs devised the word *uranian*, which referenced Plato's *Symposium*; the word described 'man-manly love' and a transgendered or 'third sex' social position (Kennedy 2005). Indeed, all queerness was reduced to a biological disorder – and queerness literally meant anything that challenged social roles. Researchers built upon Ulrichs' ideas. The medical community described uranians as 'mental hermaphrodites' while, conversely, being born intersex entailed mental deviance. Prostitutes, feminists, and even working-class women were considered biologically different (Smith-Rosenberg 1985). Indeed, as late as the 1940s, in the United States the term 'lesbian' meant 'masculine woman'. A couple was comprised of a lesbian and *her girlfriend*. When asked whether or not their lovers were also lesbians, some found the question bizarre – of course their girlfriends weren't lesbians (Kennedy and Davis 1993). As butch/femme culture developed in the mid-century, both partners began to view themselves as lesbians, except when they rejected the lesbian label altogether because it seemed to now refer to the middle-class white lesbians who opposed gender on principle (Feinberg 1993).

The term 'queer' emerged as a move away from the biologically grounded homosexual identities of 'gay' and 'lesbian' towards a more inclusive political movement. It was also an alternative to the awkward alphabet soup of GLB or LGBT, or even more awkward constructions such as lesbigay,[11] where only four possible sexual orientations are possible: gay, lesbian, bisexual, and heterosexual. Redolent of the radical feminist prohibition on gender, the term 'lesbigay' erased trans[12] people from the political equation. It is important to note that one need not adopt an idealist, anti-materialist position to see the social parameters at work here.

The term lesbigay did not accidentally exclude or overlook trans inclusion. The exclusion was intentional. On the other hand, some trans people did not necessarily want to be included in the lesbigay club; the homosexual struggle was a sexual struggle, whereas theirs was a struggle over gender and no more about sexual desire than the mainstream women's rights movement. Later, some intersex conservatives and their families disputed inclusion in the term LGBTQI because intersexuality was a physical condition present at birth, not a 'choice'.

As the term grew longer (into LGBTQQIAA: lesbian, gay, bisexual, trans, queer, questioning, intersex, asexual, allies), many were still not included in the potentially infinite taxonomy. For example, where would the cisgendered partners of trans and genderqueer people fit in? Others argued that survivors of testicular cancer might necessitate the addition of an 'E' for eunuch as genital and hormonal changes sometimes produce a change in self-definition (Aucoin and Wassersug 2006). As a default, queer became a popular umbrella term, a clear way to articulate that an antagonism existed: there were two politicized categories of people in the world, straights and queers. This new cross-class dichotomy wasn't simply a linguistic clarification; it was born out of a decade of AIDS activism. As gay men were dying – sometimes in a matter of weeks – anti-gay oppression was a more visible and immediate threat to existence for many than the system-wide extraction of surplus value; homophobia within the working class and the decline of American labor amplified this trend. Radical feminist separatism no longer made sense for those middle-class and white lesbians who had just participated in a decade of direct action standing beside gay men. But this new cross-class unity did more than blur class antagonism; it also assumed that a queer political identity was more fundamental than other political antagonisms such as race, which put whites in the position of defining the terms of the American queer movement.

Since the decline of AIDS politics, a new definition of the word queer has competed with the idea of the queer umbrella. This new sense of queer emerged from Lisa Duggan's term *homonormativity*. Queer was a moniker that embraced a working-class or poor, radical, and anti-capitalist identity in opposition to 'homonormative' middle- and upper-class gays and lesbians who were perceived as seeking acceptance from heterosexuals. But unlike the era of butch/femme, which was tightly tied to *actual* class position, gender queerness and anti-capitalist ideology were no longer situated in the realities of class; rather, anti-capitalist radicalism became a badge, a militant identity disconnected from the material world: plenty of working-class and poor gays and lesbians were 'normative' and a good chunk of queer-identified 'gender radicals' were middle and upper class. What's more, the primacy of the queer/normative antagonism was global in theory only; in practice, the Anglocentrism of language-intensive politics isolated the Anglo-American queer movement. The fact that most global politics involve class, immigrant, and anticolonial struggle left all but middle-class Americans at the periphery of the queer movement. I will later argue that *homonationalism* (see Puar 2007) develops within this set of political parameters regardless of the behavioral norms of individuals (see 'Beyond homonormativity and homonationalism' in Chapter 3).

Sex and social gender: dichotomy or dialectic?

Twentieth-century queer theory emerged, in part, as a response to the anti-gender thrust of second-wave radical feminism. Women were defined as people with a particular biological heritage suffering violence at the hands of patriarchy. Femininity was considered a weapon to keep women under patriarchal control. Gender was no longer considered to be an essence emerging from a specific body type; rather, it was a cultural construct, a form of ideology and therefore *unnatural*. The goal of a good portion of second-wave feminism was to liberate the female body from the idea of the feminine. Thus, to behave in a feminine manner was to be atavistic, anti-feminist, co-opted. To behave in a masculine manner was evidence of internalized self-hatred and a violation of women-centric social norms. For lesbian separatists divorced from the social and material conditions of compulsory heterosexual life, 'masculine' and 'feminine' behavior became highly policed abstract pejoratives. Everyone was expected to be 'free' and 'genderless'. A queer backlash emerged from the impossibility of the project.[13] Queer theory flipped the script: it was sex that was constructed by gender, the latter being inscribed into social reality through repetition.

Since the turn of the millennium, narratives between trans women (who are certain of their womanhood despite their imposed social identity) and queer theorists (who argue that both womanhood and femininity are social constructs and therefore unstable) have started to reproduce some of the hotly contested sex/gender debates of the 1970s, but with the arguments reversed. The new contention highlights the fact that both queers and radical feminists consider gender to be a construct; the two positions are divided only on the social meaning of the construct. Radical feminism considers gender to be an expression of internalized patriarchy and views the body as an irreducible fact – with the distinction between male/female bodies indeed constructing the political dynamics of everyday life. For radical feminists, women's responsibility for childbirth and women's vulnerability to rape produce conditions for the rise of patriarchy. Radical feminism's definition of womanhood as a situation defined by the social consequences of having specific reproductive organs put its proponents on a collision course with trans politics. Deducing politics from sexual dimorphism and reducing gender to ideology, trans-exclusionary radical feminists have militantly insisted that not only are trans women *not women* but that they are the most violent men of all: men intent on colonizing women's bodies; men so intent on raping lesbian women that they are willing to transform their bodies to carry out their sinister plans.[14] Trans-exclusionary radical feminists (referred to here as TERFs) have aligned with the religious right in their attempts to keep trans women from using bathrooms reflecting their lived gender. Leading TERFs have created websites designed to ridicule trans women and trans men, and they have even tried to dissuade the United Nations from acknowledging trans rights.[15] Yet despite this antagonism, both TERFs and many trans women insist that women's bodies are definable and grounded in biological fact. The difference is that those who wish to exclude trans women from womanhood insist upon the presence of visible 'birthright' biological markers that would determine an individual's social trajectory: particular clusters of secondary sex characteristics, particular genitals, the experience of menstruation. Trans individuals, however, unlike queer activists, do not necessarily root their experience of womanhood outside biology; instead, some maintain that there are invisible biological factors at work – neurological differences or exposure to hormones in the womb. But here, biology is a series of material processes independent of social ontology.[16] After all, the presence of ovaries and the experience of menstruation are not grounds for womanhood. If they were, it would mean that some trans men should automatically be considered women and cis women with amenorrhea would not be.

Unlike TERFs, queer activists tend to be trans-supportive; in fact, since sexual orientation is distinct from gender identity, there is an overlap between queer and trans community membership. But queer politics is anti-identitarian and predicated on social construction: in queer theory, no one is innately a man or a woman, and anyone can perform masculinity and femininity. The queer theoretical attitude towards gender identity is also marked by a politicized voluntarism: here, irreverent self-construction of the gendered body is the key to subverting the disciplinary apparatus of power. But politicized gender also implies consciously choosing to be a gender outlaw and this is precisely what the trans community argues individuals should not have to be. Trans men and women are not the only ones who sit uncomfortably within the political paradigm of gender transgression. While the idea of the queer emerged as a response to the radical feminist exclusion of working-class butch/femme culture, queer thought has never been fully comfortable with butch/femme as a stable pattern of desire.[17] But the trans criticism of queer theory's trivialization of gender identity does not stand as the final word. Because intersex bodies fall somewhere along a sexual spectrum, the reassertion of the truth of sexual dimorphism that emerges within certain sections of the trans movement erases the complex embodied experience of intersex persons. Moreover, the argument that there is an antagonism between trans and cis identities leaves intersex people without a political location.

Debates about definitions internal to queer culture would not necessarily be of immediate political interest to Marxists (or at least not to Marxists outside queer and trans communities). However, there is a fundamental difference between disputes over language and the antagonism between working-class lesbians and lesbian CEOs, or between trans people and those who wish to wipe them off the face of the earth. The imprisonment of CeCe McDonald, a Black trans woman imprisoned for the death of a white supremacist who assaulted her on the street, highlighted the need for cisgendered, heterosexual Marxists to understand trans politics. Talking to people in ways that do not make them feel utterly alienated is a baseline requirement for solidarity.

A final word on queer language

My understanding of language and identity in this book will undoubtedly be imperfect; but nonetheless, as a realist who does not believe that language makes communication impossible, I will try to use terms that reflect the expressions most common at this particular moment (in the Anglophone world). I will try to use the most general pronouns whenever possible, including the singular 'they', 'them' and 'their' as both a pronoun for gender queer persons and a universal pronoun; however, when I am using the work of feminists who are referring to women, I will use the pronoun 'she'; when I am referring to historical individuals identified as men, I will use the pronoun 'he'. There will be times, however, when I intentionally use feminine pronouns to underscore the existence of women and gender non-conforming people within domains commonly associated with masculinity. The term 'cisgendered' is widely used for non-trans people who move through life with a body that matches their gender presentation. 'Cissexism' will be used to describe the systematic exclusion and erasure of trans people. However, even among trans allies, the term cisgender does not avoid contention. As mentioned earlier, some intersex people feel that the cis/trans binary reinforces the two-sex model and that intersex[18] people are hence written out of language. The term also fails to describe (or is used unevenly to describe) many queer people who face discrimination and violence for transgressing gender assumptions, regardless of whether or not they are trans.

The word 'queer' itself also contains a number of meanings. When queer is an umbrella term with a meaning roughly synonymous to LGBT, I will call this *queer in the 'queer umbrella' sense*. However, queer has always had another referent: those who are not heterosexual nor cisgendered but who do not fit neatly within the LGBT classification. I will call this *queer in the LGBTQ sense*. The concept of homonormativity created another sense of queer – queer as a transgressive anti-identity in opposition to gay and lesbian identity. Because one of the symbols of this movement is a transformation of the equal sign[19] into a greater-than symbol, I will call this *radical queer* because it sees queerness as both a defining political problem and a moral-political solution.

The explication of these terms is not a detour away from 'real politics' into 'identity politics' but a clarification of meaning and an attempt to affirm the right to self-determination. Marxists are no strangers to paying attention to language. We have spent generations debating whether or not the Soviet Union was a degenerated workers' state or a deformed workers' state, or whether it was 'really existing socialism', and even longer debating the term 'proletarian' itself. In the chaos of struggle, it is standard practice to map the terrain of the battlefield and locate its borders and edges. When people's lives do not make sense within the hegemonic order, words will be invented. It is not a concession to some phantom of identity politics to embrace the language of the oppressed. It is not a concession to post-modernism or linguistic constructivism (the theory that language creates the material world) to use words that arise from worldly experience. In fact, doing so reflects a materialist approach to language.

II. What is capitalism?

One of my biggest challenges here is to describe the Marxist critique of political economy in a way that is clear without being reductive. My strategy is to outline the skeletal points of the Marxian view of capitalism as a system of social relations. There is considerable debate about what Marx intended (exacerbated by the fact that *Capital* was intended to be six volumes long but Marx died during the writing process), what Marx got wrong, what is a legitimate method to prove Marx right or wrong, and at what point abandoning or adding to Marx's ideas subverts Marx altogether.

This book rests on a number of propositions about capitalism, all derived from some of the least contentious elements of Marx's thought among Marxists:

1. capitalism is not a plutocratic conspiracy but an impersonal system – as a functioning whole, it is not immoral but rather

amoral or beyond morality since it is not a conscious entity –
and, because we are dealing with a process and not persons,
moral fist-shaking and appeals to capitalism for mercy have
been and will continue to be fruitless;

2. capitalism is not a broken system – on the contrary, it generally
functions in accordance with its own laws;

3. capitalism's optimal functioning entails the rational extraction
of profit from commodities – particularly commodified labor –
despite irrational consequences;

4. capitalist production processes are a threat to the global ecosystem and they immiserate the world's majority;[20]

5. crises are a general feature of capitalism but the presence of crises
never directly suggests that capitalism is collapsing or coming to
an end through purely mechanistic contradictions (see Henning
2014: 17–42; Kautsky 1910; Bernstein 1961)[21] – capitalism
can end only through intentional political intervention;[22]

6. capitalism should be supplanted via such an intentional political intervention.

The following is a brief sketch of the development of capitalism
out of feudalism, followed by the rudimentary tenets of Marxian
economics. Almost every statement that follows is subject to
scholarly debate, and references to these debates will appear in
the footnotes.

The origins of capitalism

Marx's *Capital* outlines the system of capitalist social relations,
showing that such a system is an entity that emerges dialectically
from European feudalism[23] and through its colonial expansion to
the so-called New World.[24] European colonization was, in part,
inspired by the hopes of finding precious metals (i.e. gold and
silver) that were already valuable on the existing world market

(Bozorgnia 1998) as well as locating a swifter route to Asia to facilitate trade. As with Columbus, whose original goal was to reach India, European colonizers were looking for a shortcut to reach *economically developed* Asian territories (Anievas and Nisancioglu 2013) in order to bypass the intercontinental network of trade routes over land that emerged after the Mongol invasion (see Abu-Lughod 1989: 352–72; for the impact on the theory of uneven and combined, see Anievas and Nisancioglu 2013). Several reasons have been argued for England's leap from relative under-development to becoming a fruitful location for the expansion of capitalism. The most commonly cited reason is the Enclosure movement, whereby emerging capitalists usurped land from the serfs (Marx 1978a: Vol. I, Chapter 27; Marx and Engels 1996) and created a class of landless people – proletarians – who were forced to survive by selling their labor. It has also been argued that England was ripe for capitalism to develop not because it was so developmentally forward, but because it was isolated as a result of the Habsburg Empire's preoccupation with the expansion of the Ottoman Empire (Anievas and Nisancioglu 2013: 92–7). Another reason proffered is that Europe was able to develop before Asia because more advanced regions, such as China (ibid.: 88), had been gutted in the Mongol invasion. So, it was not so much the specialness of the British themselves that led to the development of industry in Manchester, but rather a confluence of conditions born out of the effects of intercontinental relationships.[25]

The texture of life was transformed in the move from feudalism to capitalism. As we will see in the following chapters, this change in the mode of production transformed gender and sexual relations. Feudal society typically consisted of a patchwork of agricultural domains, each one controlled by a local lord and by a local church parish. Serfs – themselves divided into freemen, villeins (origin of villain), and cottagers – lived on and farmed their own land and also depended upon their access to the commons. Serfdom was hereditary and right of access to the homestead generally passed through descendants over the course of generations: since knowledge about paternity affected inheritance rights, control of sexuality – particularly women's sexuality – was a matter of survival within the social order for serfs as well as lords. Serfs were not paid arithmetic wages. In exchange for the right to exist, lords required that serfs hand over a fixed portion of their yield, or required them to work on the lord's private demesne for a fixed period of time. Outside this requirement, peasants generally produced material for their own sustenance at their own pace. Although the lord lived off serf labor, he had limited methods at his disposal to keep serfs in line: the lord did not own the land in a modern sense – before capitalism, land wasn't perceived to be a commodity – so neither eviction nor destitution was generally available as a motivational threat. Church ideology and direct violence were the most widely used means of social control.[26] Over the period of a few hundred years in England, with change accelerating and becoming normalized in the sixteenth century and continuing into the nineteenth century, the new class of 'townies' (the bourgeoisie) wrested much of the feudal land from the major landholders, the royals and the clergy. This coup was achieved politically by law, through the establishment of parliament, through theft and occupation, and through revolutionary upheaval.

The privatization and enclosure of the land robbed common people of their capacity for self-reliance: they no longer had access to their own land, nor access to the commons where they would pasture their animals and gather the wood and water necessary for survival (see Marx 1978a: Volume I, Chapter 27; Marx and Engels 1996). They were hence referred to as the proletariat, or 'propertyless people', those who did not own the means to reproduce their existence.[27] The lands they had tilled for centuries were transformed into pasture for wool production and fields for cash crops. With nowhere to turn, these former serfs, now the proletariat, had little choice but to go to the city to work in the newly emerging workshops and factories for something called *a wage*. Begging was also an option. For many, the choice of begging was preferable to the bizarre, claustrophobic world of factory labor. Refusal to work became such a problem that the first anti-vagrancy laws emerged in the form of England's Poor Laws.

The first step towards alienation under capitalism occurs when the peasant laborer's tribute to the local lord is replaced by the worker receiving a wage for their time. Marx emphasizes that the wage system is a social relation, one that hides expropriation beneath a veil of abstraction. Serfs had their own land and, while they were required to give a fraction of their labor, they knew precisely how much they were required to give to the lord and how much they were permitted to keep. But under the wage system, those ratios were impossible to fathom. The profits that owners amassed from proletarian labor were largely a mystery, as was the logic behind the amount returned in wages. Wages obscured exploitation, and therefore they also obscured social relations between the new order of master and servant, between the bourgeoisie and the proletariat. *Exploitation under capitalism is not the description of a negative emotion or a synonym for mistreatment; it is the fact of an economic ratio, one that is always in flux.* The distance between the terms of this ratio depends, in large part, on class struggle. This antagonism is not between a master and servant but between two free equals in the marketplace: those free to sell their labor and those free to buy it.[28] By agreeing with free market proponents that wage laborers were free and equal to their bosses Marx exposed the emptiness of terms such as 'freedom' and 'equality' when divorced from a sense of material justice. (The insistence that freedom equality and justice' only have meaning in context has been a critical feature of second-wave and third-wave feminist thought as well.)

While waged exploitation led to alienation for the incipient proletariat, a new type of madness arose from the commodification of goods: unlimited wealth (Marx 1978a: Volume I, Chapter 4; Marx and Engels 1996). No doubt, royals and emperors had demanded the fruits of others' labor since the dawn of civilization. But the profit system changed the meaning of accumulation. In earlier modes of production, wealth could be vast but it was always limited. For example, a king or lord might demand that a peasant give him a hundred turnips, or a thousand turnips, or even ten thousand turnips; however, the limit of a king's demand for turnips was the high-water mark of use value. The idea of a hundred million turnips, or a billion turnips, would have been absurd. Not so under capitalism. Extracting a profit of ten million is wonderful, but extracting ten billion is always better, but never as good as a hundred billion. It was the number that suddenly mattered, not the noun. Production was now developed with exchange value in mind. The bottom line purpose of the production of any particular commodity was no longer its use. The new bottom line was profit.

The basics of capitalist exchange

The philosophers of the Enlightenment, like the Western philosophers who came before them, pondered the human condition as an unchanging truth. Philosophy's abstract human was outside history and (perhaps with an exception for Plato) always imagined as a freeborn male. Enlightenment philosophers, continuing their disregard for context and history, projected Man into an imaginary apolitical past using thought experiments styled after Defoe's novel *Robinson Crusoe*. Since the titular protagonist figures out how to survive from scratch in isolation from other humans, classical (and now neoclassical) economists treat the book as if it were an example of foundational economic processes: if you want to understand economics, imagine a solitary man on an island trying to produce the requirements for his existence. Marx considered such 'Robinsonades' to be both ridiculous and thoroughly useless for explaining the mechanisms of capitalist development. Robinson Crusoe economics were little more than bourgeois academics imagining themselves to be ingenious, self-made men. From a Marxian perspective, Robinson Crusoe microeconomic models fail on a number of points. The whole of any economic system is not the sum of its parts. In this case, the world is not composed of seven billion protagonists, each living on their own desert island, laboring for their own personal sustenance with open access to natural resources (Marx 1993: Introduction; cf. Marx 1978a: Volume I, Chapter 1, Section 4; Marx and Engels 1996). Not only does the model fail to grasp how quantity transforms quality, it imagines that individuals can be plucked from the market economy and imagined as stable abstractions. Nor is it a problem for classical and neoclassical models of economics that the character Crusoe, the prototype of Economic Man, was a slaver who went on to occupy 'cannibal territory', later Christianizing one of his victims into a personal servant. The influence of Robinson Crusoe is a reminder that colonization as a process is not separable from the early development of capitalism.

The economic model of the Robinsonade is a romanticized version of barter, the direct exchange of commodities for other commodities. Marx formulated this economic model as commodity exchanged for commodity, in code, as a C–C relation. But Marx noted that pure barter economies were untenable. Say I have a thousand turnips and you have forty chickens. I want forty chickens but you can't stand turnips. You want an ox. I don't have an ox. My neighbor has an ox, but they don't want turnips either. They want ten woolen coats. Due to the unwieldiness of the barter system, money developed early on as a mediating abstraction. Marx formulates this social relation by the syllogism C–M–C, which translates as 'commodities are exchanged for a special commodity called the money commodity, which is then exchanged for different commodities'. This manner of exchange is the logic under which most people live their lives. But Marx shows that capitalists operate under a different logic. The capitalist does not exchange one commodity for the money to buy another, but advances his money to buy commodities in order to get more money. This is the logic of the M–C–M' (M–C–M prime) formula.

The existence of this simple economic inversion transformed the material organization of human life. In each formula (C–M–C or M–C–M'), the middle term is just a means to an end. In the life of working people living in the C–M–C circuit, money is the 'vanishing mediator', the thing that has no intrinsic value in itself but that exists only as a means to an end. In the C–M–C worldview, a person sells their labor power, gets a paycheck, and buys sustenance for themselves and their loved ones. If the same person's paycheck disappeared but they still had the same access to goods as before, the loss of money would mean little. Money is just a way to get the stuff you need. A capitalist, however, is defined as someone who takes the money and buys 'stuff' (i.e. widgets, oranges, labor power, narcotics, weapons, children, etc.) for the purpose of getting more money. Here, *the commodities are the vanishing mediator with no intrinsic value*. To capitalists, commodities exist primarily for exchange value, for their capacity to yield more money, money that will be used as *new capital*. The use value of a commodity, in itself, is of no systemic interest. This is how an individual capitalist grows their wealth. Such unlimited growth is historically unprecedented. Who creates this wealth and who collects it becomes the story of modern social relations.

The extraction of surplus value

The individual of the Robinsonade is still in many ways the subject of neoclassical economists.[29] His individual consciousness is thought to be the engine of the economy. While labor was considered the source of value for classical economists (such as Adam Smith and David Ricardo), contemporary neoclassical economists do not locate the value of commodities in the labor time socially necessary to produce them. Instead, they locate *price fluctuations* in commodities based upon supply and demand; the idea that commodities have value is considered apocryphal. This position makes psychological sense, since commodities have no inherent meaning for capitalists: they signify only the possibility of profit. Skepticism about value is a defining feature of neoclassical models of economics; it is also a feature of the various post-Marxisms[30] that undergird queer theory's anarcho-liberal intellectual milieu. Some Marxist thinkers themselves began to take on neoclassical ideas when they embraced theories of monopoly capitalism.[31]

Marx never argued that supply and demand were absolutely irrelevant to economic theory; he argued that supply and demand could not explain economic growth. If supply and demand were relied upon as the engine of growth, the system could not expand: capitalism would be a zero-sum game (Marx, *Value, Price and Profit* in Marx and Engels 1985: 101–49; 1996; 1997; Marx 1978a: Volume I, Chapter 25; Volume II, Chapter 4). For Marx, labor is a special commodity in that it generates the value of other commodities. Workers are hired to either bring forth or create all commodities, including the machines that produce objects and the factories that produce the machines that produce objects. Because capitalists are competing with other capitalists, they do not necessarily profit from sticking a high price tag on commodities; their prices, generally speaking, must trend down. This means that, to maximize profit, the costs of the commodities used to make other commodities should be as low as possible per unit, which in turn reinforces the necessity of low prices. Whereas dead labor – i.e. machines (which are produced by living labor) – distributes into each commodified unit an irreducible amount of its cost, living labor, because it is waged and not bought outright, can be forced to work longer and faster for less, reducing the cost of each widget produced. The limit to the reduction of living labor costs is the minimum required to keep the worker's body and mind on task.[32] The drive to lower the cost of labor – i.e. the cheapening of human life – has immense effects on the production of social gender. Unwaged childcare and eldercare, often provided by women, keep labor costs low. In this way, surplus value – value that labor has created beyond its own recompense – comprises the time and effort donated by workers to those who hire them. From this surplus value, profit is derived. This is the 'more money' part of the M–C–M' economic perspective. Money is spent to buy labor for the purpose of making more money. Capitalism benefits from such uncompensated labor, as the free care that maintains families and individuals before and after they are able to work keeps capitalists' profits high.[33] Moreover, contradictory forces are at work since new machines make short-term gain possible but lower the *rate* of profit in the long term because of the reduction of living labor in the labor process.[34]

Marx noted that there have generally been two ways for capitalists to extract profit from labor: absolute surplus value and relative surplus value. Absolute surplus value is extracted through the extension of the working day. If workers produce one thousand widgets per hour, five additional hours of labor per day gives the capitalist five thousand more widgets per day, giving them more units to sell, an increased capacity to drive prices down to gain market share, and a lower cost of dead labor per unit by keeping the machines running. To access relative surplus value (surplus value relative to other capitalists), a capitalist calculates the *abstract labor* of the output of his workforce compared with the workforce of the competition, then either makes workers produce faster than the competition or pays a lower wage to gain an advantage. A capitalist might also accelerate production by investing in new machinery before other capitalists do. For this particular capitalist, it is a short-term windfall, as machinery systemically slows the rate of profit over time.[35] Lower prices lower the cost of living, and this lowers the cost of the labor commodity itself.

But isn't the workforce the consumer base for a lot of these commodities? If their wages drop but prices don't, wouldn't consumption also drop? Aren't industrial capitalists, as a group, not just consumers of luxury goods but also consumers of the raw materials and machinery needed for their factories? Doesn't the short-term gain of one sector (offshore drilling in the Gulf of Mexico or American corn crops, for example) affect the long-term disadvantage of others (oyster harvesting in the Gulf of Mexico or Mexican corn crops)? The answer to all these questions is yes. Since commodities are produced as quickly as possible to reduce unit costs, under-consumption of a commodity or set of commodities can reduce the volume of production, which reduces the consumption of commodities used by the factories involved (called 'productive consumption'), which in turn affects the profits in those sectors. When factories go under, they are cannibalized by remaining industries; this produces a glut of used machinery and a slowdown in the production of heavy machinery.[36] Once the bust cycle begins, profitability must be restored, and this is done through absolute and relative surplus value extraction from labor: in short, during these periods, workers work harder and receive less. And when the pressure is ratcheted up on working people, the anxieties and pressures are not gender neutral: more work means less time for childcare and eldercare, and workers fall under more pressure to conform to (cis)gendered expectations in the labor market.

The goal of this rather crude economic summary is not to argue the finer points of Marxian economic thought but to give a reasonable overview so that readers interested in feminist, queer, and trans politics can make sense of the discussions about gender and economics in Chapter 2.

III. Philosophy and the Marxian roots of queer political thought

Once upon a time, political economy was a subject embraced by philosophy. But Marx's ideas threw classical political economy into crisis: not because Marx disagreed with Smith and Ricardo, but because he used their key ideas (such as the labor theory of value and the equality between exploiter and exploited) to undermine their assertions. His affirmations of their analyses were, in fact, refutations of their arguments: yes, labor was the source of value in the system, but not only did the system fail to result in *universal opulence*, as Smith imagined, it clearly produced an antagonism between the new variety of master and servant. The bourgeois intellectual desire to sidestep Marx's criticism of capitalism led to what Christoph Henning terms 'Marx avoidance' in academia. In order to avoid Marx, the intellectual world had to separate economics from sociology, sociology from economics, and both from philosophy (Henning 2014). This mechanical separation of the disciplines cleansed social philosophy from having to analyze the manufacturing and distribution of goods – such mathematical drudgery was for the new professional economists. And philosophy and sociology became disciplines in which tracking commodity manufacture and circulation was outside disciplinary bounds – requiring calculations beyond the ken of a mere philosopher or sociologist.

If Marx's object of study is society itself, as Henning suggests, then the cost of Marx avoidance is the destruction of society as an object of inquiry. Society becomes something layered on top of economics, rather than constituted from it. Social activity and the laws of motion become hopelessly detached spheres (ibid.). This post-Marxian thinking splits the world into binaries – humanity versus the environment, the sociopolitical versus the economic, the Idea versus The World. Such thinking reaffirms Cartesian dualism, where mind and body are separate substances that cannot be reconciled. Insofar as queer theory and other poststructuralist disciplines partake in this split by avoiding economic analysis, they actually reinforce the Cartesian thinking they claim to reject as a Western excrescence. However, in some respects, queer theory is a response to – and even a transformation of – the intellectual heritage of Hegelian variants of Marxism; so, the two conceptual paths are bound together through both real-world political activities and the history of philosophy.

Marx and philosophy

Greek materialist thought was Marx's original scholarly focus;[37] later, he would become influenced by Ludwig Feuerbach, who argued that the divine was a projection of externalized human qualities. However, Marx and his co-author Engels considered Feuerbach's materialism to be too static to properly explain how the world worked. For this, they turned to Hegel's dialectics, which described the world as a process of unfolding. The concept of dialectics is by no means specific to Western philosophy,[38] but Hegel was influenced by the pre-Socratic philosopher Heraclitus, who saw the universe as a flowing river, as an ever-changing flame and an ongoing struggle. Heraclitus's dialectical conception of the world was criticized by another pre-Socratic philosopher, Parmenides, and his student, Zeno, who argued that the world was eternal and unchanging and that the feeling of motion was an illusion.[39] Both pre-Socratic philosophers influenced Plato, who saw Socratic dialogue as a form of dialectical movement towards Truth. Hegel's philosophy understood history as a metaphysics, as an Absolute Idea unfolding through conceptual antagonisms reconciling themselves; this reconcilement was not a matter of merger and compromise, but *sublation*, a decisive victory in which the idea of the world moves to a more advanced level. Whereas

Plato understood dialectic as a dialogue, as philosophical intercourse uncovering the truth about an eternal world and moving thought to a more advanced level, Hegel's dialectic, like Heraclitus's, occurred through a vital unfolding.

Debates about dialectics are beyond the scope of this book, but I choose to give an overview of the term because it is useful for understanding both Marx and the influence of Hegel on queer theory. Also, the dialectic is less complicated than it sounds.[40] Whether or not one treats dialectics as an ontological process or as an intellectual process within a complex and changing universe, dialectics corrects the empiricist error of treating every object as if it were a fractal, as if discrete aspects of a phenomenon's unfolding could represent the whole. In the language of informal logic, it protects against the fallacy of composition where qualities belonging to only the parts of a thing are mistakenly attributed to the whole. Henning (although he is thoroughly anti-Hegelian and considers dialectics mystical) explains this error as two people arguing about a car indicator light with one insisting that the light is off and the other that the light is on. Both positions are nonsensical because the object of inquiry is only understood in duration, in its motion (ibid.). Moreover, unlike the blinking light, as day turns to night turns to day, the second day is not a return back to or a repetition of the first day; it is a new day, a return to daylight at a more advanced stage in the calendar. The Romantic poet William Blake's *Songs of Innocence and of Experience* describes another dialectical motion: there is innocence, then experience, then innocence after experience – a return to innocence. Dialectics implies that historical time moves in one direction, that it is never possible to reverse its course towards an earlier stage of history. Hegelian dialecticians imagine the world moves in a spiral formation: what might look like a return is actually an advance – like starting at the beginning of a higher level of a video game. When I use the term, I will generally be indicating that we have arrived at a point where I feel that it is important to look at the big picture and to consider antagonisms within situations, and/or that the long-term unfolding of an event is not reducible to any one moment within that unfolding. The opposite of dialectical is eternal and ahistorical (the term 'natural' also often signifies ahistorical).

Marx is an epistemological realist – he believes that the world exists independently of the human mind, that the world is not just an idea or a spirit unfolding, that the world is material and not a reflection of ideas. As a consequence, this worldview asserts that antagonisms happen in the real, material world and therefore that change happens in reality. This does not mean, however, that Marx operates as a *naïve realist* – as someone who believes that our senses present us with perfectly reliable knowledge about the world. In fact, scientific thinking implies that there is a gap between truth and appearance. For example, even though it feels like the earth is still, we are actually moving at a thousand miles per hour. Our ability to acquire knowledge is always checked by our limited vision, our imperfect attention, and the fact that material existence is always in flux. To this, Marx adds a new social element to the critique of naïve realism: perception is perspectival.[41] Not only is the world filled with appearances, which require reason to determine their truth or falsity, but what one knows about the world is conditioned by one's position within social relations: different classes have different experiences within the totality of such relations. In this sense, Marx is a critical precursor of standpoint epistemology, the latter being a cornerstone of the feminist critique of Enlightenment rationalism. So, Marxian thought is not expressing some mystical totalitarian togetherness where all difference is absorbed into the One. Totality for Marx is a recognition that the world functions as a system of internal connections and processes. Meaning is not static – what is sold today as a work shoe might be a child's toy tomorrow, a doorstop the next day, and part of a sculpture in a museum the day after that. Likewise, yesterday's peasant may be today's proletarian, who aspires to be tomorrow's petit bourgeois. A commodity moving within the C–M–C circuit has a different existence compared with one in the M–C–M' circuit. This does not mean that the commodity has changed metaphysically. Rather, the same object in a different context is perceived differently, used differently, and is shaped by history in different ways, leading to different outcomes. If two children, one poor and one rich, are switched at birth, their future selves will not be identical with who they would have been had they not been switched. Their lives will be shaped by their experiences. There are no reasonable grounds for imagining that gender, sex, and sexuality should remain some sort of primordial, spiritual truth. A change in the mode of production will produce fundamental changes in people's lives – including changes in gendered bodies. The world changes and we change with it. In this way, Marxist standpoint epistemology *does not* collapse into identity politics.

Marxist standpoint epistemology is not grounded in identity; it is grounded in position. The Marxist subject, class, is a fluid aggregate of persons existing globally, across cultures and genders. In most regions, people are declassed and re-classed – for example, moving from the peasantry to industrial work, and back to peasant life. Relying upon waged labor for survival defines one as a worker; however, in political terms, the class itself is the broader section of the population supported by working people, including the elderly, the young, and unemployed adults. The unemployed[42] are also operationally within the working class because they serve as a destabilizing force. To be clear: I am not implying that the unemployed are 'unstable' as people. They are simply workers intentionally positioned within the system to politically weaken the labor force through structural unemployment. Racism, traditional sexism, and oppositional sexism[43] function to reinforce Adam Smith's moral mythology that capitalism is a system in which the good and strong produce wonders and the lazy and weak feed off them. Building this morality into stable identities splits the working class into hostile segments that can be pitted against one another. But people cannot be reduced to some sedimentary mass of permanent characteristics that shape a fixed understanding of the world. Just as money serves as a form of payment for those in the C–M–C circuit and as capital for someone in the M–C–M' circuit, people are neither self-made individuals nor reflections of a cultural collective spirit, nor reducible to permanent 'things', but conscious points moving and changing within a system.

Epistemology revisited

Where Marxist and feminist epistemological commitments differ noticeably is in: 1) their opinions about the role of phenomenology; and 2) their thoughts on the existence of objective truths. Cultural feminists argue that science lacks insight into lived phenomena; it cannot see or know what the individual body sees and knows. The objective analyses offered by Marxist theory assume a gap between truth and appearance, but this is not necessarily at odds with feminist epistemology. The idea that the masses suffer from false consciousness is not part of Marx's own work.[44] The proletariat is systematically alienated from the material world it produces and working-class people are intentionally misinformed by the ruling classes and often blocked from access to genuine education, but there is no sense in Marx that working people necessarily *misinterpret* their *own* experience due to a false understanding of themselves. The gap between truth and appearance is a matter of social science; it does not occur at the level of individual consciousness.

In Western feminist thought, however, patriarchal ideology misshapes women's own relationship to their bodies and identities; this creates a rupture in women's experience of their own psyches. In fact, without the concept of false consciousness, it is difficult to explain how women inculcate gender expectations, body anxiety, and sexual shame in other women. Feminism outside the Euro-American context is often less interested in false consciousness and more geared towards collective action involving concrete demands – be it striking home-based women workers in Pakistan, the Maquila Solidarity Network, Mothers of the Plaza de Mayo in Argentina, media women's alliances in Uganda and Tanzania, or anti-rape organizing in India. For Western feminists, truth emerges at a personal level when false consciousness gives way to a correct understanding of one's self-worth. Science – the usual method of confronting appearances that defy reality – has little to offer the pursuit of the feeling that one has an authentic self. In fact, because it developed alongside industry, science has been misused to marginalize the experience of women and is viewed by cultural feminism as a tool of patriarchy. It is true that, throughout the world, women are treated as if they exist in a combative relationship with truth: women do not say what they mean, women are irrational, women are superficial, women are superstitious and easily duped by appearance. Alternatively, women's irrationality is imagined as providing them with terrifying powers and forbidden knowledge in the form of witchcraft (Federici 2003). But, generally speaking, women are perceived as failing to understand not only the world around them, but also their own intentions and experiences. Traditional sexism insists that women are stupid, childish creatures; feminism – particularly second-wave cultural feminism – argues that traditional sexism operates as a false consciousness that makes women ignorant about their true selves. This has led to the particularly unhelpful creation of the image of the 'female chauvinist pig' (Levy 2005), whereby 'false-conscious' women are characterized as an enemy that is simultaneously pathetic and sinister. Of course, such female chauvinist pigs are notable for their collusion with the cosmetics industry, fashion industry, and sex industry (through their consumption of products or through their labor), and, apparently, only more misogyny can combat this fifth column. But it is not only feminists who are concerned with women's 'false consciousness'. The image of the dreaded childlike dupe, the working-class high femme, has sometimes found her way into the imagination of the American Marxist left as well.[45]

The debate as to whether or not women can be trusted with their own self-perception takes an enormous toll on women's health. Women are medically misdiagnosed because their symptoms are dismissed or ignored. While a woman's words are considered particularly unreliable, her body is said to speak volumes but in poetic language.[46] This is, in part, why the idea of sexual consent is treated with so much suspicion despite superficial political support. If a man says that a woman has consented to sex and a woman says that she did not consent, it is a considered a toss-up as to who is telling the truth about what she wanted at the time. There are two ways to look at this: either she is an irrational child-fool incapable of knowing at any given moment what she wants (in this scenario consent is impossible) or she is vindictive and evil (in this scenario consent is a trap). This objectifying and infantilizing also forms the core of *transmisogyny*, which affects both trans women and people who fall along the transmasculine spectrum. It is no wonder why feminists are skeptical about claims of objective knowledge, no wonder why there is a call to validate truth claims based on articulations of women and gender non-conforming people's experience.

But we should distinguish between two subtle meanings of the word 'objective' here, although the two are closely related. In one sense, objective means the knowledge of objects and conditions that can be gleaned in a way that does not depend on personal experience: for example, we can have only objective knowledge of the sun's dimensions. This is rational objectivity. The other meaning of objective is the capability of knowing an answer to something – i.e. *judging* – without resorting to personal bias. Let's call this the claim to interpersonal objectivity. When a doctor fails to properly interpret a woman's[47] medical symptoms, it is not because the doctor is blinded by scientific objectivity; in fact, the doctor is being absolutely unscientific when engaging in such behaviors. It is scientific objectivity itself that is being blocked by the failure of interpersonal objectivity. When someone seeks help from medical professionals, they are hoping for relief based on objective, scientific answers: t-cell counts, the size and shape of platelets, the presence of leukocytes, the absence of cancerous cells. When a woman's voice is silenced by medical professionals, the problem is not that the woman wanted someone to affirm her feelings; the problem is that she has been denied access to medical care. Trans patients, generally speaking, have an even greater difficulty obtaining appropriate healthcare than cis women. Sexual assault prosecution is often plagued by the reverse problem: objectivity – both interpersonal and scientific – is used to reject the subjective claim of non-consent. Demanding evidence of non-consent is absurd. It either requires the violation of consent to coincide with assault or requires that the victim's character be put on trial.

Global economics, on the other hand, is understood only through scientific objectivity. It is impossible to understand global economics *solely* by patching together one's own experience. One might intimately know the hardships of unemployment or have witnessed the bizarre behavior of the filthy rich, but one cannot gather from perception alone the macroeconomic movement behind these phenomena. This is why Marx referred to his project as scientific. Not because he was trying to swap Hegelian metaphysics for scientific experiment, but because his project consisted of going beyond appearances in order to understand the processes beneath the surface. The world is more than what we experience, though not in a mystical sense. Scientific objectivity does not undermine the value of subjectivity; by definition, it aims to discern what we cannot know from pure experience. But this does not discredit experience. It only limits its claims. If knowledge is limited to personal – or even collective – experience, we can know nothing outside human consciousness.

Changing words or changing worlds?

Whether Marx is a philosopher, political economist, or dialectician is another matter that is contested by both Marxists and anti-Marxists. The reason for this ambivalence is Marx's critical stance towards philosophy, political economy, and idealist dialectics. Although Marx's thought was inspired by Hegel's method, Marx was not a Hegelian; he was a *critic* of both the Hegelian dialectic and Hegel's followers. He studied philosophy but ultimately criticized it, particularly German philosophy, for its detachment from real life. And while Marx intended to write six books on capitalism (he finished one – the other two were cobbled together posthumously), he called his work not political economy but a *critique* of political economy. There have been extensive attempts to purge Marx of any trace of Hegel,[48] while others have worked to draw out the Hegelian legacy in Marx's work.[49]

The discussion of whether or not Hegel influences Marx is not just philosophical squabbling; it's a debate about how change happens – and processes of social change are hardly irrelevant to socialist and internationalist politics in general, or to queer, trans, and feminist politics in particular. Theoretical discussions about change are politically meaningless only when they are divorced from the world, when they float above real political activity and the material conditions of life. Dismissing theory in favor of pure practice, in the expectation of spontaneous social transformation or with the idea that feelings of human connectivity will triumph over 'difference', is as chiliastic and mystical as it is anti-intellectual. When the middle and upper classes make accusations that working people cannot understand theory, this is only an expression of their own arrogance. For hundreds of years, workers have been engaged in debates over the opaque poetics of the Bible and the Koran, but for some reason discussing cause and effect is simply beyond regular folk! The argument that working people are patently uninterested in theoretical matters reflects a metaphysical and moral understanding of class in which class position is imagined to be determined by the inherent characteristics of individuals. The belief that regular people have the capacity for superior reasoning and political wisdom is what drives Antonio Gramsci's argument for the primacy of organic intellectuals – intellectuals who emerge from within a struggle grounded in real life. Such organic intellectuals synthesize their experience of social conditions with rational objectivity, and they can articulate this synthesis to a broader audience. Organic intellectuals can integrate subjective and objective knowledge in such a way that knowledge is both produced and transmitted.

So, the relation between subjects and objects has real stakes. Another way to put this is: who or what is the agent of change in a situation (the political subject)? Who or what is being changed (the political object)? And what is the relation between the two? One concrete application of this is the question: 'Can people intentionally change the world?' If the answer is yes, other questions emerge: for example, does the exchange of ideas itself change the world or is intentional action upon the world required? Lastly, if people (subjects) can change the world (objects), does the fact that people are also part of the world (all subjects are also objects) affect what is politically possible?

Before Hegel, Kant argued that the actual objects of the world were beyond human thought, that all we could know about objects was our sense perceptions of them and our rational capacity to order those perceptions: the objects themselves were beyond our knowledge. This articulation of subject–object relations sees an unbridgeable rift between human understanding and the things understood, as if we are each surrounded by an invisible force field, unable to really touch the world. One implication of this is that knowledge of an object does not change that object. I can know about the sun without changing the sun. I can know about a person's existence without it affecting the person. Hegel criticized Kant's subject–object split and suggested that subjects and their objects form a unity. In this conception of subject–object relations, subjects *can* affect objects – people can change the world, not just their impressions of the world, because there is a unity at work. For example, public knowledge that someone is a criminal affects the criminal's capacity to act even if no other action is taken against them. But the collapse of knowing and being also implies that our assessment of a situation will be muddled; this is because, when we remove conceptual distance between subjects and objects, objectivity disappears. When objectivity disappears, sometimes knowledge is mistaken for change. Economic problems are a good example: if everyone in a city is aware of the city's rates of child poverty, does that knowledge in itself change the situation? If everyone in a city is aware that a river is being polluted, does such knowledge change the river? The lack of conceptual distance between subject and object does not necessarily mean intimacy or awareness. It can also mean cognitive dissonance or obliviousness. A drought's effect on a lake often makes a greater impression on someone who passes by once a year than someone who passes it each day.

The difference between these two ways of imagining human knowledge has surprising meaning for political organization. Aside from the fact that if Kant's epistemology is correct we cannot really ever know for certain (beyond our organs of perception) that the material world is affected by our actions, Kant's model gives us the requisite distance to observe a situation. Hegelian unity leads to a collapse of distance between subject and object, which means that we are both that which transforms and that which is to be transformed. In this model, analysis itself has the capacity to change the world. But this can easily devolve into the political belief that you can 'be the change you want to see in the world' – that by changing yourself, you change the world. Becoming aware becomes a political act in itself. Changing language changes the world.

Both models lend themselves to political individualism, but in different ways. Marx rejects Kant's denial of certainty about objective reality and, of course, the ultimate authority he affords the autonomous individual mind. But Marx also rejects Hegelianisms that confuse a change in consciousness with actual change. He criticizes political activists who focus on fighting language with new language, noting that they change only the phrases of the world, not the world itself.[50] Against both Kant and Hegel, Marx famously asserts that philosophers have only interpreted the world when the point is to change it (Marx 1978d). The stakes for gender politics should be immediately recognizable. In the media-saturated regions of the global North, the fight to change the language about and representations of women, queers, trans people, and colonized populations has nearly trumped all other political aspirations (see 'The queer Marxist critique of postcolonialism' in Chapter 3). This certainly does not mean that Marx would consider language irrelevant to material social relations. Declarations, in the sense used by J. L. Austin (1975),[51] are linguistic acts with real-world consequences: pronouncing someone 'guilty', signing a contract, and designating a gender marker on an ID are examples of such language. But to argue that changing how people think about the world is a recipe for changing the world gives us a politics where problems are solved through awareness of those problems. Politics no longer constitutes political action, but political thinking. A global network of performance artists decrying capitalism on street corners becomes equal in political weight to the organization of a mass strike. But the reason why the mass strike is a more effective tactic is material: the latter stops profit flows.

The political subject/object question boils down to defining political problems, what needs to be done about them, who can do the doing, and to what extent the doers should do what needs to be done. The banality 'we can all make the world a better place' is seriously obscurantist despite its simple language. Is change made by the people who suffer under the current conditions, those who do not suffer, or those who actually cause the suffering? And does it matter who makes political change, so long as change occurs? What constitutes changing the world for the better? Do small changes lead to larger social transformations, or do they prevent them? One's answer to the question of who should have political agency generally hinges upon one's ideas about the meaning and value of the experience of struggle. Does the experience of struggle make a political subject 'fit to rule'?[52] Is solidarity a precursor to struggle, or is solidarity forged in struggle when disparate groups unite around common interests (see Marx 1973)?[53] Is a subject's location within capitalist production strategically important (as in a strike) or does the election of candidates representing one's interests suffice? Is a therapeutic environment or 'safe space' necessary for or a barrier to creating change? Who, if anyone, is excluded from a struggle and by what criteria?[54] Finally, is 'political subject' a legitimate category[55] or are we not so much a collection of rational individuals as networked flows of being (Deleuze and Guattari 1987)? Answers to the above questions determine one's position on political reforms and how they relate to revolutionary change.

Marx was a realist and a materialist who approached the world as if it could be changed directly; however, unlike the utopian socialists (see 'Sex and the utopian socialists' in Chapter 2), he insisted that social change did not happen through the readers of political tracts implementing the ideas baked into utopian fiction – amorous armies, and seas turned to lemonade (Fourier 1996).[56] Change happens, but only out of the possibilities contained within the real situation at hand. People are in a metabolic relation with the world and with one another: we are both subjects and objects, but subjects who can act and be acted upon. To change the way we think about the material world cannot in itself change the material world, and history is not a conscious entity forging its own course: there are no transcendental gods or spirits, no *élan vital* driving social change. History is simply the name for the material legacy of struggle. How working people would fight and win was not something Marx addressed substantially – and intentionally so. The materialist outlook is inappropriate for making tactical recommendations for future material conditions. This is a sensible omission, but an omission that made the practical success of Marxist theory contingent upon the activity and ideas of future Marxists. This battle for hegemony among future Marxists shaped twentieth-century global politics, and that includes gender politics.

The separation of politics and economics

For Marx, humanity acts upon and transforms the world but is also transformed by it. This understanding of the human metabolic relation to the world is distinct from Enlightenment philosophy's preoccupation with (individual) Man's capacity for reason and the tendency to imagine human rationality as an entity floating above the baseness of nature. The conception of a metabolic relation between humans and the environment assumes that people are part of the active content of the world, not sculptors imposing form on whatever content they happen upon. But despite Marx's break from Enlightenment individualism, twentieth-century critics associated him with a myopic scientism. Marx was at once identified as a masculinist Enlightenment humanist and an inhuman pro-industrialist. While critics of the Enlightenment opposed Marx's supposed scientism, inheritors of the Enlightenment tradition, particularly in American academic life, criticized Marx as utterly unscientific, the progenitor of political hysterics born from Hegelian irrationalism.

The problem is, in part, that critics conflate Marx with subsequent political movements claiming Marxist roots. But if one dismisses Marx because one rejects political movements that claim Marxist roots, one is unable to assess whether or not those movements actually reflect Marx's ideas in the first place. This circular reasoning leads Western intellectuals (Henning 2014) into an even more overreaching and sloppy gesture: the rejection of Marx as a 'totalitarian' thinker, perhaps even spiritually akin to fascists. Here, because Marx critiqued epistemological individualism, any politics that puts the collective above the individual would be considered a variant of Marxism, whether or not the notion related to Marx's actual economic critique. Later, this motivated Western Marxists to attempt to 'rescue' Marx by rethinking his work.[57]

Christoph Henning makes a compelling case that anxiety over the interpretation of Marx's work began immediately after his death, compounded by the distortions resulting from the German Social Democratic Party's (SPD's) need to polemicize and popularize his economic theory (ibid.: Chapter 2, 'A Genealogy of Misconceptions', particularly pp. 17–42). Marx was no stranger to criticizing the party (Marx and Engels 1989: 75–99) or intervening in its affairs. The SPD was the largest and most influential socialist party of the late nineteenth century, and was therefore an automatic heir to Marx's work. Henning traces the matrix of errors attributed to Marx to the influential Erfurt Program (Kautsky 1910), which was developed by the leading theorists of the SPD, Karl Kautsky and Eduard Bernstein, after the repeal of the anti-socialist laws in Germany.

Henning argues that the Erfurt Program simplifies the ideas found in *Capital*, but instead of being understood as a pragmatic party-building polemic, its rhetoric came to be treated as an instance of theory in practice. Because it needed to connect Marx's theory to the political moment, it reduced what *Capital* describes as complex processes and general tendencies into crude empirical claims that could lend the program a sense of urgency (for more, see Henning 2014: 41–3). Henning gives this example of the slippage: the declassing of small craft labor into proletarian labor is a *general tendency* in Marx, not an iron-clad rule that suggests that one will always and everywhere see a mass exodus from the middle classes to the working classes. A general tendency only unfolds over time. It is not something present at every instant that can be relied upon to build political rhetoric. Nor can one claim that a theory is invalid simply because there are counterbalancing forces at work. Henning uses another metaphor to describe this: the existence of butterflies does not refute gravity. But, unable to account for the failed predictions of the Erfurt Program, Eduard Bernstein decided that *Marx himself* was to blame. He revised Marx's work (Bernstein 1961). This analysis would become the foundation of what came to be known as *revisionism*. So, in *Evolutionary Socialism*, Bernstein claims to refute Marx by refuting the Erfurt Program; this is not Bernstein refuting Marx, but refuting *his own* earlier distortion of Marx's ideas (Henning 2014).

The Erfurt Program had presented a rather apocalyptic vision: capitalism was causing and would continue to cause a rapid economic decline among the German working and middle classes. Bernstein revised his earlier Erfurt arguments with new arguments based on a new *empirical* reading of *Capital*: he insisted that not only would there not be a revolutionary transformation of capitalism into socialism, but that capitalism had overcome its crises, that it would all be smooth sailing from here on, and that capitalism would evolve into socialism bit by bit, reform by reform. Bernstein famously argued that the end of working-class organizing means nothing and that the movement is everything. And so Immanuel Kant replaces Marx.

Bernstein's revisionism caused an uproar in the SPD. Stalwarts joined Karl Kautsky and rallied round the Erfurt Program as if saving it meant saving Marxism itself. By doing so, Kautsky doubled down on the legitimacy of Erfurt, including its naturalism, determinism, and implied predictions (Henning 2014: 41–52). This positivist, teleological Marxism used Engels' *Dialectics of Nature* (Marx and Engels 1987a: 313–58) to interpret Marx's materialist critique of Hegel literally: revolution would unfold from the laws of nature itself. Kautsky's side of the debate would come to be known as *orthodox Marxism*. The spat between the two teleological interpretations produced a mountain of political distortions, and both sides would be used to justify racist colonial expansion, which Marx quite clearly opposed (Anderson 2010). Such distortions ultimately led the members of the Second International to vote that socialist parties should back their respective nations in World War I. This, of course, contributed to the deaths of millions of workers and peasants and undermined the International itself.[58]

Predictions of working-class decline were not the Erfurt Program's only problem. Erfurt further confused the matter by combining revolutionary fervor with demands for modest reforms (including universal suffrage and the right to bear arms), none of which were clearly explained in terms of their relation to capitalism (Henning 2014: 23–9). Unfortunately, this is still common practice in the Marxist left today: groups and activists often polemically condemn a social ill as a product of capitalism without clearly explaining how capitalism produces it. For example, when Marxists connect the issue of gay rights to capitalism by simply highlighting the fact that modern industrial capitalism has facilitated the development of a gay identity[59] or reduce the problem of homophobia to its instrumental use by ruling classes, the explanation skirts any clear link between socialist economic change and the eradication of oppositional sexism. Lack of clarity negatively affects the development of political strategies, and it leaves people unconvinced about the value of the larger Marxist project in ending specific oppressions.

At the time of the Erfurt Program, linking social reform to the capitalist mode of production could not even be assumed since the state was a monarchy. In fact, there were, at certain points, even alliances between the Social Democrats and the monarchist state (ibid.: 37).

Marxism became, on the one hand, an ethos in search of normative foundations, and, on the other, a materialist version of millenarianism. Henning criticizes Lenin for compounding the matter by unnecessarily inventing a new phase of capitalism: monopoly capitalism (ibid.: 78–120). He argues that 'rethinking' capitalism as the product of national aggressions undermines the labor theory of value, the economic foundation of Marx's work. This debate often pivots around the role of capitalist accumulation.[60] Henning calls this shift away from understanding economics *the primacy of politics*, where politics and economics are conflated so that an ethicized 'political will' comes to trump economic analyses. The working class then becomes a spirit that can emerge triumphantly during any economic conditions, but this argument forgets that: 'Man makes history, but not under conditions of his own choosing' (Marx 1913).

This will-based Marxism comes to full fruition in the philosophical tradition of Western Marxism where György Lukács analyzes the notion of class consciousness, Jean-Paul Sartre isolates the politically committed existential subject, and Herbert Marcuse argues for a politics of refusal. Marcuse's Great Refusal (Marcuse 1964) in particular is a clear influence on queer theory's style of resistance politics. Bernstein's assertion that 'the movement is everything; the ends, nothing' takes form in queer theory's conception of politics as a critique of everyday life and a resistance to imposed norms, a conception that only glances at capitalism. So, the historical context of the emergence of queer politics and queer theory, along with the search for a foundation in normative ethics, is shaped by both capitalist development and the overall trend of Marxist politics in the West.

From Western Marxism to poststructuralism

Both queer theory and third-wave feminism developed from poststructuralist thought, which itself arose as a response to Western

Marxism's concern with the need to rethink twentieth-century politics. Western metaphysics (that is, philosophical debates about the form, shape, and movement of objects and existence itself) began with pre-Socratic, proto-scientific questioning. Plato followed by adding a social component to the ontological distinction between truth and appearances. Descartes brought the West into modernity by submitting medieval thinking to radical skepticism, stripping away all presuppositions and rebuilding knowledge on a stable axiom that would be paradoxical if it were not true. ('I think therefore I am' was what he came up with: an individual consciousness thinking about its existence must exist in order to think about itself.) From there, Descartes rebuilt the truth of the world based on proof of individual consciousness. It is easy to see how the Cartesian emphasis on the individual mind can be an asset to capitalism, which was still in its earliest stages during Descartes' life.

Since Descartes, philosophers have been mesmerized by subject–object relations: how do we know that what we are seeing is really there? How can we trust our senses? Phenomenology came along at the turn of the twentieth century and reacted to metaphysics with a shrug: so what if we can never perceive the 'real' thing? If we are looking at a cube and, outside collective perception, it is something other than an object made of connecting squares, who cares what it 'really' is as long as it is a stable object of our perception? Phenomenologists argued that reasoning through perception and experience is key to understanding. The argument is not that experience should be used to calculate what's 'really there', as the empiricists did, but that perception should be the center of philosophical inquiry. Although this position is anti-Cartesian in its rejection of metaphysics, it reasserts the individual mind at the center of knowledge. Phenomenology became the grounds for variants of standpoint epistemology: if a phenomenon seems real, then it is real enough. A Marxist vision of standpoint epistemology, on the other hand, does not privilege individual perception as the arbiter of reality.

Marx is not only criticized for trying to understand objective conditions, he is also criticized as a linear thinker for even imagining a historical process that moves from past to present. But it is no more possible to return to medieval feudalism than it is to return to yesterday. We can simulate medieval feudalism and we could even potentially arrive at social and material conditions that echoed earlier aspects of the feudal mode of production, but we cannot return to medieval feudalism because it has already been surpassed. It is one thing to say that historical return is impossible; it is quite another to say that forward motion entails inevitable improvement. Acknowledging the simplest facts of historical movement is not determinism or teleology.[61] Moreover, there is nothing 'linear' about trying to think about the interconnections of an entire system. There are no simplistic claims of cause-and-effect relationships in *Capital*; rather, there are considerations of how subjects and objects circulate within the whole. The fact that Marx is criticized for being at once linear and totalitarian shows the ideological nature of these dismissals. Looking at the world as a historically fluid totality does not entail forcing the whole of humanity into matching jumpsuits.[62]

The existentialist critique of orthodox Marxism

Existentialism, an offshoot of phenomenological thought, emerged, in part, as a response to the ethical crisis posed by the French capitulation to the Nazis. Building on the nineteenth-century ideas of Nietzsche and Kierkegaard, Jean-Paul Sartre challenged adherents to take responsibility for their destinies, to break from the herd, and to pursue freedom to the point of death. Existentialism shared phenomenology's disdain for metaphysics.[63] Its mantra *existence before essence* proposed that a radical human freedom was possible despite the fact that the world had no fundamental meaning and no telos. Existentialism would prove critical to Western feminism: Simone de Beauvoir's tome *The Second Sex* was the first philosophical work to treat the idea of Woman as a social creation. If Platonic or Aristotelian conceptions of essence were not the guarantor of meaning, then there was no such thing as an innate essence called Woman either – hence de Beauvoir's famous quote: 'One is not born, but rather becomes, a woman.' De Beauvoir was the first to separate gender from biology, but while she described womanhood as a historical, political phenomenon, the body became a dumb and meaningless thing. Although de Beauvoir's work is foundational to modern feminist philosophy, Descartes' mind/body split is still palpable throughout her work, and this dualism would be criticized by later feminists, especially third-wave feminists and queer poststructuralists.

Sartre's existentialism was grounded in Marxian commitments. He was a staunch critic of colonialism and of Soviet expansion, and a defender of the National Liberation Front in Algeria; he supported the Cuban revolution but strongly opposed Castro's persecution of gays. But Sartre's understanding of Marxism was hotly contested by classical Marxists,[64] in part because of the voluntarism that undergirded early existentialist thought. What changed the world according to Marx wasn't the moral decisions of individual minds but the intersection of historical-material circumstances and collective social action. Here we see evidence of Henning's criticism that post-Marxist philosophy's preoccupation with the moral constitution and right action of individuals over-rides an interest in the general movements of society and history. After Khrushchev's secret speech, Sartre published *Critique of Dialectical Reason* as a criticism of Soviet thought under Stalin; however, the book was also an attempt to bridge the gap between existentialist commitments and real conditions, between the human agency required by existentialism and Marx's emphasis on objective reality. Sartre tried to achieve this by expanding his

Hegelian distinction between a subject *in-itself* and a subject *for-itself* to include a problem he called the *practico-inert*. To summarize this lingo: a thing *in-itself* is its factual existence; a thing *for-itself* is when the thing in-itself engages in conscious self-determination (Sartre 1957). For example, the argument between trans-exclusionary radical feminists and trans women is one over the *in-itself* – over who gets to be considered within the subset of womanhood. The subject *for-itself* would be the self-conscious self-organization of women for women. Another way that this can be conceptualized is through the problem of tokenism. Adding a few visible minorities to a group changes the group *in-itself*; but if the new additions consciously come together to change the overall dynamic of the group, this is a collective subject organizing *for-itself*. The problem of tokenism is that it uses minor changes within the composition of the group in-itself to short-circuit the possibility of such conscious change.

The political subject in *Critique of Dialectical Reason* is not the individual of *Being and Nothingness*, but rather a collective spontaneously arising in response to a particular historical condition. Sartre affirms that the spontaneously emerging group can shape history, but that, after history's transformation, the subject's energy dissipates, structures ossify, and bureaucracy emerges. Sartre's analysis thinks through the questions commonly posed by Marxist theorists grappling with the decomposition of the Russian Revolution into Stalinist bureaucracy. Why did the state flourish instead of withering away after the heat of revolutionary activity? Why did the early experimental attitude of Soviet culture decline into conservatism? What was inevitable – if anything – and what was contingent in Stalin's ascendancy? Put into the language of a feminist epistemological framework, can the proletariat think beyond its lived experience of subjugation? How does the proletariat become aware of its own potential to transform the global economic system? Was Hegel correct when he argued that understanding always tails history?[65] If so, how can human activity get in front of history, so to speak, to change it? In other words, how can a political subject intentionally transform the world into something it has never experienced?

The *practico-inert* is Sartre's response to these questions. Insofar as groups are active, creating, revolutionizing, and transforming an object, whether it be a painting or a political milieu, dialectics are at work. However, as soon as there is no more spark, no more active principle in the totality, the thing is overtaken by the *practico-inert*. While the active principle creates history, the practico-inert is nature's entropic, anti-dialectical, and oppositional pressure that always eventually undermines human agency: a person becomes a corpse, a painting disintegrates, a revolution ossifies into bureaucracy and mindless routine.[66] One problem with this pessimistic social ontology is that it disengages creativity from consequence and meaning. In the end, it's all going to fall apart – which provokes the question: 'So why bother?'

While it is one thing to criticize blind historical telos or teleological conceptions of nature, it is another to ignore the fact that purpose and meaning – even self-created meaning – are important motivators of human activity, especially political activity. The assumption that the practico-inert is inevitable is a concession to liberal democracy's insistence that any revolutionary fervor is a terror that necessarily devolves into orthodoxy and dictatorship. One would expect the liberal democratic position to mean that uprisings against kings and slavers – the French Revolution, the American Revolution, and the Haitian Revolution, among others – would necessarily produce a less free world. (In some ways, the Frankfurt School's criticism of industrial society does just that.) The neoliberal thinker Francis Fukuyama's book *The End of History* (1992) found another way to resolve the problem: Fukuyama made capitalism the final stage of history and therefore exceptional. The argument that no good comes of revolutionary activity leads us to two political impasses: 1) overt nihilism, which is certainly palpable in the developed world today; and 2) a conception of politics reduced to making the most of our brief reprieves from the practico-inert. The latter boils down to political activity for its own sake, a joyful nihilism complete with hippie be-ins, parades, celebrations, political marches that are ends in themselves, art projects, creative self-expression, personal development, potlucks, communes, and so on. Such events might make a dreary life worth living, but such activities cannot transform the capitalist system of production.

Sartre was not only responding directly to Marx. His conception of existentialism both borrows from and attempts to refute the ideas of early twentieth-century Hungarian Marxist György Lukács. Lukács was grappling with questions of political consciousness at the height of Bolshevik revolutionary activity. While liberal pluralist thought takes the form of airy musing, philosophical questions that emerge in the middle of revolutions intend to solve urgent problems. Lukács' questions centered on the relationship between class consciousness and history, particularly the problem of the gap between material history and consciousness. He argued that the valuable developments from Marx were not the maxims of Kautsky's orthodoxy and certainly not Bernstein's revisionist, 'weak Kantian', anti-revolutionary position, but rather the dialectical materialist method itself; so, for Lukács, criticism of Marx's own ideas would still count as Marxist thought as long as the line of inquiry was dialectical materialism. Once again – and independent of whether or not we find Lukács' work valuable – we can see an opening for the rejection of Marx's critique of political economy within Marxism itself.

Lukács argued that Engels' naturalistic explication of dialectics was incompatible with the understanding that the proletariat is the subject–object of history (see Engels, *Anti-Dühring* and *Dialectics of Nature* in Marx and Engels 1987a; Lukács 1972). According to

Lukács, the revolutionary party becomes the intellectual apparatus that *imputes* consciousness to the class *in-itself*. Theories of imputed political consciousness rely heavily on who is doing the imputing, an elitist bureaucratic agency or a vanguard of activists and organic intellectuals immanent to the class. However, whether external or immanent, imputed consciousness is a denial of standpoint epistemology proper. Imputed consciousness means that standing in a particular location does not guarantee the capacity to interpret experience; rather, only the understanding of one's standpoint in relation to the whole can produce an accurate analysis of one's position. While it is easy to scoff at the idea of codified intellectual leadership, it addresses a question that proponents of political spontaneity cannot address directly: how does spontaneity happen and how does it lead to change? Given that the ruling ideas of any period belong to the ruling class, how does the collective political subject overcome obscured frameworks and facts so that it can act? How does it suddenly know what to do? How does an amorphous subject spontaneously know how to unite diverse groups and rebuild cities?[67]

Sartre's practico-inert gets around the problem of imputed knowledge. It is impossible for the state to wither away (Lenin 1992) because the withering away of the revolution *implies* the ossification of the state. For Sartre, the mistake of Marx and Lenin lies in their invention of the idea of the 'dictatorship of the proletariat'. Sartre's contention here is not so much the idea of dictatorship as the idea that a special group called proletarians should run it. By marginalizing the role of labor in Marx's philosophy, Sartre is left with a concept of revolution that is only tangentially related to political economy. The proletariat becomes a metaphor for the oppressed 'whoever' and the bourgeoisie becomes the equivalent of an existentially evil empire. This refashioning of the proletariat as a metaphorical stand-in for any oppressed population moves socialist politics from the political to the moral.

The structuralist critique of existentialism

Structuralism, particularly the structuralist Marxism of Louis Althusser, emerged as a response to existentialism's focus on individual agency. Its critique hinged on a number of points. First, it kicked the human individual from its pride of place at the center of the universe. The idea of Man, the conscious protagonist of existentialist philosophy and phenomenology, set up a false dichotomy between the individual and the world. For structuralists, the idea that the conscious subject thought himself (and the subject was indeed a 'him') into existence seemed ridiculous. Clearly, the *world* is prior to the individual. Second, structuralism was interested in locating invariance, laws, and conceptual infrastructure. Third, it was not explicitly concerned about human experience or standpoints; it was interested in the unconscious relations between terms within a system. Fourth, structuralists, like the poststructuralists who would later refute their work by expanding the logic of structuralism to the point of implosion, were critical of history, philosophy, and the idea of meaning. Historical materialism would be forever tainted by Hegelian notions of progress and the arrow of time.

The structuralists were suspicious of meaning understood as the correspondence between words and the world; meaning was instead located in the relations between concepts. In this way, structuralism assailed the entire architecture of existentialism: its inward gaze, its angst, its stoic political morality. Not everything boiled down to Man's quest for meaning, the radical freedom of his choices, or his feelings of alienation. For Althusser, science would replace philosophy – not the empirical science of industry, but a new kind of systematic scientific thought predicated on a new reading of Marx, one that considered Marx's interest in human alienation a youthful error that had been corrected by the publication of *Capital* (see Althusser 2006). Whereas the publication of Marx's early writing on alienation inspired Sartre and Marcuse, Althusser dismissed the newly available work as having about as much weight as one might give the unpublished writings of a young scholar.

In fact, for structuralists, the very concept of Man was something to be abolished. Conversely, the concept of Woman was not abolished. Since those organized under the term 'Woman' were never the subject of history, structuralism agreed with de Beauvoir that women were not born but made; however, what made and unmade women would always be structural law and not personal development. This resonated with Marxists because it was a critique of the individualism of liberal feminism, including its pressure on individual women to be 'revolutions in one body'.

The poststructuralist critique of structuralism

The students of the major thinkers in the structuralist movement developed sharp criticisms of their professors' theories; their body of work became known as *poststructuralism*. Later, a variant of post-structuralist thought dubbed postmodernism debated the meaning of the conditions of post-industrial life in the West, particularly the conditions of its arts and technology. The 'post' in poststructuralism, postmodernism, and postcolonialism (see 'The queer Marxist critique of postcolonialism' in Chapter 3) reflects the negation embedded in each theory, that the affirmative cannot be named, that history has passed. At its most angst-ridden pole, to paraphrase postmodernist Jean Baudrillard, the body of the world is dead and it is only an illusion that history, like the hair and fingernails of a corpse, still grows (Baudrillard 1994: 116). At their most hopeful, the 'posts' are articulations of survival: survival of colonization, survival of the Holocaust, survival of the expanding bureaucratic machinery of contemporary life. Post-al philosophy disavows belief, commitment, and, as Alain Badiou puts it, 'the passion of the real' (Badiou 2007) as inexorably leading to terror. Likewise, it is skeptical about the possibility of concrete experience, and moves towards language and image as the secret locations of power where experience is distorted by invisible hegemons. Since poststructuralism and postmodernism directly gave rise to queer theory's major tenets, we will now examine three of their most important theorists: Derrida, Foucault, and Lyotard.

Derrida and deconstruction

Beginning with *On Grammatology* in 1967, Jacques Derrida challenged nothing less than the whole of the Western canon, from Plato to phenomenology. Derrida's major contention was with what he called the metaphysics of presence; however, his critique of metaphysics was substantially different from the phenomenological critique. Derrida was not just wary of ontological questions – questions regarding whether or not objects of our experience exist outside the mind – he, like the structuralists before him, was bothered by philosophy's navel-gazing humanism. By the term 'metaphysics of presence', Derrida referred to: 1) the sense of self-presence behind Descartes' *cogito*, as well as the logic attributed to the cogito (logos); 2) Western philosophy's privilege of voice over writing through the figure of Socrates (which he termed phonocentrism); and 3) obsession with the phallus. In other words, the metaphysics of presence could be summed up in Derrida's neologism *phallogocentric*, an adjective that connotes what can crudely be described as 'like an arrogant man-mind who is obsessed with his own existence and the feeling of empowerment that he derives from hearing himself talk'.[68]

Against phallogocentrism, Derrida wanted to privilege writing over speech. By writing, Derrida did not mean the empirical act of writing, but the interconnectivity of language as a whole, or *intertextuality*. By privileging writing over voice, we can see here the *trace* (to use another Derridean term) of structuralism's influence. But Derrida criticizes structuralism in three important ways: 1) he rejects the value of binary oppositions, which structuralists enjoyed for their seemingly stable, law-like properties; 2) he argues that words are *under erasure*, a concept he developed from Heideggerian phenomenology and psychoanalysis; and 3) instead of accepting structural relations as having explanatory power or scientific value, Derrida posited the concept of *différance*, whereby relations between terms are slippery and difference implies an interminable deferral of meaning; thus, interpretation is an infinite process and not even the analysis of relations between terms provides stable truths. What's more, for Derrida, language is a sort of prison with no relation to the things referenced. Words do not correspond to the world, they only correspond to one another. Or, as it is commonly put: 'There is no outside the text.' This critique of structuralism and phenomenology emerges in a theoretical procedure he calls deconstruction. Deconstruction involves a close reading of a network of signs – or, in the language of deconstruction, the *text*. The deconstructionist's job is to tease out the moments where the text's overreliance on logic threatens a total collapse of meaning, where ambiguity and undecidability emerge, where binary oppositions assert themselves with an aggression that masks authorial insecurity.

Derrida argues that all logic rests on binaries organized in such a way that the second term is always a negative subjugated by the first: nature/culture, good/bad, positive/negative, man/woman, young/old, up/down, hot/cold. Deconstruction as a practice seeks to show how the first term relies on the second for its identity. This aspect of deconstruction rewrites Hegel's famous dialectic of master and servant. As the Hegelian parable goes, while the master considers himself a self-made man, the servant internalizes his own insignificance, until one day the servant realizes that the master is nothing without him, that the master is like an infant unable to care for himself, completely reliant on the know-how of others for his survival. In Hegel's dialectic, the situation is resolved when the servant gains a deeper sense of self and respects the value of his own knowledge. Of course, Marx changed the outcome of the master–servant dialectic to a materialist one. In Marx's version of the story, the master and servant start in the same position as in the Hegelian framework; however, once the servant realizes the absurdity of the situation, the servant resolves the dilemma by abandoning the master and letting him figure out how to cook his own meals and shine his own shoes. But, for Derrida, there is no dialectic, only aporia, a permanent dance of language that never resolves into stable meaning. Deconstruction points out how the privileged term in the binary works by flipping the relationship. Now, bottom dominates top, down is raised above up, negative is more valuable than positive, *absence decenters presence*. The point of deconstruction is to do the work of flipping the binaries, or, in the language of bumper-sticker slogans, to 'subvert the dominant paradigm'. This task is achieved through the process of deconstruction. The problem for deconstruction is, of course, that if down were ever to actually succeed in dominating up, it would paradoxically be the new up.

The process begins with a detailed reading of a given text in search of traces that destabilize its established meaning. Erasure is never complete; a trace of what an author tries to suppress always remains. Here, Derrida refers to the Freudian notion of the palimpsest, where, when one writes on a soft surface, an almost invisible impression of the word remains beneath the page. This is a common plot point in detective stories. The detective finds a writing pad with a page removed and, by rubbing a pencil gently across it, the clue written on the removed page is revealed. In this metaphor, psychoanalysts and deconstructionists are like the detectives who know the right techniques to read the trace. A simple way to think of 'under erasure' is to use the pop psychology experiment 'try not to think of a pink elephant'. As soon as the words 'pink elephant' appear, the 'try not to think of' command is nullified – one cannot help but picture the pink elephant one is instructed to disregard. This suggests a radical ambiguity in language. Words contain traces of their opposites. Likewise, words are affected by their relation to other words in a given grammatical sequence and in a larger metaphorical sense. When Alexander Pope says 'Hope springs eternal', the word 'eternal' is conditioned by the terms 'hope' and 'spring', where 'spring' brings forth images of springtime and buoyancy; moreover, the sarcasm of the poem is also often 'under erasure' since the whole of the quote is 'Hope springs eternal in the human breast; man *never is*, but always to be blessed.' Thus, for Derrida, there is no such thing as unequivocal language. The political consequences here are quite significant.

The fact that language contains subtext is not in itself hostile to a Marxist materialist dialectic. We know that when Golden Dawn's Nikos Michaloliakos insists that he does not give the Hitler salute, we know that the subtext is that he most certainly honors Hitler. Slavoj Žižek often tells the story that, in the mid-twentieth century, letterheads in the Soviet Union featured lionized profiles of Lenin and Stalin, but after Brezhnev's secret speech, when Stalin's crimes were revealed, the Lenin–Stalin letterhead was replaced by a double-profile image of Lenin. Here, one could say that Stalin is 'under erasure' since the second image of Lenin is a clear stand-in for Stalin. But merely *noting* irony or equivocation is not the point of deconstruction – for deconstructionists there is no such thing as unequivocal language – the point is to reveal how ambiguity undermines authority.

Derrida's notion that there is no unequivocal language is deeply problematic for Marxist politics. It is one thing to say that the word 'spring' has equivocal connotations in a poem. Poems, like jokes, are not arguments or declarations; they use equivocation for aesthetic ends. But equivocation has serious consequences for political speech. In deconstruction, the reader is the writer, author be damned. In this way, deconstruction, as a form of radical skepticism, doesn't just subvert the dominant paradigm, it subverts *everything* – the dominant and the dominated alike – it elevates

subversion itself to a politicized ethic. But the permanent postpone-
ment of any ultimate meaning seems to be predicated on a sort of
psychological distance from the examined texts. For example, one
can deconstruct the meaning of a novel in which the protagonist
is sexually coerced by the son of a wealthy industrialist. But the
stakes are raised if we are on a jury and we are reading accounts
of an accusation in a lawsuit where a worker has actually accused
her boss's son of rape. Here, the language performs a task; it is not
just a description. We could 'deconstruct' both documents, and
we could try to find gaps in the logic that undermines each document's claim to 'truth'. If we see the plaintiff and defendant on the
stand, we will have the 'texts' of body language to add to the list
of signs open to analysis. But what does it mean to call the interaction between the worker and the boss's son itself a *text*? Are we
comfortable saying that there is no right or wrong interpretation
of *that* text? A third scenario reveals a deeper conundrum. Let's say
that we are the worker under assault. When we say 'No', should our
statement be open to interpretation? Will our words, like Zeno's
Achilles, never arrive at their destination, lost in an infinite play of
interactive 'discursivity'? Sure, we can insist on *our* interpretation of
our words, but it would always be just one possible interpretation
barred from that 'Eurocentric' notion of objective truth. Our boss's
son's interpretation of our 'no' as a 'yes' would be just one more
interpretation. This is nothing new to women. Self-deconstruction
is already a staple of girlhood. Girls are trained to be polite and
indirect, but they are also trained to internalize this indeterminacy
as a personal failing.

The above scenario is not meant to accuse deconstructionists of a callous disregard for the agency of victims of violence.
In fact, on the contrary, deconstruction is quite preoccupied with
logic's inability to address the indescribable. Language's inability to
capture memory, nostalgia, pain, hallucinations, and the sublime
terror of the disaster are recurring themes. When Derrideans say

that there is nothing outside the text, this is not the same as saying that awareness of phenomena is an impossibility. It is more like saying that language cannot refer to something outside language. This does not mean that something extra-linguistic did not occur or is irrelevant; it means that it cannot be represented or known. If one allows for authorial intention, we can easily point out that Derrida is himself a mid-century French Jew coping with the specter of the Holocaust. So whatever critiques of deconstruction we wish to make, ad hominem attacks on the callous relativism of deconstructionists distort the project's best intentions. Deconstruction, along with psychoanalytic theory, often elevates the fragmentary and disrupted language that results from subjugation. Whereas Western logic categorizes hysterics and 'mad women' as illogical and beneath philosophical thought, deconstruction opens up a space for *écriture feminine*.

So, there are many ways in which the project of deconstruction responds to the scenario of the third worker, the worker who says no to her boss's son. One way a deconstructionist could respond to the problem of an equivocal 'no' is to focus on the boss's son's account as a 'privileged term' in the binary where hierarchy itself scripts the violence. In other words, whatever workers say or don't say is irrelevant because workers are outside the hegemonic discourse: the boss's son's discursive bits are going to intercourse with whomever he pleases because he is the boss's son. The fact that the worker's speech is not the text in question could even provide consolation – the violence done to her was not a result of her failure to make herself clear. Such skepticism also means that, while the boss's son has a right to his own interpretation, it will also always be open to question, undermining the ruling class's desire to transform its interpretations into objective law.

My disagreement here, however, is that *I think unequivocal language is actually possible.* What if the celebrated elliptical language of the mad woman is not a powerful critique of phallogocentrism, but an effect of having one's unequivocal 'no' endlessly perverted into 'yes'? Isn't the poetic language of the mad woman a language in which recourse to logic has been denied so systematically that the speaker has resorted to an indirect form of communication? Contemporary feminism uses the term 'gaslighting'[69] to identify the act of making a sane person appear crazy to others and themselves. This is, of course, not just a matter of women's speech. When Michael Brown said 'Don't shoot' to the police officer who killed him, I'm quite confident that he said this because he did not wish to be shot. That he put his hands in the air was a non-verbal reinforcement of his desire not to be shot. I firmly believe that such a wish can be unequivocally communicated. It is precisely the denial of such simple, rational demands that provokes social unrest. It is not logic in the abstract that is the problem here, but the conditions under which logic is defined. It is one thing to say that the poetic language of the traumatized deserves the ear of philosophy, but it is another to say that language is by nature equivocal or that the language of trauma is always more authentic than direct speech. Deconstruction, then, like the things it deconstructs, has its own moment where it collapses under its own logic, its own method of internal coherence. (Even Derrida noted that his ideas were being subverted by the American academy to support institutional dominance.)

Lyotard and the grand narrative
In the 1980s, a discussion about the social sensibilities of advanced capitalism began to cohere around the publication of Jean-François Lyotard's book *The Postmodern Condition*. The term postmodern is layered. It refers to the rise of technocratic power and the problematic ethics of pure efficiency. It also refers to the aesthetic sensibilities of such a world, the flight from modernism in art and architecture, and the flight from Enlightenment reasoning. It is true: bricolage, pastiche, repetition, and kitsch in art and architecture replaced the

high design of modernist architecture at the end of the twentieth century; aesthetic life was displaced from paintings in the museum to commodities at the mall. Fascination with New York, Paris, Cairo and the cosmopolitanism of the modern age collapsed into fascination with their simulations in Las Vegas. Disneyland became the model for everyday life. Irony, sarcasm, and snark replaced naïve appeals to authenticity. The notion of the postmodern condition flows from what (Frankfurt School Marxists) Adorno and Horkheimer termed *the culture industry*, and from what Herbert Marcuse put forward as *one dimensionality*, the feeling that contemporary life in the centers of capital accumulation is flat and empty, punctuated by bursts of violence and intensity – it is easy to see how Marx's early work on alienation resonates with these ideas.

Lyotard argues that postmodern society flows from Enlightenment rationality, particularly the shift from narrative meaning to scientific explanation. Truth is displaced by efficiency and bureaucratic legitimization. Ironically, this scientific discourse is grounded by a perversion of narrative proper according to something that Lyotard calls *grand narratives*. A grand narrative is an overarching story or explanation of how the world works. My earlier explanation of the development of capitalism would be an example of such a narrative. According to Lyotard, all grand narratives strengthen ideological dominance. Here, he affirms the existence of the Platonic concept of the noble lie while morally rejecting it. Grand narratives include religious explanations to existential questions, but mostly Lyotard is using Nietzsche to attack Marx by accusing him of Hegelianism.

Lyotard's attack on Marx is not an argument about theories of labor or exchange value. For Lyotard, Marx's sins begin with his connection to Hegel's philosophy. Hegelian logic is an idealist (spiritual) and progressive view of history based on the precepts of pietist Christianity, where both the truth and God himself unfold over time and where the resolution of conceptual contradictions moves truth towards an absolute. Hegel's idea of 'forward' contains teleological connotations – history moves forward like an unfolding spirit intent on improving itself. Marx took Hegel's logical reformation of dialectics and applied it to the material organization of society: social forces conflict and that conflict moves history forward in material terms. It is hard to refute – absent a sci-fi scenario where amnesiacs repopulate the earth after cataclysmic devastation – the assertion that human history is not likely to go back to an early hunter-gatherer society with no memory of farming techniques or textile manufacturing.

Certainly, we have a fictional interest in describing potential returns to these states, but they are *fictional*. And even when we imagine such dystopian scenarios, they are never returns to the social relations of the past, but futuristic, often post-apocalyptic takes on early forms of social organization that serve as a commentary on present conditions. In other words, we might fantasize about a neo-feudal order where robot overlords force humans to serve them or about a post-apocalyptic world of roaming hunter-gatherers going from city to city raiding pharmacies and supermarkets, but we never imagine a future that is an exact replica of, say, Mexico's war of independence against Spain. When we do imagine participating in the latter, it is usually via a time machine with which we *return* to an exact time and place. We do not go to the future in our time machine and encounter the past. We intuitively know that the arrow of history moves in one direction. Even if elements of the past are incorporated into the future, they will be incorporated in ways that would have been impossible in the past.

In Lyotard's view, what I suggest above would fall under the category of grand narrative. There is no 'human history' moving in time; there are only local explanations and interacting individuals, small narratives longing to be free from the imposition of ideas such as historical time, science, and progress. Narratives of emancipation are particularly dangerous in Lyotard's view. The guillotine always leads to the gulag. Marx inexorably leads to Stalin. Narratives of emancipation are tools of the state. They are a cover for the tyranny of a new technocratic regime. Here, once again, we see the theme of Sartre's *practico-inert*: ashes to ashes. As mentioned in the previous section, this nihilism reflects the liberal democratic worldview. So what does one do to oppose dystopian technocracy? Lyotard's solution is a general fatalism: reject calls for political liberation, focus on small narratives and the diversity of local community, pursue aesthetic intensities, reject science and the university, and oppose experts. None of these solutions challenge capitalism as a system of economics. Lyotard supports a return to the localization of pre-industrial life, but also the ironic, pleasurable use of technology. Perhaps the biggest contradiction in Lyotard's thought is that it is itself the new grand narrative, the new explanation of modern society.

This appeal to reject grand narratives affects gender politics in a number of ways. The incommensurability of narratives means that gender politics in Texas, San Francisco, and Tokyo cannot genuinely connect. This is not an argument that the political situations of gender-diverse and sexually diverse people are different, but that these differences are *incommensurable*. It would be surprising if the demands of cis women in rural China were indistinguishable from those of trans women in London. Political demands are situated in real material history. But such an argument differs from claiming that these demands are necessarily incommensurable. For example, if incommensurability is real, then just because queers want to be treated with respect in the United States, it cannot be assumed that *kuchus* in Uganda desire the same. It is hubris to think that there is a universal figure of a person who does or doesn't want to be treated with respect. There may be whole communities that enjoy violence and denigration. Welcome to the seedy underbelly of relativism. In postmodern politics, assumptions of solidarity are, in fact, considered a precursor to technocratic oppression. In this view, one should be as local and specific as possible, and one should strive for self-development and monad-like solitude.

Foucault and the powerful power of power

Foucault is without doubt a key progenitor of queer thought. His rejection of broad historical analysis in favor of the forgotten pockets of history established grounds for research into queer lives. Gender non-conforming people had always been beneath the shadow of history's rainbow arch. Foucault's genealogical method promised to focus on the margins, on the exceptions that would *disprove* the rule.

Traditional historical analysis starts at the past and shows how the present develops from it. Genealogy instead takes a concept and traces it backwards until a glitch is discovered, an epistemological break with the past that explains the present. Foucault's interest lies in the epistemic shift's capacity to change the stable meaning of the present. What causes the past to be different from the present is not necessarily relevant for Foucault. What is relevant is the fact that such a shift is possible. Given the chasm between past and future, there must be something generating the appearance of social stability in the here and now. Foucault rejects classical Marxist explanations of ideology, although his later work shows the influence of Louis Althusser's concept of ideological state apparatuses. Foucault writes as if there were some sort of mysterious abyss generating the social present. The phantom he battles finally emerges in his later works, *The Archeology of Knowledge*, *Discipline and Punish*, and the three volumes of *The History of Sexuality*. The name of that phantom is power.

Foucault's political goal is to legitimize silenced discourses, to make the obscure visible in order to transform our sense of the present. But he doesn't just devise a new scholarly technique (or, more accurately, merely revise a Nietzschean concept), he argues that linear, forward-moving historical analysis is part of the

intellectual moral wrong that creates those pockets of 'invisibilized' categories and people in the first place. Foucault is interested
in the form and function of bureaucracies. The fact that both the
democracies in the West and the failed revolutionary projects
of the East were highly structured bureaucracies was no doubt
influential. However, Foucault's project is in no way an attempt
to think through the legacy of the Russian Revolution or any
other Marxist paradigm; indeed, his work belongs to neither the
left or the right.[70] Instead, he locates the problem of bureaucratic
disciplinary violence in a power that requires the eradication of
difference and the creation of 'Others' in order to perpetuate
itself. Power marginalizes. Power desires – power itself has a will
to power. Power is refracted throughout the whole of society via
hierarchies structured by power. But power for Foucault is not
prohibitive, it does not restrict liberty. For Foucault, power is
generative. It produces subjects, forces them to internalize its discipline; it does not condemn subjects to silence but forces them to
confess. This is perhaps most succinctly and brilliantly expressed
in Foucault's analysis of the panopticon, a prison with a guard
tower at the center capable of seeing all prisoners at all times, but
where the guard's line of vision is obscured so that the prisoner is
unsure of whether or not the guard is watching, resulting in the
prisoner's own self-discipline. Foucault's point here is that when
social discipline is internalized, violence becomes unnecessary to
maintain order; and that this is, in fact, the preferred mode of
discipline for the modern state. (There is certainly some empirical
evidence for the latter at work in the ideology of lean production.)

But what is this 'power'? Foucault does give some shape to the
term. He speaks of judicial power, strategic power, disciplinary
power, bio-power. Indeed, Foucault has a nominalist understanding
of power, meaning that there is no universal form of power but
only local instantiations of power. But what is power? If we break
down the disciplinary mechanisms of Foucault's panopticon, we

find that power collects itself in the form of the state, then disciplines its worker-organs symbolized here by the prison guards, who then transmit the effects of power on to the prisoner. The prisoners discipline themselves and, if they were ever to be released, they would continue to spread this discipline to others. The political project of Foucauldianism, then, is for each individual to examine how they themselves have been disciplined by power, to reject that discipline, and to inspire the rejection of power in others. Each individual body resists power's colonizing ... power.

But doesn't this political trope actually predate Foucault? Two Hollywood film classics come to mind: *The Blob* and *Invasion of the Body Snatchers*. In *The Blob*, an amorphous and unstoppable monster consumes individual citizens, expanding its scope by incorporating them into itself. With a slight twist on the narrative, in *Invasion of the Body Snatchers*, aliens use human bodies as generating pods. These 'pod people' are physically identical to their former selves, but have become mindless zombies who do the bidding of alien forces. Pod people root out remaining humans and collectively impose an alien existence upon them. Power dissolves them into its mass (the blob) or colonizes them and establishes a false consciousness within them (pod people). In other words, Foucault's political lessons match those of American Cold War cinema. The alien powers in *The Blob* and *Invasion of the Body Snatchers* are, of course, symbols of communism and communist agents respectively. Communism is cast as a diabolical project to dissolve human agency and individual difference, massifying everything into a nightmarish collective where unique and precious human individuals are sacrificed for the good of the whole. Here I find assertions of Foucault's conservatism compelling; Foucault's political schematics, despite their radical patina, contain no necessary epistemic break from liberal ideology. We see the Foucauldian subject everywhere, whether running from communists, Nazis, witches, zombies, Satanists, android housewives, or 'mean girl' cliques in high school. In fact, in American culture, the trope of the lone individual struggling to resist interpellation into an uncannily inhuman collective is itself oddly inescapable. But this analogy isn't quite right. For Foucault, we are not sovereign Enlightenment individuals resisting a colonizing force. We are always already colonized by power, always already its subjects. The sci-fi horror sequel is a better analogy for the political crisis described above. Movies entitled *Escape from the Blob* and *Rise of the Snatched* would function as better parallels, movies in which the organs and cells of power awaken and immanently begin processes of personal resistance. As a logical consequence, Foucault's final work focuses on the care of the self.

The postmodernist condition

Poststructuralism, broadly construed, is the theoretical expression of a politically vague anti-authoritarian communitarianism. The left variant of this tendency opposes the bureaucratic power of the state, the commercial corrosion of intellectual life, and the alienation of people from one another and from the land. The right variant of this trend, well represented by 'patriot' talk radio stations in the US, denounces what it calls (idiosyncratically) *corporatism*, a society dominated by large multinational corporations.[71] This corporatism is alternately characterized as a fascist or communist threat to liberal democracy. In opposition to this inhuman blob-like communo-fascist corporatism, with its big-box stores, invisible international factories, and sinister currency regulations, today's right communitarians posit the ideal of genuine capitalism. This (white) melancholy for the past is nostalgic over the loss of family farms, family-owned shops on the town square, and social cohesion (also known as family values). This nostalgia is rendered palpable by the concept of the nation: the flag symbolizes the belonging and comfort of a recognizable and therefore easily navigable set of rules and customs. The spread of this reactionary yearning is instructive in two ways. First, it means that there is mass disaffection with capitalism in general and neoliberal society in particular, and not just among progressives; even among the system's most strident proponents, the social effects of capitalism must be blamed on something, be it modernism (Bell 1996: especially Part One) or 'the unionized homosexual-Black-Muslim-immigrant-poor' (the all-powerful blob feared by the social conservative movement in the United States). Second, it means that there is little understanding of the mechanisms of capitalist production and its social effects.

IV. Conclusion

This chapter has been an overview of the territory, stakes, and debates within Marxist history that led to the rethinking of the materialist dialectic and the subsequent poststructuralist erasure of that dialectic. The disaster of Stalinism provoked a rethinking of the revolutionary project while New Left street politics identified new political subjects who appeared to transcend class. Queer theory – in both its academic and popular incarnations – developed from within this intellectual ecosystem. On the surface, these newly awakened social movements seemed to be a critique of Marxist politics because they were a critique of the nineteenth- and early twentieth-century proletarian 'Mallet Man' protagonist. The combination of Marx erasure and the poststructuralist fascination with text and image has produced a strange sort of double consciousness around gender and class. Everyone knows that women and girls in Asia and Latin America are manufacturing the world's clothing, fabric, toys, and electronics. Yet when someone invokes workers' power, the knee-jerk feminist and queer reaction is often a head shake, if not a fist shake – don't replace discussions of gender politics with discussions of Mallet Man! But a great portion of those with their hands on the levers of production are the same political subjects addressed by feminist and postcolonial theory:

the women of the global East and South. Labor has been globalized and feminized. Feminist politics, queer politics, and trans politics are not external to these debates because women, queer, and trans people are not external to the global economic system.

The goal of this book is the development of an internationalist and materialist feminist, queer, and trans-inclusive politics grounded in the fundamental insight of Marx's political economy: that capitalism operates through the expropriation of surplus value from labor. This basic economic truth has been either avoided, abandoned, or forgotten. Because of this abandonment, capitalism appears in contemporary politics as an ineffable spiritual blight that weighs upon the world, that clutters it with mass-produced bric-a-brac to titillate and distract the faceless masses. Commodities are treated as the indecipherable message of mysterious forces. But the antidote to commodity fetishization is an understanding of the way in which capitalist production works. When we pull back the curtain, we don't find the Great Oz, we find labor networks processing ore, earth, and water, not for the purpose of creating useful things, not for the purpose of bamboozling the masses, but purely for the profit of capitalists. While it is fine to theorize a communist hypothesis based on a radical egalitarianism, without connecting inequality to capitalist production it is easy for anti-capitalists to find themselves lost in irrelevant liberal projects that *seem* to promote equality, such as the microfinance scam or the localization of manufacturing.

Phenomenologist Emmanuel Levinas bases ethics on 'the face of the Other' (Levinas 2011: 187–219). This is a fundamentally flawed ethical model for capitalist social relations. Capitalism forces the interaction of billions of faceless people: the Other is always faceless. The liberal humanist solution of 'buying local' is an attempt to uphold the ethics of the face: 'I cannot be ethical to you from afar, if only I could see your face ...' Once again, the flaw here is that ethics replaces politics. But nor can politics be disengaged from economics. Egalitarianism cannot be brought about without understanding the actual mechanisms of inequality. To demystify the economic realities under which we operate, it is necessary to analyze production for profit within the actual market and the labor that sustains the production process.

While equivocation appears as playfulness in the poststructuralist canon, it derails political debate. Such equivocations often come wrapped in abstraction. Just as a commodity can be either a use value or an exchange value depending on the way it is employed in concrete situations, political meaning shifts according to context. And abstraction can cover a multitude of sins.[72] For example, Michael Hardt and Antonio Negri's concept of 'immaterial labor' considers everyone to be engaged in productive labor: factory workers in China produce the coffee cups, and baristas in Seattle and London produce smiles. University professors produce ideas, which, since they originate in common language, are a common property of the multitude. We now all work for one another, and, as with Eduard Bernstein a century earlier, Hardt and Negri imagine that through subsumption[73] capitalism will eventually wither away and allow for some bright new paradigm. Proletarian class struggle in this formula is beyond passé. In fact, for Hardt and Negri, working-class antagonism is actually thought to *strengthen* capitalism. So, when we rip the term 'production' from its context and replace it with a dictionary definition, suddenly everything counts as production, and so everything also counts as labor; meanwhile, the sort of laborers who directly *produce capital* are erased – or even vilified as a political subject.[74] If value production for capital includes everything that strengthens the system, then almost everything could be 'productive labor', from the maid who cleans Donald Trump's bedroom, to the web designer employed by a non-profit charity, to a creative writing class offered for free at a public library, to planting an herb garden in your backyard.

But productive labor in classical economics is labor that produces *more capital*, not labor that produces a use value. Simply put, 'productive' means *productive of capital*. In the M–C–M' formula, the commodity (C) that serves as the vanishing mediator to get more money (M') is productive labor. Unproductive labor is labor that does not produce surplus value for a capitalist. A capitalist hires a maid to clean bathrooms in his mansion, but he does not sell what is produced by the maid, he merely enjoys it. For it to be productive labor, the capitalist would have to be selling access to the clean bathrooms of his mansion. The terms 'productive labor' and 'unproductive labor' are no reflection at all on the maid, her work, or her social value as a worker.

Anti-capitalist struggle cannot be limited to proclamations of equality or commitments to emancipatory politics. It actually has to understand its capitalist present in order to plan a path towards an anti-capitalist future. This book suggests a bold new approach: the old, unfashionable approach of Marx's materialism, complete with the even more unfashionable call to reinvest in the centrality of working-class organizing in order to *begin* a revolutionary transformation of social relations. The social movements championed by Hardt and Negri are critical to this process, just not for the reasons they imagine. For all who are affected negatively by capitalism, inside and outside the working class, protest is necessary for survival. The value of Zapatismo is that it contributed to the survival of the people of Chiapas, gave voice to the indigenous populations of Mexico, and inspired marginalized people around the world. Such struggle is critical. However, despite the creativity of this movement, its expansion alone could never *end* capitalist production. The armed occupation of lands can slow capital, it can damage capital, but, in the end, capitalism and its states have the motility and the weaponry to squash such protests. While access to the earth and raw materials is critical for production, productive labor itself – labor that produces a profit – cannot be forced from human laborers since capitalism relies on the obfuscation of the wage, the ideology of free labor, and human desperation to maintain production. Mass strikes can stop the flow of *generalized* profit – not just the flow of profit to one capital or one nation of capitals, but system-wide. Solidarity *of* labor and solidarity *with* labor are, then, practices that are critical to revolutionary anti-capitalism. It is therefore necessary to demystify production, abandon the 'mindfulness' and 'teamwork' of capitalist ideology, and engender solidarity by protecting one another in struggle. While early twentieth-century Austrian economist Joseph Schumpeter exalted capitalism's capacity to self-revolutionize through the serial destruction of old products, destructive downsizing, and war economies, revolutionary creative reconstruction is not a matter of destroying material objects; it is a matter of changing social relations for the purpose of remaking the world. The constructive force behind this social transformation is a solidified anti-capitalist force, with labor as its fulcrum. The solidity of this creative principle is the practice of solidarity. Revolution is the principle that destroys old social relations, and solidarity is the embryo of the new within it.

CHAPTER 2

Marxism and gender

I. Don't be vulgar ...

The term 'vulgar Marxist' is often attributed to those who immediately and unthinkingly reduce the direct cause and effect for every event to capitalist processes, if not to the dark intentions of capitalists themselves, regardless of the actual causal mechanisms at work. Should a tragic mountain climbing accident occur, the vulgar Marxist will mutter about how capitalism facilitates the shoddy production of equipment and will lose interest in the topic if it turns out that mere inclement weather sealed the climbers' fates. The response is vulgar not just because it uses disaster to cheaply score a political point; it also ignores the real conditions of the given situation; such crude leaps of logic are ultimately unconvincing, more evangelical than explanatory, more dismissive than rooted in solidarity or even basic human concern. This is not really vulgar *Marxism*, though. Marx took decades to outline the mechanisms of capitalism; he didn't just assign random blame to it in a quasi-religious fashion. It is true that the capitalist mode of production produces myriad obstacles despite the procession of supposedly helpful gadgets it unleashes upon us. Still, it is important to investigate how the mode of production *actually* affects real social phenomena and events. It is true that economic conditions affect law, art, media, and institutions. But they do so in direct and indirect ways with complex relations of cause and effect.

Women's liberation has been subjected to similarly reductive readings in the name of Marx. This is not a matter of economism (i.e. economic reductionism); actually, quite the opposite: these particular reductionist readings tend to hinge on the reduction of political economy to analyses of consumption, where the culprit of gender anti-freedom is the consumer-hungry capitalist who robs you of your self-esteem in order to sell it back to you in a tub of hair gel or in a tube of lipstick. Of course, this accusation is not *incorrect* – any angsty teenager can attest to that. But anti-consumerism is not the same as understanding the complexities of the conditions of capitalist production and reproduction. Anti-consumerism ends up being a sort of grumpy disdain (or sometimes benevolent pity) for the consumer herself. Coextensive with the development of mid-century Western feminism, the birth of mass advertising subjected women to new product lines that shaped their bodies for the job market and the marriage market. Second-wave feminism's answer was, in part, the creation of a movement of women who were skeptical of gender, gender being understood after the publication of Simone de Beauvoir's *Second Sex* as a socially manufactured femininity theoretically separate from the body. But this mode of consumer resistance was better suited to middle-class college-educated women than secretaries and waitresses, and better for whites than ethnic minorities, for whom 'good grooming' was a form of personal resistance against racist dehumanization.

The intra-party debate on cosmetics within the American Socialist Workers' Party (Hansen and Reed 1986; see also note 71 in Chapter 1) is a perfect example of disdain for feminine consumers and how such disdain sits poorly with working-class women. In a lead article for the group's newspaper, the document's male author waxes lyrical about the days of yore when all women needed was a little strawberry juice and rice powder to pretty themselves up before the dance (Bustelo 1954, reprinted in Hansen and Reed 1986: 29). Nostalgia for pre-industrial village customs has nothing at all to do with Marxism; in fact, it takes more from Justus Möser, the eighteenth-century conservative political economist who lamented how international capital destroyed local mores and handicrafts, than from Karl Marx. Not all anti-capitalism is progressive. However, this is not the only conservatism underlying the beauty debate. The shift in analysis from reproductive and productive labor to beauty regimens turns a political and economic question into a moral question where painted ladies come to signify both the 'cheapness' of working women and the frivolity and shallowness of the rich. Ultimately, middle-class Western feminism would tolerate neither group. As a consequence, the critique of beauty (both products and their consumers) slid into a critique of sexuality itself at the onset of the so-called sexual revolution. Political moralizing became moral panic and American feminism devoured itself in the morose 'sex wars' of the later mid-century.

The two sides of the sex wars' circular firing squad (a strange geometry indeed) have been remarkably stable for decades: on one side are the second-wave, white, middle-class feminists who rail against pornography and popular culture, and who have a strange obsession with protecting the sanctity of lesbian sex from gender queer, femme, and trans people; on the other, there are the queer and trans-affirmative third-wave feminists who the second-wavers consider to be collaborators.[1] Second-wave feminism's foremost goal is ending the sexualization and objectification of women's bodies, and asserting that women are more than just bodies at men's disposal. Third-wave feminism is also concerned with the commodification and sexualization of women's bodies, but also with how the maintenance of the 'good woman' narrative condemns sexually non-conforming and non-cisgendered women to the status of slutty monstrosity; the third-wave goal, then, is for women to create their own imagery, to reclaim sexuality for themselves, to break out of the aporia of the pure/impure woman paradigm. The radical lesbian movement within the second wave tried to combine both arguments through the development of lesbian separatism: the creation of a politicized society comprised only of women in which they would be able to create an exploitation-free sexuality. However, by the time third-wave feminism emerged, the lesbian separatist movement had dissipated. Feminists would have to 'create space' within the mainstream, without fantasies of a separated economy, and without the fantasy of a sexuality divorced from mainstream symbols, including symbols of social gender. These symbols would become incorporated into women's identities, not as elements of popular culture to be consumed, but as elements of straight culture to be transformed and turned into one's own, i.e. *queered*. As cultural rewriting rather than separatist utopianism became the mode of political resistance, the social aspects of biology came to the fore: not only was social gender constructed, but biological sex typing was discovered to be more arbitrary than previously admitted. Men and women were not like apples and oranges, or like dogs and cats; they were one human form existing on a spectrum. So, even though queering demanded *spaces* for self-exploration, health initiatives, and cultural development, separate and policed biological spheres for women that excluded queer men and non-cisgendered people were no longer an option. Woman-identified queers had more in common with man-identified queers than with *heteronormative* women or men.

So where do Marxists fit into all of this? Surface anti-consumerism suggests that the second-wave approach is a collective, more militant course of action, where women bond together to struggle against capitalist hypersexualization; it is easy to see how the queer model could be read as a form of individualistic self-absorbed liberal feminism. Given this reading, it would seem that the right approach for Marxists would be to continue with the second-wave tradition against the third wave. I would like to argue that the paradigm can easily be flipped on its head: in an integrated society devoid of separatist fantasies, an extension of the second-wave approach can promote only the politics of respectability. The third-wave approach, although not without its limitations, better addresses the problem of women's commodified sexual expression; it is only through the *collective choice* of individual self-determination that women can break free from the exchange economy and assert their own existence as actual human beings rather than as objects to be traded for sex, household labor, and mothering. The assignation of women as pigs and collaborators for their sexual choices reinforces the idea that it is women themselves who are ultimately responsible for devaluing one another. To worry that others will 'cheapen' you if they 'sexually sell themselves short' is the logic of someone who has hopelessly bound their personal worth to a libidinal economy. Men do not wring their hands over the sexual imagery or sexual behavior of other men because men consider themselves to be the sovereign subjects of their own lives, not objects in a social exchange. They are threatened by the fantasy of other men's buying power being greater than their own, but it is hard to imagine a political movement of men who rail against other men for buying into masculine sexual stereotypes. Alternatively, men's fear of emasculation is not some weird, existential taboo about homosexuality but exists precisely because such feminization means being an object of exchange. So long as they are not turned into woman-objects, men could not care less about other men's sexual behavior or style of dress. This is because they are purchasers with cash in hand, not objects with rising and falling values.[2]

It is only through collective insistence on the right to self-determination, including the right to decide on trivialities such as clothing and make-up, and the right to sexually express herself or to refuse to do so, that a woman can disrupt her position as exchanged object and assert herself as self-possessed. This self-definition by no means requires the purchase of consumer goods; however, the market certainly exploits women's desire for self-determination as it exploits all desire.

The claims that women who wear the veil *and* women who wear provocative clothing are harming *all* women are two sides of the same argument. Women who wear revealing clothing are collaborators who give men what they want without ties or commitments (i.e. for 'free'), while women who wear the veil are collaborating with men by affirming that women's bodies exude sex. Neither is considered a legitimate choice because, at least according to Eurocentric middle-class standards, such choices are choices against oneself. But this doesn't answer the question: *how does one choose oneself?* Another dimension of the 'neither burka nor bikini' feminist political line is that both sexualize women. In the first situation, women are considered so sexually overwhelming that they must be covered; in the latter, women are socially pressured to radiate sexuality. But as anyone from the 'neither burka nor bikini' camp will vigorously tell you, they are hardly prudes, they love sex, and so on. So what, then, is the problem with expressing sexuality? The problem is that they interpret the sexuality of both veiled and unveiled women's bodies as a pure reflection of male desire. The woman is erased by both the veil and nudity, replaced by the male gaze itself,[3] or, as Lacanian psychoanalytic feminism puts it, *the* gaze, since all desire is coded as male (Campbell 2004). When it is not considered an eternal truth about gender or biology, but instead a description of bourgeois life, the argument 'all desire is male' does seem to reflect assumptions within the modern libidinal economy – and clearly 'neither burka nor bikini' feminists agree. So, there is nothing remaining but a bind. There is no legitimately feminist public revelation of sexuality: to wear a burka is to submit to the patriarchal idea that a woman is super-sexy under all that fabric; to wear a bikini is to reveal this sexuality. Being interpellated (i.e. socially inscribed, regardless of one's desires) into public sexuality is a frustrating given.

Feminist practice inspired by the second wave attempts to disrupt this in two ways: 1) via the politics of respectability and middle-class professionalism, complete with the policing of public sexuality and/or a rejection of what queer culture calls 'high femme'; or 2) through a militant nudity where women disrobe to prove that the body is a sexless thing of nature, a mere biological tool for pissing and childbirth, just the shell with which one experiences the world – I will strip naked for you, but only to prove that there is nothing to see but my biology. Indeed, this practice is effective for disrupting patriarchal assumptions (albeit it through doubling down on cisnormative assumptions.) *But, once again, where is women's sexuality?* Women's sexuality is still relegated to privacy and secrecy – mysterious even to women themselves – and completely invisible. Roland Barthes once famously said, 'In the United States, sex is everywhere, except in sexuality.' Neither-burka-nor-bikini feminism corrects this problem by demanding that sex be nowhere except in the sex act, which happens in the sanctity of one's home with one's boyfriend or husband or perhaps with a group at a lesbian separatist retreat. Men's desire rules the streets, and women's sexuality expresses itself at home: the general dynamic remains unchanged.

Third-wave feminism was particularly concerned with going beyond this impasse. Its solution has been the celebration of all that is as it is – instead of rejecting the burka or bikini, to queer the burka by sewing feminist band patches on it,[4] and to queer the bikini by having it become an acceptable choice regardless of a woman's size, shape, or body hair. The third-wave goal was freedom of choice; not the *correct* choice, or the *legitimate* choice, but random, meaningless choice, existential choice. It is random choice that collectively pushes women into the position of self-determined subject regardless of the object of that choice. This is the reason why non-Muslims in even the most 'sex-positive' corners of the queer community do not rail against the hijab as if it were some sort of shameful concession to patriarchy.[5] The hijab is a choice like any another other, and it is the choice that counts. Third-wave feminism is correct in understanding that the root of all misogyny, including transmisogyny, cannot be that women are objectified, are the object of some subject's gaze. Intersubjectivity means that everyone is always potentially the object of some subject. The root of misogyny, on the other hand, is that womanhood itself has an exchange value that can be enhanced or diminished by veiling or unveiling, by keeping sex sacred or by foolishly giving it away cheaply. Because women are collectively defined by the value of their sexual and emotional services, the insinuation that all women must keep to a common set of so-called dignified behaviors in order to keep the collective's value as high as possible does not break with patriarchal logic. Simply put, the political logic of second-wave feminism is that all (cis) women must come together as a class and act 'in solidarity' with one another to keep up the collective's emotional, libidinal, and even market value: or else it must flee into the forest. For this reason, the political enemy is not men – as so often assumed by conservatives – the political enemy is women who won't get with the program. In fact, men may even add their feminist voices to the critique of women's behavior and sexual expression.[6]

This criticism surfaces most sharply in debates over sex work. Nowhere is the pity/hatred paradigm more evident. Sex workers are dichotomized into absolute good victims (trafficked women, bodies animated by pure abuse) and absolute victimizers (women who sell their sexual labor freely, thereby perpetuating the sexualization of women). The other category of absolute victimizer is the trans woman, who trans-exclusionary radical feminists (TERFs) often conflate with sex workers. This is a clear instance of what proponents of psychoanalysis refer to as a metonymic slide in meaning: trans women are caricatured as overtly feminine, overt femininity implies overt sexuality, overt sexuality implies cheapness, cheapness implies prostitution. Then they use the fact that many trans women are economically forced into prostitution as evidence for their case.

But what about critiques that the third-wave feminist (the queer feminist, for example) emphasis on individual choice reflects a liberal cult of the self? First, it is important to distinguish between *choices* and *choice*, or, put another way, between *objects* and *agency*. Capitalism gives us lots of choices. We can be rap stars, own yachts, eat anything on the menu, live anywhere we want. We can paint our houses blue and take up any course of study at college. But those are just the choices; they are not the choice. Despite all the choices, the vast majority of us will not become stars and we will never be able to choose a yacht. We might be able to afford to eat at a restaurant, but we have no real choice about how our food is produced. We can live anywhere, as long as we can get a job there and can afford to relocate. We can own a home but, under capitalism, we will always be at the whim of the housing market. Capitalism gives us many things to choose from, but little agency. There is a difference between celebrating a market that produces things to choose from and promoting the right to make choices.

That said, the collective emphasis on subject development leaves massive gaps in the discussion: sex trafficking goes largely untheorized.[7] However, trafficking – sexual or not – is a problem of political economy, not a problem of evil or patriarchy. The euphemism of women *selling themselves* is complicated because all laborers sell themselves. The distinction between the labor market and global trafficking is the difference between selling one's labor power and being sold as a commodity; to move from alienation and exploitation to dehumanization is to cross a thin line, although the move is a dramatic paradigm shift. No feminism can theorize modern trafficking without referring to political economy. It is not the emphasis on subject development that impedes queer feminism from doing so, nor the fact that it refuses collective behavioral discipline through respectability and pity: it is the lack of understanding of political economy that gets in the way.

Accordingly, it is not reductive to analyze the economic; reductive thinking comes from confusing the moral with the political and substituting habits of consumption with analyses of the conditions of labor within a mode of production. It also comes from the failure to distinguish between practical and theoretical reason, as with the Erfurt Program, the failure to remember that there is a gap between stirring political rhetoric and science.

II. From the woman question to the gender question

Throughout history, sexual diversity has been an existential fact. Gender variance is not a recent phenomenon, nor is it a product of capitalism; however, the significance of gender within any given society varies depending on the mode of production, the cultural and legal infrastructure supporting the mode of production, and even the institutional histories inherited after shifts in material conditions.[8] In capitalistically developed societies, strict sexual dimorphism is promoted as the foundation of all that counts for natural, but, behind the scenes, sexual dimorphism is manufactured and maintained through surgical interventions on intersex children[9] and through the production of commodities aimed at normalizing and shaping secondary sex characteristics: leg wax, eyebrow tweezers, cosmetics, bodybuilding supplements, and so on. While people have been assigned sex roles at birth throughout history, the individuals assigned to 'female' status in the twentieth and twenty-first centuries are not perfectly symmetrical to those who would have been assigned female before the development of modern medicine, let alone before the development of settled agriculture (see Wolff and Roy 1899: 288; Croom 1898–99). So, while we can discuss concepts such as the sexual division of labor at the dawn of human history, it is important to remember that such a divide would not mirror the twentieth- or twenty-first-century conception of sexual dimorphism. Certainly, sex characteristics and capacities associated with sex develop with law-like regularity: testosterone produces body hair and blemishes at puberty, XY chromosomes often predict that an infant will develop a penis and testes, having a uterus enables an infant to be carried to term. But the *social* meaning of bodily attributes depends on context. And much of that context is dictated by material social arrangements. In order to understand how peasant turnips, industrial widgets, petrol-soaked oysters, and the destruction of Mexican corn crops relate to homelessness among queer youth, violence against trans people, or the expectation that women are naturally good caretakers, economic thinking must go beyond analyses of commodity consumption. For this, I propose a queer, trans-inclusive reading of Marxist-feminist social reproduction theory, an anti-capitalist critique that goes beyond simply criticizing the consumption habits of the gay middle class.

Marxist-feminism occurred during the second wave of Western feminism, but it never fulfilled its project of transforming and enriching Marxist analyses of gender, in part because a serious discussion of social reproduction theory was interrupted by the onset of neoliberalism. What's more, Marxist-feminism has only recently begun to incorporate queer and trans subjects into its analysis. It will take a new generation of Marxist economic thinkers to correct this mistake. And, to reiterate, Marxist-feminism would do best to move away from the faux collectivist moral tone of middle-class variants of second-wave feminist practice and instead embrace the (still collective) subject-forming practices of the feminist third wave.

Much of the pre-twentieth-century literature I review below pays heavy attention to women's role in the development of capitalism in industrialized Europe. This is due to the part played by Europe in the shaping of global capital (see Chapter 1). However, Marxist-feminist scholarship is by no means limited to analyses of European women; Marxist-feminists have also analyzed the American slave economy's effect on eighteenth- and nineteenth-century Black women, the role of the housewife in mid-twentieth-century America, and the role of women in radical social transformation from Latin America to Asia. Since I do not wish to project a modern conception of gender and sex into the past, here I will adopt the use of the word 'woman' by mid-century Marxist-feminists, defining it as the sociological category of people who were assigned to live as females at birth and who were expected (and pressured) to bear and raise children. This definition includes intersex people raised as women; however, in comparison with today's understanding of womanhood, it is only a limited subset of women. I will not call these women cisgendered or heterosexual because such words, let alone the political movements for trans and queer self-determination, did not exist during this period. That said, female-assigned persons pressured into womanhood and heteronormative arrangements still make up the majority of the world's population, and thus the material analysis of their lives is critical. As we will see later, the material conditions of women in heteronormative and cisnormative arrangements – whether or not they desire heteronormativity or whether or not they are gender variant – is a core factor in the production of traditional and oppositional sexism.

III. Marxism at the center and the periphery

Since the turn towards poststructuralism, the academic world has largely dismissed Marx's work as fatally flawed due, in part, to his insufficient attention to gender and race. This shift away from Marxism was due, to some extent, to the failure of the Old Left to sufficiently incorporate New Left demands. But the lull in movement activity following the evaporation of May 1968 in France, the Tlatelolco massacre in Mexico City in October of the same year, the decline of the Black Panther Party, the disastrous Chinese Cultural Revolution, and the demise of radical groups such as the Gay Liberation Front left a lull in the movement at the onset of what would become a forty-year neoliberal employers' offensive and the dismantling of the Keynesian welfare state. From the neoliberal era onward, the academic left began to retreat from liberation politics towards politics based on awareness campaigns, small consciousness-raising groups, utopian spaces, and communal projects. The development of digital technologies and the fact that the money commodity shifted from the gold standard to pure market equivalences inspired postmodern theorists to believe that the world had spun off its axis into uncharted territory. Moreover, Marx was obviously wrong because anything coming from the nineteenth century just *had to be* obsolete.

Political and social philosophy has now strayed so far from objective economic analysis that capitalism is discussed as if it were a collective essence, less an economic system and more a spiritual sickness born out of the ur-explanation of all social ills: the hierarchical power structure. Hierarchy implies a complex, ladder-like system where the enemy is not a particular class but a matter of levels. Kyriarchy expanded this model with a more interlinked account of oppression, showing that someone could simultaneously be the oppressor and the oppressed. While more complex, the new model makes it absolutely impossible to develop *political forces.* Everyone oppresses someone – if not systemically, then through micro-aggression – therefore the development of political forces could only affirm social oppression because forcing itself is oppression. Here, the abstract concept of power is what must be opposed. Politics becomes anti-politics. The new politics becomes anti-oppression training sessions – not just a critique of ideology or self-reflection, but actual confessionals. In other words, a religious ethic of sorts has replaced economic and political analyses within feminist practice. The only kinds of force that are acceptable are self-defense and self-protection, which, without a larger macropolitical context, becomes (of course) exhausting. The development of safe spaces becomes an anti-political project of resistance with no strategy for overcoming.

Of course, self-reflection and the criticism of attitudes, behaviors, and presuppositions *while engaged in actual political activity* are critical. It is a difficult business to work through racism, traditional/oppositional sexism, cissexism, and anti-immigrant attitudes – not to mention the myriad other ways in which we ignore one another's needs – in the middle of political organizing; but working through racism or sexism in a student consciousness-raising group, at a book club, or on social media is therapy for depoliticized subjects. Therapy is not something to be opposed; but, on its own, it brings about neither reforms nor revolutions.

The financial malaise of the early twenty-first century laid bare the limitations of this sort of small-scale subjective politics. A renewed interest in Marx's economic ideas emerged. The feminization of the new service-sector labor force had pundits in the centers of capital talking about a *mancession.* Concurrent with the return of economics, antagonism between the conservative movement and queer/trans people kept the LGBT struggle on the map. Marxists found themselves back in the conversation when it came to explaining global crises, but were at the margins of queer and trans political struggle due to the lack of a specifically Marxist theory of that struggle. But sustained attention to issues of gender and sexuality began to emerge in Marxist political activity and Marxist scholarship. Sherry Wolf's activist handbook, *Sexuality and Socialism,* dispelled the myth of gay wealth, outlined pragmatic Marxist responses to queer sexual politics, and provided a history of socialist involvement in queer struggle (Wolf 2009). Lise Vogel's critical *Capital*-based analysis of social reproduction theory was rereleased (Vogel 2014). Heather Brown produced new scholarship analyzing Marx's writing on women and gender, while carefully examining his *Ethnological Notebooks* on pre-feudal family relations (Brown 2013). Kevin Floyd expanded analyses of industrial history and culture to include the creation of desire as a commodified 'thing' and its role in the development of gay male identity in *The Reification of Desire* (Floyd 2009). Peter Drucker developed an expansive historical materialist outline of how economic shifts have affected queer history around the world, openly calling for a queer Marxism (Drucker 2015). The growth of Marxist-feminist and queer Marxist scholarship makes it possible to begin thinking in terms of a unitary theory incorporating international queer, trans, and intersex perspectives into Marxist materialist analyses of sex and gender.

But this return to Marx is fairly recent. The radical feminism and cultural feminism that dominated the second-wave and early third-wave movements described Marx as a masculine thinker who sought to overthrow nature (which cultural feminism problematically aligns with 'the feminine') on behalf of a male-coded proletarian. As described in Chapter 1, teleology is the idea that history is linear and marches inevitably towards a meaningful conclusion: as if humanity were standing on the conveyor belt of history. Things happen to it and humanity responds according to its biological imperatives, but people have no agency to either hop off the conveyor belt or redesign it. Evidence of Marx's determinism usually consists of quotes from *The Communist Manifesto,* such as 'What the bourgeois ... produces, above all, is its own grave-diggers. Its fall and the victory of the proletariat are equally inevitable,' and his comments in the *Eighteenth Brumaire* 'that men make history but not under circumstances of their own choosing' and that 'the consciousness of men does not determine their being but their being determines their consciousness'. But the vision of Marx as an Aristotelian teleologist grossly simplifies Marx's project. Humanity is not a mere passenger riding atop the engine of history. The language Marx uses is more metaphorical than causal. He does not say that social life is *caused by* economics; rather, the argument is that life is conditioned by and arises from material facts. That is not the same as claiming causality. Less commonly cited are the passages where Marx puts agency at the forefront – 'the starting point ... is real living individuals themselves' – and comments such as 'circumstances make men just as much as men make circumstances'[10] can only be understood dialectically: people make history makes people makes history. Neither the chicken nor the egg 'comes first'.

Marx is not arguing that life advances predictably, step by step, but rather that life is conditioned by the organization of the world. Ideas are developed in historical context, and changes in consciousness do not come out of the ether and suddenly change the world; rather, our consciousness is shaped in response to the world, and from those changes we act upon the world. From this perspective, the tactics currently in vogue in gender politics – the awareness campaign, the development of personal consciousness and collective consciousness – cannot effect substantial change in material and social conditions. As far as the seemingly determinist comments in *The Communist Manifesto* go, it is, in the end, a *manifesto*, a political document intended to propagandize not ontologize. Indeed, capitalism produces the conditions for its own destruction by creating a collective workforce with the instruments to overthrow it. But Marx also argues the possibility of the mutual ruin of contending classes. The move from capitalism to a classless society is not a given; mutual ruin is also a possible outcome.

Awareness campaigns about environmental destruction have been very successful at helping individual consumers and whole nations understand that a crisis is at hand. But mass awareness has had no significant impact on the environment because ecological destruction is not the product of human consciousness; it is a product of the inherent demands of the capitalist cycle.[11] Since productive labor produces surplus value, the amount of socially necessary labor time embodied in an individual commodity drops as a product is produced more quickly. The faster production moves, and as more products are used, the more profits expand. This is the unavoidable logic of the system.[12] The individual capitalist who ignores the demands of the system will not be a capitalist for long. The weakness of the awareness campaign as a political strategy is not that making people aware is inherently useless or that human consciousness is irrelevant to global development. In a war of position,[13] building hegemony is a part of a political sequence geared towards social transformation. In the awareness model, the struggle for ideological hegemony is the whole of the war. All that is necessary to change the world is the awakening of the masses; their individual behaviors will transform the material world. In other words, we are at a loss for solutions. Like Smith's invisible hand of the market, modern politics relies on the invisible hand of ethical conscience.

Marxist ecologists have done the most to dismiss claims that Marx was a teleological thinker. John Bellamy Foster and Paul Burkett have shown evidence (Foster 2000; Burkett 2014) that Marx's ecology does not suggest a war-like struggle between humanity and nature, but rather that humans and the natural world are locked in a *metabolic relation*: people interact with and consume their environs, in the end transforming them, and in turn they respond to the changes their existence provokes. Humans are not opposed to nature, because humans are not detached spirits floating around nature as if it were some kind of maze. Humans exist within and develop from nature. Moreover, all that exists does so within history and as history, and therefore all that exists undergoes transformation. Even feminists critical of Marx have recently conceded that Marx's thinking was driven by disdain for the Enlightenment mind/body dichotomy. By placing material life and embodied reality above abstract rumination, Marx opens up a space within the history of philosophy where women's existence can be considered (see Leeb 2007). The relation of body to mind, of humanity to nature, of subject to object are interrelated. Nothing exists *as such*. Everything is shaped by interaction with the environment, including the environment itself; this makes for a world that is not linear or teleological, but a world filled with contingencies of all sorts, even within a world of natural laws.[14]

IV. Marx on women

Early in his writing career, Marx remarked that the health of a society is indexed by how it treats its women. Feminists have dismissed this as merely echoing the sentiments of the utopian socialist Charles Fourier, but Heather Brown argues that this comment is integrated into Marx's developmental understanding of the relationship between nature and culture: 'for humanity to reach its full potential, this biological factor must be superseded. A new unity between humanity and nature must be reached. This, for Marx, is only possible if the gender-inequalities stemming from social organization are overcome' (Brown 2013: 31). Brown shows that Marx addresses the problem of sexual violence against women in a refreshingly non-moralistic way through his analysis of the characters in Eugène Sue's *Les Mystères de Paris*. Sue's novel, published as a newspaper serial, contains an early critique of forced prostitution using the character of Fleur de Marie to describe the situation of many working-class women in mid-nineteenth-century Paris. Far from the passive victim that Sue sees in his character, Marx describes her as 'a girl that can vindicate her rights and put up a fight' (quoted in Brown 2013: 37). This is no abstract literary analysis. Marx is well aware that the streets of industrializing cities were littered with poor people forced to resort to the sex trade due to unemployment or low pay. The financial pressure to prostitute oneself within the working class was such that, in France, working men called the prostitution of their wives and daughters 'the nth working hour'.[15] Brown argues that Marx is clearly insisting here that morality is not an abstraction for the working class, nor is it based in sexual purity; rather, it is based in thoughtfulness towards others and pro-social acts. In the end, Sue saves Fleur de Marie by putting her in a nunnery, where Marx reads her as experiencing an even deeper level of alienation. She is forced to trade the difficulties of her real life as a prostitute for an imaginary piety. Soon after she becomes a nun, she dies. Like Fleur de Marie, another of Sue's characters, Louise Morel, is forced into servitude, raped and impregnated by her boss, then is charged with murder when the infant dies in childbirth.[16] The heroic nobleman who tells the stories of the poor remarks that laws ought to be passed to protect servants against violence. Marx states that, of course, neither the protagonist hero nor the book's author question why on earth the character is a servant in the first place.[17] Marx is solidly aware here that sex work is *work*, and that non-sex work for women – domestic service, for example – is often sexualized into a form of de facto sex work.[18] While feminists (even self-described Marxist-feminists) debate whether or not sex work counts as work, Marx's economic analyses give us a much clearer answer: if you work for a wage for someone who profits from your labor, you're a worker. If you live off the revenue brought in by those you do not pay, you are a slaver. If you live off the profits of the commodities produced by workers, you are a capitalist. If you are an object traded by other parties for sex rights, you are a slave and a commodity. If you receive a wage from your boss in exchange for sexual favors given to a client, you are a worker. If you are a woman who owns a brothel, you are a small capitalist (petit bourgeois). The fact that an economic transaction is sex-related does not magically transform the way capitalism works. It doesn't throw the relations of production into hopeless confusion.

In keeping with his early inquiry into alienation, Marx published an essay on the politics of suicide in the journal *Gesellschaftsspiegel* which mainly dealt with the suicide of bourgeois women (Brown 2013: 44–8; Anderson 1999). Marx quotes a suicide investigator: 'The [French] revolution did not topple all tyrannies. The evil which one blames on arbitrary forces exists in families, where it causes crises, analogous to those of revolutions' (Brown 2013: 46). The first case is that of a young woman who commits suicide after having been humiliated by her parents for having sex with her fiancé before marriage. Brown notes that Marx highlights the systemic nature of the problem in this article: bourgeois parents subject their children to discipline and humiliation just as the market disciplines and humiliates them. Discussing the case of a woman who commits suicide due to marital rape and confinement, Marx notes that, instead of a union based on the 'spontaneous feeling of the lovers', the current social conditions allow 'the jealous husband to fetter his wife in chains, like a miser with his hoard of gold, for she is but a part of his inventory'.[19]

During his time as a journalist during the 1850s, as the chief European correspondent for the *New York Tribune*, Marx took a particular interest in the gaslighting of a noblewoman by the men in her family, who did so to terminate her property rights. Lady Rosina Bulwer Lytton was married to a Tory politician, Edward Bulwer Lytton; after the marriage dissolved due to her husband's behavior, Lady Bulwer Lytton went on to become a novelist, disguising her husband among the characters. When Bulwer Lytton disrupted her husband's re-election proceedings to denounce him, her husband and son had her committed to an asylum. Marx wrote two scathing articles criticizing the British establishment journalists for refusing to expose the situation: 'For aught the chivalrous knights of the inkhorn would care about it, Lady Bulwer would have remained forever in a lunatic asylum' (Brown 2013: 107). He also attacks the low requirements for having someone cast into an asylum in Britain. For Marx, this exposes the shallowness and hypocrisy of Britain's belief in liberty. Liberty for propertied men, but asylums for women who want to keep their property (ibid.: 105–12). The feminist accusation that Marx is a narrow, class reductionist falls short of grasping Marx's actual political activities and interests. Marx saw that capitalism had ill effects on oppressed groups, whether or not they benefited from capital accumulation and expropriation.

V. Marx on gender and labor

Despite the fact that Marx showed concern for the situation of women under capitalism, he never endeavored to write a systematic breakdown of the origins of the devalued position of women in society; so, unfortunately, the legacy of Marx's position on women's oppression is not fully developed. In their early works, Marx and Engels trace the origin of the history of property relations to the patriarchal family, where 'wife and children are the slaves of the husband'. They continue: 'This latent slavery in the family, though still very crude, is the first property, but even at this early stage it corresponds perfectly to the definition of modern economists who call it the power of disposing of the labour-power of others' (Marx, *The German Ideology*, in Marx and Engels 1975c). It would be close to four decades before Engels used Marx's notebooks to explain how the state developed to protect private property through the creation of the patriarchal family. But as early as the publication of *The Communist Manifesto*, Marx and Engels analyzed how industrial production was transforming gender relations. Less physical exertion was needed to produce commodities – what used to involve chopping and hauling now required only the capacity to manipulate machinery. Workers became 'merely instruments of labour which cost more or less according to age and sex' (Marx, *The Manifesto of the Communist Party* in Marx and Engels 1976). So, in one sense, industrial labor 'ungendered' nineteenth-century workers, since certain physical characteristics were no longer required. The entire family could be swept into the factory's folds, children and all. But those who owned the means of production also used sexual divisions to hyper-exploit populations who were vulnerable because of their social gender (women) or because of their legal dependency (children). Women and children entered the labor market at a bargaining position below male workers, yet the invention of machine technology made it possible to hire women and children to do the work previously done by men. Call it the nineteenth-century *mancession*.

What makes labor a special commodity is that its value is dependent on human subjectivity, particularly on desperation and the capacity for suffering. Oppressed populations – so long as they are free enough to sell their labor – can be more profitable than populations with better options. While commodities that promise self-esteem are lucrative, a self-confident labor force is not. Relative surplus value – the fact that capitalists can make extra profit by driving down the cost of labor power relative to other capitalists – means that human labor can be more profitable than animal labor. An animal must be purchased. As a piece of property, it must be maintained by its owner. But wage labor costs a fixed amount per hour paid to any capable laborer available. This laborer can be worked to death and replaced by another wage laborer with no cost to the capitalist. The limit to how hard an animal can be worked is measured in terms of how much it will cost to replace it. The limit to how hard labor can be worked is dependent on the size of the labor pool, the degree to which workers have organized in self-defense, and their ability to have criminal legislation passed and enforced to protect their health and safety. For this reason, an attack on the perceived social value of a set of workers rationalizes the lowering of their wages. Assigning low value to women, racial and ethnic minorities, immigrants, and gender non-conforming people is also a literal lowering on the labor market.[20] For this reason alone, solidarity with women, queer and trans people, immigrants, Black people, and the disabled[21] should be the task of all who are on the side of labor.

Unfortunately, there are all too many examples of relative surplus value extraction driving wages into oblivion. Marx notes in *Capital* (Volume I, Chapter 15) that in Britain women were still employed to do the job of hauling canal boats instead of horses. This is because 'the labour required to produce horses and machines is an accurately known quantity, while that required to maintain the women of the surplus-population is below all calculation'. He notes that such hyper-exploitation has nothing to do with low levels of technological development. In fact, the shift from using machinery to hiring surplus populations to do physical labor is one contradictory feature of industrial advancement. 'Hence nowhere do we find a more shameful squandering of human labour-power for the most despicable purposes than in England, the land of machinery.'

We can make more sense of this by examining recent industrial history. During the earthquake in Mexico City in 1985, employers saved the sewing machines, not the seamstresses (Poniatowska 1995: especially 237–8). The sewing machines had a definite cost that had already been paid (or, if bought on credit, carried a debt). But the dead seamstresses could just be replaced by a new crop of women the next day. Similarly, in the 2012 factory fire in Pakistan, workers were ordered to stay in the burning building to help rescue the clothes. The clothes had a definite value determined by the labor power already used to create them. The workers, on the other hand, could be replaced as long as there were others desperate enough to take the job at the same pay. Workers are the interchangeable and disposable parts of machines; their birth is a gift to the owners of factories, mines, and workshops everywhere.

But the extreme levels of exploitation in Victorian England limited Marx's ability to fully consider the problem of social reproduction under capitalism. Marx and Engels assumed that the family form would soon be completely eroded by factory work; it seemed that wages and conditions were becoming so bad that the class itself might reach a point where it could not replace itself. He and Engels could not have predicted the interventions Keynes developed after the Great Depression, but welfare state interventions only underscore capitalism's inherent rapacity. Those who own the means of production can disregard the needs of their current wage workers as long as a reserve army of labor is available. However, that 'surplus population' must be available – be they women, children, immigrants, or the disenfranchised (former convicts, gender minorities, the disabled, the homeless). In fact, the notion that one can 'drop out of society' and live an 'alternative lifestyle' in an 'alternative community' fails to pose a challenge to the system: 'drop-outs' are always already factored in as unwitting members of the reserve army of labor. The struggle of the working class to maintain itself reveals the flatness of the argument that being radically queer is inherently anti-capitalist. What capitalism relies on is the unpaid reproduction and maintenance of its workforce. The only sexual politics that could end the reproduction of an exploitable class of workers would be a moratorium on childbirth, but this would be the destruction of the working class itself, leveraged to assure 'mutual destruction'. This is not without precedent. During the brutality of American slavery, women were driven to infanticide in order to stop infant trafficking. But if infanticide was not a genuine threat to the slave trade, how much less of a political challenge to capitalism is queer sexuality?

The use of women as a cheap labor source during the Industrial Revolution occasioned Marx to argue, against the Proudhonist anarchists, that women should be integrated into organized labor – after all, they were being organized into the labor force, to organize them as workers in solidarity with working men only made sense. One text that shows Marx's understanding that women ought to be political agents in their own liberation is his later work 'The Programme of the Parti Ouvrier'. The second part of the tract is co-written with Jules Guesde, Engels, and Paul Lafargue, but the first part is wholly his own (Brown 2013: 130–2). The document serves to codify demands 'arisen out of the labor movement itself' and acknowledges that it owes its debt to the Paris Commune, including its women fighters. The first section of the text discusses what a communist society might look like (one of the rare times Marx ventures into this territory) and the second contains a minimal program of reforms. Brown notes that the preamble 'makes a relatively strong statement with regard to the position of women within a future socialist society' when it asserts that 'the emancipation of the class of producers involves all mankind, without distinction of sex or race' (Marx, 'Preamble to the Programme of the French Workers' Party' in Marx and Engels 1989: 340–2). While the future demands for women are somewhat vague, the concrete demands of the program clearly benefited women. The first demand is that the part of the Napoleonic Code stating that 'the inferiority of the worker in relation to the boss, and of woman in relation to man' be struck out. This was important because, under the Napoleonic Code, husbands had the right to imprison or kill their wives for adultery. Other demands sought to ease domestic labor by including social provisions for the care of the elderly and the disabled, along with the immediate demand of 'equal pay for equal work, for workers of both sexes'. Brown notes that Marx's progressive stance on women's labor was not a given in the labor movement. Not only did the Proudhonists argue that women should not be included in the labor movement, in a pamphlet they argued that *without the family, woman has no reason for being on earth* (quoted in Brown 2013: 132).

One particular question feminists have raised about Marx's analysis of women's oppression relates to his position on the family wage. Medieval European society was a patriarchy, meaning that the father was the head of the household and responsible for organizing and disciplining the household labor of wives, children, and servants. As capitalism developed, outside manufacturing was brought into the home. Now fathers were the overseers of the cottage industries taking place in the domestic sphere. But as Marx describes in *Capital* (Volume 1), industrial capitalism dismantled the patriarchal family structure, and in doing so it upended domestic relations. While the women and children continued with the domestic labor once directed by the husband, in proletarian families men were the first to head to the factories for work. This holdover of patriarchal structure led to the assumption of a *family wage*. The male worker's wage was intended to support his entire family.

However, as family wages declined, women and children began to enter the factory. This undermined the position of men as head of the household, not to mention the logic of the family wage. On the one hand, it opened up a world of possibilities for young women, who could finally escape the patriarchal family. Moving to the cities for factory work provided new social opportunities, including the cultivation of same-sex desire.[22] Marx is not blind to the benefits of how the new order disrupted feudal patriarchy. He remarks that capitalism augurs 'a new economic foundation for a higher form of the family and of relations between the sexes'. But he also argued that from an economic standpoint the destruction of the old gender order had become an opportunity for the capitalist class to ramp up exploitation. Doing away with the family wage lowered the wages of each individual worker. The hook would be that the collective wages of father, mother, and child would surpass the earlier family wage, but each individual would earn less; in this way, wages in general would drop across the board. In economic terms, the end of the family wage allowed employers to expropriate even more absolute surplus value, as more workers meant more working hours for capitalists as a whole.

Feminists have criticized the language Marx used to describe the economic hardship of the loss of the family wage, sensing an underlying sexism in his tone. 'Machinery, by throwing every member of that family onto the labor market, spreads the value of the man's labor power over his whole family. It thus depreciates it.' But, as Heather Brown notes, *this is an empirical, not a normative claim* (emphasis mine). Also, a good way to completely misread *Capital* is to imagine normative moral claims where Marx is simply expressing scorn for empirical facts. Given his work as a whole, Marx's comment is not a tacit celebration of the family wage.[23] Here, we can see how the anti-woman sentiment among the Proudhonists has clear economic roots. Men, as a general bloc, not only wanted to maintain the value of their labor, they wanted to retain their identities as the heads of their households. Either way, the capitalist class benefited. The family wage maintained male supremacy, thereby upholding the social order and putting the women of the reserve army of labor in a position of weakness. On the other hand, the abolition of the family wage meant an immediate increase in profits.

The problem of the family wage would later become a sticking point between feminists who criticized the oppressive structure of the nuclear family and some socialists who felt that the fight for the family wage, even the fight to protect the family itself, was a way to protect the working class from further exploitation. But while the family wage may have been a rallying cry in the nineteenth century, industrially advanced regions in the twentieth century saw an increase in female-headed families. The family wage was, of course, not extended to them, and thus the family wage was detached from the notion of support for dependent children. Once women entered the workforce en masse, a family wage simply meant higher wages for men. What's more, equal pay for equal work has not, generally speaking, raised the wages of women, but instead has provided a negative equality by lowering the wages of men. However, Marx and Engels were expecting changes in the family form. Ripped from its sentimental veil, the family was just a unit for material production. As Marx emphasizes in *The German Ideology*, 'one cannot speak at all of the family "as such"'. In other words, there is no such thing as the essential, eternal family. Families are a response to economic social relations.

But how do Marx and Engels fare as personal champions of the queer? To be blunt: they don't. In fact, to his discredit, Engels even managed to work some homophobic snark into one of his letters to Marx (Weeks 1975).[24] Using Julia Serano's schema, where women's unequal treatment is described as *traditional sexism*, and where the demand that feminine qualities be housed in female bodies and masculine behaviors in male bodies is called *oppositional sexism*, while there is a strong case to be made that Marx and Engels were not traditional sexists, they were certainly, in many ways, oppositional sexists – along with the vast majority of Victorian Europeans at the time. While the beginning of a gay identity and a gay rights movement emerged only at the end of Marx's life, oppositional sexism is the most likely candidate for why Engels failed to recognize the validity of queer politics. Engels would go on after Marx's death to write a book about the origin of women's oppression using Marx's notes. Engels' work would simultaneously chart a materialist path for women's liberation and inscribe an unfortunate and completely unnecessary element of heterosexism into twentieth-century Marxist politics: unnecessary because, as we shall see, other early socialists had no problem getting the question right.

VI. The major works: Marx's *Ethnological Notebooks* and Engels' *The Origin of the Family, Private Property, and the State*

In 1884, one year after Marx's death, and while in the middle of preparing the unwritten volumes of Marx's *Capital*, Engels put together *The Origin of the Family, Private Property, and the State* from Marx's anthropological notes. The book instantly entered the socialist canon and has been interpreted by many as a summation of Marx's thoughts on women's oppression and therefore as the key text for orienting oneself as a Marxist on the question of women's liberation. Engels uses a historical materialist approach to describe the fate of women through different periods of human social and material life: from group marriages, to marriages within clans, to lifelong monogamy. The analysis shows the transformation of family relations throughout history, underscoring his and Marx's comment in *The German Ideology* that an eternal, ideal form of the family does not exist. His work describes how family formation is affected and transformed by larger social and political arrangements based on, 'in the final instance, the production and reproduction of immediate life' (Engels 1973).

Engels uses Lewis Henry Morgan's anthropological schema to tell a story: at the beginning of human history, before settled agriculture, societies were matrilineal and women had social power. However, after sedentarization – permanently settling in one location instead of moving when resources became thin – the gender landscape was thoroughly transformed. During the hunter-gatherer phase, it was critical to keep the tribe to a low number.[25] But settled agriculture required populations to tend to animals and crops produced at a volume that would be enough to provide the community with extra food and materials for surviving hardships. Whereas, in the past, they would simply move to another location, settled tribes had to cope with maintaining and protecting surplus goods.

The struggle for control over these surplus goods gave rise to class-stratified societies. Parents now sought to pass their surplus property on to their children exclusively; however, the only way a man could know if a child was his offspring was for women's sexuality to be tethered to his own. Women's chastity became a key factor in property relations. Whereas women's labor had once included gathering food and developing plant medicines, women's tasks became exclusively tied to pregnancy and childrearing. Engels refers to this social transformation as 'the world-historic defeat of the female sex'. Gradually, after generations of male domination, women became commodities for trade.

There have been many criticisms of Engels' analysis. The first is tied to Morgan's own weaknesses. For example, the terms matriarchy and patriarchy are not as accurate as subsequently invented terms such as matrilineal and patrilineal (describing the path of property inheritance) or patrilocal and matrilocal (describing physical locations of people within a group). However, Morgan's work is not entirely wrong – and not only because it laid the basis for further anthropological research. Empirically, the historical necessity for the creation of surplus goods does seem to lead to a struggle over who gets to control the surplus, and patrilineal families are by and large more repressive towards female sexuality.[26] Morgan's work also shows how social life develops from a mix of new inventions, changing ideas about government, changing family forms, and shifts in property distribution. Engels also adds a layer of moral evolution to Morgan's work that does not exist in the original. Here, Engels is quite teleological: early civilization leads to the family form being corrupted by the transfer of family property. The communist future of the family will bring about individual fulfillment based on what he calls 'individual sex-love', and the very unromantic notion of marriage as a duty based on inheritance rights would end. This, however, echoes Morgan's sense that the shifts in family forms – from open sexuality to intra-family marriage, to marriage between cousins, to paired couples living in larger clan households, to heterosexual monogamy – correlated to the progressive freedom of individuals. (Of course, freedom only for those individuals assigned to live as males.)

But criticism of Engels' *The Origin of the Family, Private Property, and the State* has not been wholly from outside the Marxist camp. Marxist-feminists have outlined the pitfalls of Engels' work, not in order to bicker with the material basis of women's oppression or to reject his ideas on sedentarization, but to develop a Marxist theory of sex and gender that is more informed by Marxist economics. Lise Vogel's Marxist-feminist analyses are sharply critical of Engels' shortcomings. Vogel's first critique is the one most obvious to even untrained feminist ears: Engels squarely puts the responsibility for reproduction of the household onto women. Of the two, Engels was certainly a much less nuanced writer and thinker than his intellectual companion. Despite his strong disapproval of patriarchal violence and the confinement of women, and despite his vision of a collective future where men and women would work together as equals, Engels' oppositional sexism limits his analysis.

Vogel criticizes Engels' work in three important ways. Her first critique is from a Marxist perspective, an insight from the work of Clara Zetkin: Engels' universalization of family development forgets to distinguish between the development of women's position in ruling classes and in subordinate classes. The working-class family does not hinge upon relations of inheritance. More often than not, there is no inheritance to bequeath. Vogel argues that the primary social function for the existence of the working-class family is to reproduce the working class. In other words, Engels' weakness is that '[p]roperty, not exploitation – the appropriation of the surplus labor of the producing class by another class – becomes the implicit object of class struggle' (Vogel 2014: 91). Marxist political economy isn't about the distribution of wealth, but rather the extraction of value from one class of people by another. Vogel's second and third criticisms come from a more specifically feminist angle but emerge from her first point: Engels does not explore a material basis for male supremacy in the *proletarian* household (ibid.: 88). Without a material explanation, one must resort to assumptions about ideological conditioning. This leads to Vogel's third critique of Engels' work: that it 'vastly underestimates the ideological and psychological factors that provide a continuing foundation for male supremacy in the working class family' (ibid.: 89). In other words, women's political decline during the shift to structural patriarchy is one thing, but understanding why men without property continue to abuse and demean women is another, especially if one is trying to develop a unitary theory of gender and sex oppression.

Heather Brown criticizes Engels from another perspective. Channeling Lukács, Carver, and Dunayevskaya, Brown argues that Engels' work is less nuanced and more deterministic than Marx's work and that the views of the two on gender should be disentangled. While Marx locates the kernel of the new in the shell of the old, Engels views history as a forward march, one in which society reacts to material developments and maintains its shape until the next development occurs. Where Marx dives into the concrete and rises with new theoretical models, Engels tends towards abstraction and fails to see subjectivity and objectivity as a unity of opposites.[27] Brown backs up her critique with significant scholarly work that carefully examines Marx's *Ethnological Notebooks*. Legend has it that Engels crafted *The Origin of the Family, Private Property, and the State* through a close examination of the final notebooks left by Marx upon his death, but Brown points to Engels' lack of fidelity. Marx's notes do not cover just pre-capitalist gender relations in Iroquois society but also gender relations as they developed in Italy, Ireland, and India (see Brown 2013: 133). Engels uses Morgan's anthropological research as a sort of map, while Marx was contrasting the work of Morgan against that of other prominent nineteenth-century anthropologists. Brown surmises that it is even likely that Engels did not intend for his work to be granted canonical status, and that perhaps he even meant the book to be a Marxist explanation of Morgan's anthropology, which Engels considered to be as definitive to anthropology as Darwin's work was for the theory of evolution (ibid.: 163–75).

In fact, Brown makes the claim that, in Marx's final years, his notebooks show that he was beginning to subtly revise his political theory. He remarked that revolution was not necessarily dependent on the levels of productive development so long as larger states followed suit.[28] Perhaps the most surprising revelation is Brown's evidence that Marx was treating the working class as a diverse political subject, partially composed of women, who were also considered to be revolutionary political subjects (ibid.: 133–62). For Marx, history is not broken into two halves, where women once experienced freedom only to be followed by a world-historic defeat. Marx paints a more complex picture in which the roots of sexism are visible within primitive communism and where women can emerge as self-possessed revolutionary subjects even after the development of patriarchy.

VII. Early Marxist and socialist feminism

Who is the woman in the woman question?

It is important to clarify what is meant and who is being referred to when the word 'woman' is used. By treating the collective subject 'woman' as transparently obvious, Marxists and (second-wave) feminists have still left us with a subject whose ontological boundaries are universal and ahistorical: women undergo changes, but who is and who isn't a woman is eternal. Yet it is circular reasoning to say that women are naturally inclined to fulfill particular social roles, since how we read and sort bodies depends on how we construct gender categories, and such gender categories are constructed in line with how bodily functions fulfill social needs. No, the body itself was not some sort of pure social construct without materiality in nineteenth-century Europe; and, no, sexual aspects of human bodies themselves have not changed in fantastical ways since antiquity. But the norms used to read and socially interpret physical characteristics change over time, and that interpretation is partially influenced not only by previous social gender norms, but by the subtle shifts in social meaning surrounding assumptions about the body inflected by a given society's level of material development: the way it creates race, its class relations, and the gendering required for the maintenance of those classes and races.

We only know the gender *categories* of various time periods. We do not necessarily know which bodies were, empirically speaking, assigned to those categories. For example, in the twentieth century, sex was assigned at birth based on the social opinions of the medical establishment. In the West, if the phallus of an infant with XY chromosomes was too small, the infant's penis might be reshaped into a clitoris and the child assigned to the 'female' camp because the assumption was that it is better to be a woman than a man with a small penis. In the Middle East, however, any child who could reasonably pass for male, including XX children with enlarged clitorises, would be raised as male (Fausto-Sterling 2000). Although he had a romantic heterosexual telos in mind, even Engels noted that Ancient Greeks constructed a particular sex category called 'eunuch'. Eunuchs have had distinct histories in Greece, Byzantium, and China; in India and Pakistan, some *hijra* still use the term. So we can construct a thing called women's history, but we cannot presume to know the biological reality of the people living inside and outside of it. This means that intersexed and trans people are not 'outside' of history or new to history and that women's history of the nineteenth century is not merely cisgendered women's history.

In the book *Making Sex*, Thomas Laqueur shows how Greek assumptions about sex categorization affected social gender until (and in some ways even after) the Enlightenment. Greeks imagined that there was only one universal human body – a masculine body – with heat and moisture levels affecting how the body was shaped. This is distinct from later Western assumptions of male and female as opposite sexes with no possible continuum. In the latter paradigm, sex is like a left hand and a right hand; there is no 'middle hand' of sex. But this is a fairly recent concept in the West. The sex system of Ancient Greece functioned as a hierarchy grounded in metaphor. Strength was conceived as hot and dry and weakness was thought to be cold and moist. As a consequence, females were imagined to be biological males whose penises inverted due to their inability to generate heat. Gender was assigned on a scale running from hot to cold, with masculine men at the top, followed by feminine men, viragos (masculine women), eunuchs, boys, women and girls. Medical drawings throughout Europe show this conception of womanhood lasting until the sixteenth century (Laqueur 1992).

This conception of sexual development had social consequences. Since women were inverted men, it was assumed that their pleasure was required for the conception of children. As a result, women's sexual pleasure was treated as socially valuable. However, there was a down side to this affirmation: since women's pleasure was essential for procreation, pregnancies resulting from rape were evidence of the woman's enjoyment, contributing both to the myth of rape as a potentially enjoyable experience (ibid.: 126–7) and to the myth that women's unconscious selves secretly signal sexual consent while women's conscious minds deny that consent is given. This is why, even today, when a woman says she was sexually assaulted and a man says that sex was consensual, it is called a 'he said/she said' situation. The notion that his claim about her state of mind is equal to her claim about her own state of mind suggests one of two things: either she is a malevolent creature who lures men into sex in order to make accusations against them, or she has a secret self who consents to sex without her knowledge. That she is a person who can clearly articulate sexual consent and that he is lying to save himself from criminal prosecution is only a possibility when the accused is generally disliked or in a lower class or caste than the accuser.[29]

If heating and cooling were thought to have the capacity to change bodies, then gender identity could not have been stable. While Aristotelian essentialists believed that sexed bodies determined human behavior, the 'heat theory' implied that human behavior determined sex.[30] One example of gender supposedly determining sex is the case of a youth named Marie who sprouted a penis after jumping over a ravine while chasing pigs and afterwards grew into a man with a 'thick red beard' (ibid.: 161–3). Because surgical 'correction' of intersex infants did not exist until the mid-twentieth century, bodies were more diverse. In fact, early medical taxonomists could not determine the definitive distinction between male and female. Patients varied in secondary sex characteristics – some women were more hirsute than some men. Some men menstruated and bore children. Some women were discovered to have testicles. Our contemporary impression of 'extreme difference' between sexed bodies cannot be disentangled from the invention of plastic surgery, hormone replacement, and depilatories. Since there was more body diversity before the twentieth century, in addition to (in many parts of the world) non-binary gender categorizations, we can assume that, while manhood and womanhood are constant constructs, the people living in these categories would not necessarily fit contemporary expectations. Our understanding of what constitutes male and female has shifted radically over time: the West first assumed that bodies were gendered through external environmental factors (i.e. heat, moisture), then it adopted an understanding that males and females were taxonomically distinct creatures, then from the mid-1950s to the turn of the millennium it was thought that all fetuses were female until they triggered an activity that transformed the generic fetus into a male (Fausto-Sterling 2000: 202–5). All manner of ideological frippery was layered onto this genetic assumption: for example, it was thought that this proved that the female was passive material, while the male was active in distinguishing himself; the XX of the female was described as a form of 'lack', while the XY chromosome was human agency itself.[31] Current discoveries in cellular biology disrupt this narrative. A recent article in the journal *Nature* (Ainsworth 2015) shows that cells themselves are genetically 'sex-marked' as triggering XY or XX, and that on a cellular level an individual can have a mixture of XX and XY chromosomes. Sex appears to exist on a continuum, with sexual dimorphism being merely the ends of the spectrum. There also appear to be physical aspects to gender orientation; an individual's sense of where they fit on the sexed continuum correlates with brain structure and brain activity, and is not affected by hormone levels (Kranz et al. 2014). Moreover, this sort of gendered 'proprioception' is not associated with existing genitals or reproductive capacity.

Gender diversity is not some mere product of late capitalist individualism. One sometimes hears remarks suggesting that transgendered people are attention-seeking postmodern hyper-individualists[32] who think they can purchase gender as if it were a commodity. Indeed, one deep ecology group has adopted a trans-exclusionary position based on such an assumption.[33] Here, we see how the strict social constructionist position on gender serves to uphold the ideology of strict biological sexual dimorphism. Despite their acknowledgement that social gender is a construction, trans-exclusionary feminism requires a deep belief in biological truth categories. Women (i.e. cissexual, non-intersexed women defined by vaginas) remain the clear victims of sexist violence, which is something that men (i.e. cissexual, non-intersexed men defined by penises) are biologically predisposed to perpetuate. In this worldview, gender is just the social ideology that oppresses women, not as a category but as a 'class'. Whereas a truly systemic analysis of the functions and origins of sexism would examine structures of misogyny and their relation to transmisogyny, despite their lip service to fighting the so-called system, in TERF logic the perpetrator of violence is not a system but ultimately the male ability to penetrate females who cannot penetrate back.[34] But not only is scientific inquiry revealing that sex is not strictly binary, non-binary gender expression predates capitalism. In fact, it is well documented that colonial expansion enforced regimes of binary gender on indigenous peoples. Countering the belief that trans political demands are expressions of decadent Western individualism, before European contact a number of Native American tribes had a much more rational approach: children were socially ungendered, and then, at puberty, they met with village elders to reveal whether they were male, female, or a different gender altogether (Williams 1986).[35]

Social gender assignment also fluctuates at the intersection of economy and culture. Sworn virgins in Romania do not necessarily live as men because they identify as gender queer individuals, but because they are determined at birth to live as men in order to continue lines of inheritance. In *Baran*, Iranian film director Majid Majidi depicts a rural girl heading to the city to cross-dress in order to access work – not as an expression of gender identity but as a risk taken to support her family. During Western industrialization, assumptions about childbearing capacity played a larger part in social gendering than it currently does in the twenty-first-century developed world. An ahistorical perspective might cause us to assume that birthrates were relatively stable until the invention of medical contraception, but dramatic fertility shifts followed the move from hunting and gathering to sedentarized, agricultural society. This was partly because extended periods of nursing prevented ovulation in hunter-gatherer society, while settled society saw an increase in ovulation, making large families possible while restricting the perimeter of activity for those assigned to live as female (Seccombe 1995: 17).

However, even when large families were possible, birthrates varied wildly. In the sixteenth and seventeenth centuries, after the devastation of the Thirty Years' War, the mean age for a woman to marry in England was 27; in Germany it was 30. Given that premarital birthrates declined drastically in this period, in part due to the expansion of Puritanism, we can assume that it was socially acceptable for women to go through an extended portion of their lives celibate – or at least refraining from the forms of sexual expression that produce pregnancy (ibid.: 190–2). Agricultural development and the Industrial Revolution initially reversed this trend. More children meant more laborers and therefore more income for parents. In the United States, for example, by 1800 the average fertility rate for white women was seven children. The birthrate among Black women in the 1850s was 7.9. In 1870, more than 37 percent of women had more than five children, compared with the late twentieth-century average of 1.7 children for white women and 2.3 for Black women (Ferguson and Folbre 1981: 313–25).[36] With motherhood as an almost guaranteed constraint on the lives of a vast number of women, it is not essentialist to assess women's lives during the rise of industry as intensely shaped by childbirth and childrearing responsibilities.

While industrialization allowed heterosexual couples to escape the confines and financial pressures of their birth families (children were typically expected to hand over earnings to parents), it also created space for gay and gender non-conforming people to gain independence, interact, and eventually develop a political identity. Subsequent changes in pensions and the creation of the welfare state replaced (or at least heavily supplemented) the care once expected of children in the West, and access to public healthcare has lowered infant mortality. Such innovations allowed a break from restrictive gendered social expectations and, in fact, changed the meaning of gender. In other words, the use of the term 'woman' always outlines the parameters of people in a social category at a concrete point in history. It is not the description of the trials and vicissitudes of a universal gender essence, nor does it assume that the gender identity of individuals matches their social gender assignment. Industrialization also gave rise to the proletariat and its political identity: as social norms and meanings shifted, nineteenth-century socialists committed to the emancipation of labor attempted to make sense of changing gender politics as well.

Sex and the utopian socialists

In everyday language, the term 'utopian' is synonymous with something along the lines of a beautiful but impossible dream. When political thinkers call Marx 'utopian', it says more about their opinion of Marx's ideas than it does about Marx's actual thinking. In Marxist terms, to be utopian means to have an abstract program for a better world, one that does not ground its goals in material reality, and one that does not give a credible explanation of how such a world would come to be. In contrast to the utopians, Marx refrained from prognosticating; instead, he busied himself with analyses of industry and manufacturing, with the vicissitudes of real political activity and social unrest, war, uprisings, material history, and living conditions. In contrast to Marx, the utopian socialist Charles Fourier created a politics that read like speculative fiction. In Fourier's new world, the experience of life was going to be 'a continuous … kaleidoscopic explosion of rapturous joy' (Riasanovsky 1969: 60). Here, Fourier channels Plato: all that is required to build a perfect society is a perfect design. Once the design was complete, human reason would ensure that humanity would be eager to participate in the utopian project. Marx and later Marxists, more interested in developing rational, materialist assessments of actual phenomena than designing an orgasmic paradise, naturally distanced themselves from utopian thinking. However, the feminist arguments of the utopians were clearly an inspiration to later socialist thinkers, including Marx. Charles Fourier has even been credited with inventing the term *féministe* (Goldstein 1982: 91–2). And, as mentioned earlier, Marx's comment that the level of progress in a society can be measured by its treatment of women is an overt appropriation of Fourier's feminist commitment.

The two nineteenth-century utopian strains most influential in Western feminist development were those of Charles Fourier and of the Saint-Simonians. The Saint-Simonian movement preached a kind of social equality for women that managed to be simultaneously forward-thinking and reactionary. The Saint-Simonians wanted to liberate women from domestic chores, unequal property relations, sexual double standards, and enforced submissiveness. Not satisfied to simply dream, the followers of Claude Henri de Rouvroy, comte de Saint-Simon, communed together in nature and practiced their principles. In the language of late twentieth-century gender politics, they *created space*. Possibly the most heterosexist variant of feminism in history, the Saint-Simonian concept of gender equality hinged upon designating heterosexual couples as the primary social unit of production. Each couple would be assigned a single public task to work on together with no sexual division of labor, and they would be remunerated for their work, not as individuals but as a couple. But this de-gendering of labor did not mean that men and women went socially ungendered. Their utopia was founded on the principles of reason and love – terms imagined to be synonymous with science and art. Of course, reason was the domain of men and love was the domain of women. Similar to their later cultural feminist counterparts, the Saint-Simonians thought that the ills of modern society stemmed from reason's repression of love. The solution to ending *logocentrism* was to elevate women's place in society.

Yet the Saint-Simonians' oppositional sexism overshadowed their attempts to eliminate traditional sexism: the only way to elevate women to positions of power would be to wait until a better society emerged, because the evils of the current world would corrupt women's pure spirits. The Saint-Simonians found themselves in a catch-22. Elevation of women would cure society, but elevation of women was impossible until society was cured (ibid.: 93–7).

As quirky as they may seem, the Saint-Simonians were positively sober compared with Charles Fourier. Total equality for women, including equality in choosing an occupation, was only the beginning of his program. Collectivization of women's deadening tasks would lessen the time required for labor, and an unprecedented sexual liberation would ensue. Fourier's new feminist world would be called Harmony. It would be divided into towns possessing a level of industrial progress that could rival any 1950s Hollywood sci-fi flick. Deserts would be irrigated. New technologies would control the weather. And, as a response to Harmony's attempts to make the world a better place, the universe itself would help humanity by making the weather more temperate. Libidinal energy would encompass Harmony so thoroughly that the planets themselves would have sexual relations with one another and, as a result, the seas would turn into lemonade.

Aside from the unlikelihood of this political psychedelia, Fourier's feminism was also deformed by the way he envisioned his utopia would manifest itself. This is partly because Fourier thought women's oppression was caused by a generalized libidinal repression. Because the release of libidinal desire would necessarily lead to a better society, sexual fulfillment was a cure-all and an imperative. Of course, participation could not be imposed; Fourier was a voluntarist. He knew that getting co-ed troops to embark upon the project of irrigating the Sahara desert would prove difficult. So his solution was to send the most beautiful women to work beside the men. Fourier's underlying assumption was that women, freed from repression, would *naturally* be open to heterosexual sex at any given moment. Consent would never be a concern because sexuality would be understood as transcendently good; so, for Fourier, the solution to ending sexual assault was not addressing misogyny but shoring up gaps in male sexual fulfillment.[37] Women's liberation and male sexual pleasure are not only not at odds here, but fundamentally intertwined. Marx agreed with Fourier about the abolition of the family, and agreed that the measure of a society is its treatment of women; however, Marx did not share Fourier's opinions about women's sexuality and had no interest in the development of utopian libidinal armies.

Sex and the Second International

By the end of the nineteenth century, the First International gave way to the Second. The socialist movement in Germany was the largest in Europe: the German Social Democratic Party (SPD) had 1 million members, its own media, and its own party schools. Two prominent party members, August Bebel and Clara Zetkin, were next to tackle what was referred to as 'The Woman Question'.

Bebel's book *Woman and Socialism* was first published shortly after Marx's death under the title *Woman in the Past, Present, and the Future*. The publication of Bebel's work seemed to warrant enough urgency that Engels interrupted his transcription of what would become the second and third volumes of *Capital* in order to write *The Origin of the Family, Private Property, and the State*. His motive was likely to be that he wanted to bolster the scientific basis of socialist analyses in order to strengthen the revolutionary current within the SPD (Vogel 2014: 102–4). Bebel's *Woman and Socialism* was an enormous success, selling out edition after edition. The book was sectioned into three parts: past, present, and future. In the first edition, before the release of Engels' work, Bebel's assessment of women's predicament spanned the ages: men oppressed women in a uniform manner across classes and throughout history. The first section dealt with the past, and the second outlined the current economic and social oppression of women, but it was his final section about the future of gender relations that made the book a bestseller. Departing from the concrete, the third section of the book reads like a program for a future liberated society. Unlike Fourier and the Saint-Simonians, Bebel roots his program in the real world of actual relations between people. Bebel shows how collective domestic arrangements will free women from household drudgery and liberate them to pursue any career they wish. The abolition of the family would reveal the illusion of oppositional sexism, with women and men both able to develop themselves freely and choose their own sexual destinies – including non-heterosexual ones. (Bebel was an early champion of gay rights.) No utopia for Bebel, no seas of lemonade. He outlined a clear vision of what could be possible.

But visionary as it was, the non-dialectical, historically weak characterization of the relations between the past and the present and between the present and the future undermined his analysis. Despite its down-to-earth approach, Bebel's work was utopian and ahistoric (ibid.: 100–9). Bebel rewrote the first chapter of *Woman and Socialism* in order to correct its static presentation of women's history, but, as Vogel notes (ibid.: 101–2), this was only a cosmetic corrective. Past, present, and future did not connect. This rendered his radical-sounding book quite reformist. The new socialist society would be just a matter of redistributing the goods produced under capitalism, with no thought given to the restructuring of production itself. Women's oppression was, at base, an issue of dependency (ibid.: 106). In a precursor to dual-systems theory, Bebel analogized that men were to women as capitalists were to wage labor; therefore, a transhistorical patriarchy was at work alongside ever-evolving material relations. Once women were no longer forced into the position of being financially dependent upon men, women's individual fulfillment would appear on the horizon. And the horizon was the only place where women's liberation could ever be found. Any meaningful transformation for women was bound up with larger social transformation (see Lopes and Roth 2000: especially 66–85).

As inspiring as Bebel's vision was for the socialist movement, it was more a product of liberal egalitarianism than Marxist economics. Bebel did not answer the fundamental question for socialists: what is the *class basis* of women's oppression? Likewise, Engels' use of Morgan's description of the development of private property and inheritance set the analysis of women's situation on a material basis, but no one had addressed the question of women's concrete lives. In short, how can a Marxist analysis of women's situation argue that proletarian and ruling-class women suffer the same oppression for the same reasons and to the same effect? How could monogamy and family structure be explained as a matter of maintaining intergenerational property relations when the working class didn't have property to pass down?

In 1896, Zetkin remedied Engels' and Bebel's shortcomings by explaining women's oppression according to class. The situation of the wealthiest women, who she calls the Upper Ten Thousand, is a struggle over property relations and a sexual struggle against ruling-class men. Their domestic concerns are wholly carried out by other women. The petit bourgeois and middle-class women, including the intelligentsia, are sandwiched between the pressures of ruling-class domination and, for the intelligentsia, their precariousness and the proletarianization of middle-class brain work. For such women, the goal is for equal access to education and professional work. Zetkin argues that their struggle for individual rights is progressive (Zetkin 1984: 101). But proletarian women's lives, according to Zetkin, were marked by pressures distinct from the problems of ruling-class or middle-class women. Proletarian women did not need to fight for education or access to professions because the barrier to those fields was not their sex but their class. Proletarian women were often wage workers already, and if they were able to avoid wage work, they weren't banging at the gates to be exploited out on the fields or in the factories. Zetkin argued that proletarian women were not at odds with the men of their class but rather with the bourgeoisie who interrupted their ability to live fulfilling lives *as wives and mothers.*

Before addressing the shortcomings with Zetkin's work, it is important to reiterate that she was the first socialist to attempt to go beyond theories of inequality based on property relations and dependency (Vogel 2014: 119). Zetkin sets up a class analysis that considers the social experience of women in her period. Nevertheless, Zetkin's work has a number of theoretical weaknesses. There is no mention of working women's double day: that women are tasked with the domestic labor necessary to get other members of the family to the factory. The notion that proletarian women are not in competition with proletarian men for jobs can be understood only in the context that ultimately neither wish to be exploited, but to suggest that women do not compete with men in the job market is empirically untrue. And it does seem that Zetkin's comments in this case are normative and not empirical.

Even more odd are the assessments of what counts as leading a fulfilled life. Zetkin comes dangerously close to becoming so economically reductive that the horizon of what a woman should wish to become is determined by class position. It is one thing to say that proletarian women do not have access to professional work, but it is another to say that capitalism's primary injustice to proletarian women is that they have been robbed of the opportunity to be stay-at-home moms. It is as if proletarian and middle-class women are treated as substantively different beings; they are either innately different creatures or the 'cultural' identity of class has demarcated them from one another so clearly that they have categorically distinct desires. So while Zetkin's analysis is the most concrete yet, it is marked by a sentimental proletarian conservatism. While it is understandable that she collapsed the concept of womanhood with that of motherhood during a time when the average woman bore four children, in light of the progressive view of gender put forward by Bebel in the same time period, Zetkin's narrowing of the horizon of proletarian womanhood is politically problematic. In fact, far from agreeing with Marx that the goal was the abolition of the family, Zetkin romanticized the peasant family and the division of labor within it. So, Zetkin leaves us with the strange legacy of having created a class analysis of women's oppression by attempting to solve proletarian women's problems through a strange doubling down on oppositional sexism for the working class. Lesbian relations do not seem to exist; indeed, if proletarian women were as nostalgic for housewifery as Zetkin argued, lesbian desire would be external to the class.

Sex and the Russian Revolution

The Russian Revolution was the socialist movement's first opportunity to test theories of women's liberation and queer liberation in the material world. Such tests did not take a back seat to other concerns. By 1920, women had the vote and the right to abortion. All laws enforcing sexual 'morality' were abolished. Same-sex marriage ceremonies were held, and doctors worked on hormone therapy for the gender non-conforming (see Wolf 2009: 89, 97). Such gains were made despite a brutal civil war, a 60 percent illiteracy rate (Eklof 2008: 128–9), and a peasant majority organized into patriarchal households.

But the liberation of desire – in many ways an impossible and, in itself, undesirable abstraction[38] – was a more complex matter than establishing rights based on gender. Alexandra Kollontai imagined a new form of socialist love – 'winged Eros' – where individuals would sexually interact at will without ties but treating one another as equals, not as commodities to be traded or consumed. Igor Kon's *The Sexual Revolution in Russia* details the difficulties the Bolsheviks had in navigating between commitment and free love (Kon 1995: 55–8). On one hand, the old norms of marriage seemed like a throwback to the tsarist era. On the other, revolutionaries, including Kollontai, were critical of the idea of communist bacchanals, harkening back to Marx and Engels' disdain for anything that threatened to move women from patriarchal control to communally consumed sex object. Kon notes that, despite all the rumors, orgies weren't really the order of the day, with the majority of women having premarital sex, but almost all of them doing so with their future husbands (ibid.: 64).

Lenin approached women's liberation from a practical, organizing perspective, remarking that women's liberation would come about not simply from legislation, but also from making men conscious of their behaviors. In *The Emancipation of Women*, he wrote: 'Our communist work among the masses of women, and our political work in general, involves considerable education work among the men. We must root out the old slave-owners' point of view, both in the Party and among the masses' (Lenin 1933). But this 'education among the men' would not be Lenin's most-remembered position on women's liberation. Later socialists were more likely to cite Lenin's comments that there should not be a women's caucus within the party because it would split party unity in a time of crisis. While such an unprincipled stance might seem craven to modern politicos – and such excuses usually are – the Bolsheviks were holding together a fragile alliance in a civil war followed by one of the worst famines in modern history. Addressing the sexism of a highly religious, patriarchal peasantry (the two largest religions in the 1897 census were Russian Orthodox at close to 67 percent of the population and Muslim at close to 11 percent; see Institute of Demography 2015) was an immense task. What is perhaps more problematic than Lenin's opposition to a women's caucus is the Marxist movement's ongoing decision to use the argument against a women's caucus within a political party in times of lessened struggle, and the ignoring of his comments about the need for 'education among the men'.

After the revolution, Bolshevik women traveled to rural regions to unionize the *batrachkas*. However, the Bolshevik party's unresolved ambivalence towards the organization of rural women, and the *batrachkas'* skepticism about the new government's ability to make good on its promises, impacted on the overall effectiveness of the campaign.[39] The restoration of the market in the New Economic Policy (NEP), the overarching fact that so many workers had perished in either the Great War or the civil war, and the revolution's failure to spread internationally isolated the new Soviet government. In less than a decade, Stalin would take power, in part by appealing to a more conservative, nationalist sentiment. Instead of Marx's abolition of the family, the Stalinist campaign instituted the concept of the New Soviet Family. Abortion laws were reversed and gays were driven out of the Communist Party (Kon 1995: 71).

The debates in early socialist theories on how to approach traditional (and at times oppositional) sexism mirror beliefs about sexual liberation popular in radical movements today. At base are six questions: 1) should there be a unitary theory of gender oppression or does the problem of gender oppression stem from two sources: historically given class-based social structures on the one hand and ahistorical patriarchal repression on the other?; 2) what is the value, if any, in visions of liberation divorced from concrete experience, especially liberation that takes place only 'after the revolution'?; 3) can utopian enclaves outside the capitalist economy function as experiments in gender liberation?; 4) is the family form a base of solidarity and social power for the working class that needs to be protected or is it a source of women's oppression that needs to be abolished?; 5) does the abolition of the family pose a challenge to the survival of capitalism, or will the abolition of the family be a consequence of the abolition of capitalism?; and 6) do women, gays, and gender non-conforming people have a *specific* role to play in the abolition of capitalism as women, gays, and gender non-conforming people?

The first question requires revisiting the debates between Marxist-feminism and dual-systems theory in the mid-twentieth century. The second question is the old problem of knowledge and organizational practice, one that Rosa Luxemburg's dialectic of reform and revolution does a good job of addressing. The third question is a question of utopian thought. The modern incarnation of this question is the contemporary Western space-based, localist, class-irrelevantist approach to gender liberation in queer thought. The fourth question requires us to explore the contradiction between traditional communities as a site of socialist resistance and the contribution of the traditional family to the continuance of women's oppression and queer oppression. Since women from working-class families may or may not themselves be engaged in wage labor, the question also raises debates about who counts as working class.

The fifth and six questions are perhaps the questions that this book addresses most directly because they are not so much questions that have been posed but answers that have been assumed in politically radical queer thought. There is a tacit (and sometimes explicit) assumption in queer politics that queerness itself challenges capitalism because it challenges the family. It has long been the position that the horizon of politicized queerness is resistance to heteronormativity. Lisa Duggan has taken this further, suggesting that the political role of queerness is to resist not only heteronormativity, but homonormativity (Duggan 2002). In the following sections, I will explore the contradictions of this contemporary political truism, including how it assumes that the abolition of the family poses a challenge to the survival of capitalism. In order to better understand the role of the family within the reproduction of capitalist relations, an exploration of Marxist-feminist social reproduction theory is necessary.

VIII. Theories of social reproduction

Until the rise of the second wave of the feminist movement, the effect of unwaged domestic labor on capitalism was not explored with any sustained depth by Marxian economists. This is partly because, while Marx and Marxists addressed the wrongs of traditional sexism, they were muddled about oppositional sexism. Women were not inferior to men, but they were often assumed to possess different characters. The cause of gender difference oscillated between nature and historical development, but a hard kernel of sexual difference always remained. However, Engels' historical and developmental reading of gender and family relations pointed to a materialist basis for women's position; it also undermined some arguments about women's nature: for example, if the vast majority of human history has been spent living in itinerant tribes, then attributing innate domesticity to women is irrational. In fact, any concept of women's natural domesticity is a move away from Marxist analysis to Aristotelian essentialism, a move from evolution to design, from life to spirit. Engels' work clearly shows that women's position changes from equals to broodmares for agriculture. The facts that women labored in the Industrial Revolution and Marx put forward political arguments in favor of women's participation show his inclination against the idea that women are naturally tied to the domestic sphere. Yet the inverse of this position, excluding Zetkin's, is that women's liberation was a matter of being liberated from the domestic sphere into public life. Every vision of the socialist future imagined a lessening of household drudgery through the collectivization of women's labor, yet women's liberation never involved men sharing the labor of reproducing their daily lives.

Part of the reason why the reproduction of the working class fell into Marx and Engels' blind spot was that they initially believed that the level of exploitation in the working class was so high that the only thing keeping the class alive was the inevitability of sex acts and pregnancy, not maternal labor. It is also possible that social reproduction would have been covered in later volumes of *Capital* had Marx lived longer – from the *Ethnological Notebooks* we see that Marx's interests were turning towards women's oppression at the end of his life. However, feminism's biggest problem with Marx's economic theory has always been Marx's formula for how labor creates surplus value. Marx focuses on the individual wage worker and the extraction of absolute and relative surplus value from their labor. When focused on the cost of reproducing the individual laborer, Marx sometimes depicts the cost as a matter of the worker's individual consumption while at other times he invokes the family wage and ongoing costs of reproducing workers: childrearing, housework, and eldercare. But despite the limitations of Engels' focus on property relations over production relations as a source of women's oppression, his comments in the preface to *The Origin of the Family, Private Property, and the State* confirmed for many feminists that the reproduction of life was a part of the economic equation for Marxists:

> According to the materialistic conception, the determining factor in history is, in the final instance, the production *and reproduction* of immediate life. This again, is of a twofold character: on the one side, the production of the means of existence, of food, clothing, and shelter, and the tools necessary for that production; *on the other side, the production of human beings themselves, the propagation of the species.*[40]

This quote would later be used to justify both patriarchy theory and a unitary conception of the exploitation of women.

It wasn't until the development of second-wave feminism's laser focus on women's equality inside the home that Marxist-feminists began to raise the question of the double day: women might be liberated to enter the public sphere, and might be able to fight expropriation alongside other workers, but when the working day ended for men at the end of every shift, the second part of the working day was just beginning for working-class women. Women were in a double bind: if they worked outside the home they faced the double day – perhaps, at best, with their husband 'helping' but not taking full responsibility for what was supposed to be her work. Or, if the family wage permitted, the woman could stay at home and make domestic chores her total contribution at the expense of the possibility of economic independence.

It became clear to some Marxist-feminists that Marx and Engel's account of the production of daily life under capitalism did not systematically address the *reproduction* of daily life beyond waged labor. If the most determining factor of human existence was the production of everyday life, where did childcare, house-work, and pregnancy fit into social relations? When the question wasn't ignored by classical Marxists, the answers that emerged were curious; for example, it was argued that perhaps women's domestic labor was still a holdover from feudal relations or perhaps women were still existing in a feudal economy while wage-working men were in a capitalist economy. The solution of bringing women into public life did not address the problem. Rooted in oppositional sexism, the division of household labor would remain the same.

In 1983, Lise Vogel[41] published a theory of social reproduction that sought to explain women's domestic servitude in economic terms beyond Engel's focus on property. Vogel wanted to root her Marxist-feminist analysis not in property relations, but within relations of production. If property relations and lines of heredity explained why ruling-class men needed to regulate women's bodies, why were working-class women's bodies also regulated? Why would any state care, for example, about abortion rights for working-class women if the reason to control women's bodies was to control *propertied* women's bodies? Engels' argument was only a partial explanation. So what was the rest of the story?

Vogel argues that working-class women's oppression stems from the fact that the reproduction of a laborer's daily existence is the costs involved in the production of that laborer; and the cost of keeping a worker alive for work is the basis for workers' wages. If a category of people – women – innately desire to service the workforce, including past, present, and future workers, without compensation in wages from those who possess the social wealth, then this cheapens the workforce as a whole and increases relative surplus value. Of course, there are competing factors in the market: individual capitalists also race to sell products that ease women's workload and, once normalized, the use of those products increases the cost of maintaining the entire workforce. Since capitalism is an anarchic and off-balance ecosystem of contradictions, it should be no surprise that the first fact exists alongside the second.

Understanding how capitalism extracts relative and absolute surplus value is crucial for understanding the social reproduction of the working class in Marxist terms. In *Capital*, surplus value is (reductively put) the term for profit (minus costs) for any individual capitalist, and profit after the payment of wages for the capitalist class as a whole. It is the *extra* value produced by a laborer beyond what is necessary to produce themselves as a laborer as represented by their individual wage. There are two ways in which an employer can raise their own level of profit: one is by making the worker work faster – that is, forcing the worker to finish more quickly, thereby creating more surplus value for the same wage. The second is by making them work more hours, which gives the capitalist more surplus value over time. But the production of absolute surplus value has physical limitations. A laborer can pick tomatoes only so fast and can work only a maximum of twenty-four hours in a day. So another way to produce surplus value, and therefore profit, is by lowering the cost of labor power itself (i.e. wages). This is done, in part, through reducing the cost of what it takes to get a laborer to work: lowering the cost of the commodities necessary to keep the worker alive. The fact that those commodities are also produced by laborers and produced for profit is merely another contradiction within the system, one that is both eased and exacerbated by diverse state policies.

The question of social reproduction is embedded in questions about the necessary expenditures involved in getting labor to work. The question is political. It works best for the purchasers of labor power to minimize the quantity and quality of what workers need to survive: some combination of protein, carbohydrate, and fats; enough sanitation to not disrupt the flow of goods through illness or offensive smells; enough clothing to protect from injuries that might disrupt production; and some sort of shelter – be it a family home, dormitory, or homeless shelter – along with some sort of transportation. It is to the advantage of workers to insist that the wage that represents the value of their labor power require more inputs: better-quality food without fillers and chemicals that cheapen it, enough sanitation to live a good life, enough suitable clothing, suitable housing, quality healthcare, and enough extra for entertainment and relaxation to make life worth living. So the reproduction of daily life and the reproduction of workers themselves are factors in keeping the value of the working class high and thereby retaining as much quality of life as possible; from the employer's perspective, the overall goal is to reduce labor's standard of living as far as possible.[42] It is to the immediate advantage of capitalists to limit the cost of living allowance (i.e. wages) to the individual adult worker. It is simultaneously to the capitalist's advantage to deny or offset the cost of getting this same worker to the age when she can work (i.e. childcare) as well as offsetting the cost of taking care of her after she can no longer work (i.e. eldercare). If the cost of healthcare, cleaning, and schooling can also be uncompensated in wages, all the better. Of course, making the discussion of childcare and eldercare *obscene*, making it the natural duty of a subhuman group (women, immigrants, and especially immigrant women), gets all workers to buy into a lower calculation of their own wages, a lower calculation of their own worth as people.

Lise Vogel notes that domestic labor is not just an invisible boon, but an issue that is economically and politically contradictory for capitalism. Mothers are the primary caregivers for the workforce, but mothers themselves need to be maintained during and immediately after childbirth. Women outside the workforce have also traditionally served in the reserve army of labor, a workforce waiting in the wings. This workforce can be used as an expendable and flexible labor force for when there is a boost in production and a dearth of workers. It is also used as a disciplinary measure against currently employed workers, a reminder that they can be replaced if they trouble their employers too much. However, Vogel notes that women do not occupy the reserve army of labor uniformly (Vogel 2014: 166–7). *Which* women occupy the reserve army (Black, white, mothers, daughters, trans, cis) can only be understood concretely. However, Vogel points out that the growth of women's role in the reserve army of labor during the twentieth century shows that capitalism has a tendency to want all avenues of labor power to be available to it. This is an example of the contradiction between capitalism's need for workers to be both completely mobile and completely stuck, to have individual laborers work together and to keep the whole of the workforce ideologically divided.

The lack of compensation for working people's daily needs creates gaps between current workers' wages and the needs of the entirety of the working class: precarious and surplus workers, the next generation of workers, and workers who have aged out of the workforce are dependent on active workers. With no mechanism within capitalism to cover the unwaged, capitalism's surplus populations are generally cared for by women or they are not cared for at all. Where labor is well organized and capable of making demands on the state, the negative response of neoliberals is gendered: poor cis men are 'deadbeat' dads and poor cis women are too lazy to do the jobs that capitalists imagine justify their lives. The ideological line of the capitalist state is that poor men and women are negligent of the human property that came into the world as a result of their sexual expression. But the real story is that working people's children are a surplus population that will eventually become useful to capitalists; meanwhile, the advanced elderly and infirm – those who are completely unable to engage in productive activity – are an *unnecessary* surplus population that is often completely dependent on women's and immigrants' hidden labor to survive. Their existence is entirely contingent on the sentimentality of their immediate families and the class at large.

Women's and immigrants' uncompensated caretaking of capitalism's surplus populations creates exploitable antagonisms between the working class and the reserve army of the unemployed. This rift is not just based on the potential threat that the reserve army will 'take jobs' away from currently employed workers; it is easy to con workers who have scarce resources into believing that the unemployed are a burden to working people rather than members of the working class. This reinforces familial obligation, resentment towards the poor ('I can't afford to give you handouts as I have my own family to take care of', and other such arguments), and xenophobia. In other words, when employers extract more relative surplus value and suppress wages, capitalists are simultaneously able to nurture working-class resentment towards surplus populations. Enlightenment ideas such as personal responsibility and sexual morality create an ideological wedge between the overworked and the unemployed. There is always a way to trace individual destitution to some defect of the soul.

Token members of oppressed groups are used to argue that formal equality exists and to distract from systemic inequality. Women are handy targets at every turn: if they work, they have taken a man's job and have pulled down wages; if they do not work, they are social dependents; if their wages do not cover the cost of caring for their children, they shouldn't have had children – even where abortion is illegal, even when they are married or widowed. Michelle Alexander has pointed to the racism inherent in the hatred of surplus populations in the United States, particularly the criminalization of Blackness under the cover of colorblind language. Alexander points out that there is no unjustified discrimination against Black people anymore, there is only justified discrimination against *criminals*, and Black people – especially Black men – just happen to be the social construct of what a criminal is (Alexander 2012). The social marginalization of all women, Black men, immigrants, and people who are disabled is connected directly to the need to have and maintain surplus populations of workers and the need to reproduce working people cheaply.

In expanding the Marxist discussion from property relations to relations of production, and in taking on the feminist criticisms of Marx's historically constructed blind spots within the Marxist economic tradition, Vogel reconciles the issues with earlier critiques of the problem of value. First, Vogel notes that it is not a law of class societies that social reproduction occurs within heterosexual households. Capitalism can reproduce its need for labor power by establishing worker dormitories or importing an immigrant labor force. Vogel posits that three types of processes characterize the reproduction of the labor force, be it through kinship bonds, dormitories, or the importation of immigrant labor power: 1) 'a variety of daily activities restore the energies of direct producers and enable them to return to work'; 2) 'similar activities maintain the non-laboring members of subordinate classes – those who are too young, old, or sick or who themselves are involved in maintenance-activities or out of the workforce for other reasons'; and 3) 'replacement-processes renew the labour-force by replacing members of the subordinate classes who have died or no longer work' (Vogel 2014: 188). In fact, Vogel shows that it is possible for workers to be reproduced not through the restoration of their energies, but by working them to death[43] and replacing them with new bodies. However, she notes that the most usual way for workers to enter the workforce is through what she calls 'generational replacement' (ibid.: 149) – through the future employment of workers' children. However, workers are also replaced in non-generational ways by using non-immigrant surplus populations and other newly minted adult workers: former stay-at-home moms, now-impoverished sections of the petit bourgeoisie in times of heightened economic crisis, the unemployed homeless, or prison labor.

The second innovation in Vogel's work is her clarification of necessary labor as a concept. The workforce labor that produces value equivalent to a worker's wages she calls 'the social component of necessary labor'. This is the necessary labor that provides the wages that cover the cost of the commodities that sustain the laborer throughout the day. The unwaged work that renews, restores, and makes labor power available, that makes it possible to use the commodities (milk, mops, sponges, underwear) that the laborer purchases is called the domestic component of necessary labor (ibid.: 158). Vogel's intervention in social reproduction theory rescued the concept from conceptual rigidity and abstraction. The domestic labor debates reached their height in the 1970s, as middle-class Western feminists struggled to understand their confinement to the household; this theme was particularly popular in the United States, where white women who had been swept into the war economy during World War II were placed back in the home with a renewed emphasis on femininity, what Betty Friedan called the *feminine mystique* (Friedan 2001). The crux of the domestic labor debate was how to situate women's labor in the global economy, including in (arguably) non-capitalist societies such as Cuba, the Soviet Union, and China;[44] however, the debate's primary concern was the role of household labor within capitalist production. The core of this debate was twofold: 1) what sort of social product did household labor contribute to the economy?; and 2) what was this contribution's relation to the renewal of the labor force? In other words, did domestic labor directly produce value *for capitalism* or did it produce use values in the home? In the language of classical political economy, the question was about whether or not domestic labor was *productive* or *unproductive* labor.

The term *unproductive* labor outraged feminists unfamiliar with the language of Marxist economic theory. The equivocal reception of the terms 'productive' and 'unproductive' labor, value, and abstract labor are responsible for many tirades against Marxism that have nothing to do with Marxist economics. The difference between use value and exchange value is not a matter of philosophical scholastic quibbling. Use value is what a produced thing can do: a chair exists for sitting, for standing on to change a lightbulb, or as an element of an art project, among other things. How an object is useful depends on its context. The use values of a product are not inherent in the thing itself. A chair does not have to be an object for sitting on; it can also be an object stacked in a barricade or used for firewood. A commodity's exchange value, on the other hand, is the abstract quantity it can be reduced to in order to be swapped for some other commodity. Exchange values are not bound by use values. The commodities market is a good example of this. When a commodity share passes through the hands of a hundred traders in a day, its use value does not rise and fall with prices, and neither does the amount of labor it took to make the product itself. Likewise, productive labor in Marxian economic terms does not mean having a good work ethic or doing a job that is important and meaningful. Unproductive labor does not refer to meaningless labor or labor performed by incompetents. Productive labor simply means labor that is producing *surplus value* for capitalists. Unproductive labor is labor that does not produce a commodity that capitalists can trade. When a child lovingly draws a portrait of the family pet, the child's labor is unproductive to capitalists. It doesn't mean it is *meaningless* labor. Certainly, we would rather children spend their time doodling as opposed to sewing garments in a sweatshop. If you receive a wage to provide home healthcare to an elderly neighbor, that's productive labor. When you go home and take care of your own elderly grandparent, that's unproductive labor. This is why theories of 'affective labor' (see Chapter 1) that mix unproductive and productive labor are particularly unhelpful.

Another Marxist term considered by many to be troubling is 'abstract labor'. Abstract labor has been cited by feminists and postcolonial theorists as an attempt by Marx to make work race and gender neutral, rendering our working bodies meaningless and culturally blank (see 'The queer Marxist critique of postcolonialism' in Chapter 3). But abstract labor is not a normative concept, nor an empirical one. Abstract labor is the mathematical calculation capitalists use to compare the productivity of their workforce to that of other workforces within the system. Railing against the concept of abstract labor is like shaking your fist at an arithmetic teacher because there is no such thing as twelve in the abstract. Just as the question of productive labor is not a question of whether or not household labor is socially valuable, important, or performed efficiently, the term abstract labor does not mean you think of workers as mindless, disembodied abstractions any more than a comparison of the teacher–student ratios of schools in wealthy areas to those in poor areas dehumanizes teachers or students.

But not all feminists agree that domestic labor does not directly produce value for capitalists. Italian feminist Mariarosa Dalla Costa and American feminist Selma James argue that domestic labor is in fact productive. In order for this to be the case, the value of what a non-waged housewife produces must be transferred to the capitalist via her waged husband. Women are, in Dalla Costa and James's language, the slaves of wage slaves. In their 1972 book *The Power of Women and the Subversion of the Community* (Dalla Costa and James 1972), women are defined as a distinct group that is oppressed by the fact of unpaid household labor. They argue that all women are housewives – on a world scale – whether or not they work outside the home. The struggle for women, therefore, is to demand wages for the housework that sustains the system. Wages for housework would not only solve the problem of dependence, but also, as Silvia Federici maintains (Federici 2012), it would provide a way in which women could collectively organize a strike. Those who argue that domestic labor does not, in Marxian economic terms, produce value – and this includes Vogel herself – contend that, because wages are determined by the cost of reproducing the existing labor force, social reproduction (and hence domestic labor) is already factored into the equation of wages whether we like it or not, and whether it is enough or not. For something to have exchange value, it must be a commodity, and unwaged domestic labor carried out in the home is simply not a commodity (see Ferguson and McNally 2014: XVII–XL).

With echoes of Clara Zetkin's reduction of working-class woman to wife and mother (but without Zetkin's attention to the class differences in the labor performed), Dalla Costa's theory boldly claims that all women are housewives because all housewives are women. This glosses over class analysis. Wealthy women need not do their own housework, nor do they raise their own children – particularly because of those who actually do receive wages for housework: maids and nannies. Moreover, the idea that all women are housewives defines women through heterosexual kinship ties. Clearly, out lesbians of all classes, by definition, are not housewives to men. However, if this argument is taken normatively rather than empirically (i.e. all women are *expected* to be housewives as opposed to all women *are* housewives), Dalla Costa and James's concept of the universal housewife concurs with Serano's argument that oppositional sexism grounds gendered violence. If oppositional sexists view lesbians and (misgendered) transgendered men as housewives who refuse to provide free household and affective labor, their violence begins to make sense politically.

IX. Race and social reproduction

The domestic labor debates – indeed, most second-wave feminist accounts of women's labor – are woefully deficient when it comes to addressing race. The problem of white American feminists analyzing (white) women's domesticity is particularly blind to the contradictory situation of millions of American Black women. Second-wave feminist analyses of working women not only ignored Black women's very different perspective on labor, they elided the tales of immigrant women and the work of colonized women inside and outside the home.

Angela Davis addressed this distortion in 1981 with the publication of *Women, Race, and Class*. Davis concedes to Dalla Costa's formula that housework has a public as well as a private character. But Davis, like Vogel, is less convinced that women comprise a special class of workers defined by their place in the household, or, as Davis puts it, a class of 'secret workers' in the capitalist system. Davis argues that 'if the industrial revolution resulted in the structural separation of the home economy from the public economy, then housework cannot be defined as an integral component of capitalist reproduction' (Davis 1983: 234). Here, Davis points to what Vogel would later concretize further: the reproduction of the working class is not produced *capitalistically* nor does it require kinship networks to care for laborers. Davis gives numerous examples. During apartheid, Black male labor became more profitable when Black men were *separated* from Black women. Black women were often not even permitted in the cities where their husbands lived. In this way, the network of white South Africans who owned the means of production did not even see the value of a Black woman caring for her husband because Black male workers were simply units of labor power to be exploited as fully as possible until they could be replaced with other Black bodies. Examples that complement Davis's are easy to find: migrant Bangladeshi strawberry pickers in Greece live in tents on the land and are murdered by their bosses (without consequence) when they ask for a raise; Nepalese and Indian workers in Qatar live in squalid tents outside the shining, ultramodern city of Doha; political prisoners in Chinese labor camps make lingerie and even 'farm gold' by making repetitive gestures inside video games while free Chinese workers assemble smartphones while living in dormitories; Mexican women live in single-sex dormitories at *maquiladoras*; sex workers in New Orleans sometimes live in the strip club where they work; American prison labor is sex-segregated.

Living conditions in labor camps are often described as filthy and dangerously unsanitary. This is, of course, because the method capitalists use to reproduce such labor daily is not the restoration of the workforce but the replacement of workers when they wear out. The upshot of the realities of labor camps is that queer subcultural practices are simply not inherently anti-capitalist. Challenging the family is not inherently anti-capitalist. The truth is that capitalist expansion can do quite well without the family – and much of the time it does so. As Amalia Pallares points out in her research on undocumented immigrants in Chicago, the family is also emerging as a political subject capable of grounding political mobilization (Pallares 2015). Black families also have a history of struggling to stay together when torn apart by capitalist infrastructure (slavery, although not 'capitalistic production' in itself, was a product of eighteenth- and nineteenth-century capitalism's need for agricultural commodities). So, the attitude popular among queer radicals that the very concept of family is normative and thereby hopelessly reactionary ignores the realities of Black lives, undocumented immigrants, and migrant workers around the globe. Politics cannot be divorced from the needs of families when families are the structures into which capital disciplines people in order to survive, nor can it be divorced from the needs of those who suffer under the logic of family values.

In *Marxism and the Oppression of Women*, Vogel undermines the radical feminist claim that the fundamental political struggle is a war between two 'classes' called women and men. Vogel shows that women's social position is not established by men per se, but by the material needs of a world divided by economic class. Likewise, Davis shows that the foundational proposition of radical feminism – a universal sisterhood – would not find many takers in the Black community. Black women's oppression has always been tied to the oppression of Black men. With the legacy of slavery in the United States, the notion that Black men are *the* political enemy of Black women is utterly irrational. Because of the different conditions of the production of slave labor and free capitalist labor, an entirely different history of gender relations emerged in the Black community. The failure to take into account the history of Black sex/gender paradigms is not only a characteristic failing of radical feminist theory, it is also absent in the queer theoretical goal of 'deconstructing' and 'undoing' gender as a key to both personal liberation and general social transformation. Yet, the 'undoing' of Black women's gender under slavery was not only not liberating, it actually reinforced the slave system.

Davis gives examples of the contradictory outcome of Black women's de-gendering that also included the dismantling of the gendered division of labor. During slavery, while wealthy white women were hovered over like delicate flowers in stultifying hothouses, Black women worked alongside men in cotton and tobacco fields, lumber mills, factories, and refineries, and on the railroads (Davis 1983: 230). Davis notes that this *negative equality* with male workers had the effect that Black women never identi-fied housewifery as one of their problems. Clara Zetkin's campaign to allow proletarian women to be mothers makes sense in the context of Black women during and after slavery. Whereas freely laboring women exchanged their labor power to capitalists for a meager wage, Black women were exchanged *as commodities* on the market, sold for their laboring and reproductive potential. Since their husbands, children, friends, and lovers were also traded on the market, the political power of Zetkin's argument about the rights of motherhood takes on another dimension. The historical denial of Black women's right to have a family and gender expression, as opposed to being reduced to a biological sex commodity capable of reproducing other commodities, inspires political demands that run counter to radical feminist concepts of sex oppression. Whereas radical feminists argued that femininity is a mindset foisted upon women by men, the recognition of femininity and masculinity became an integral part of being recognized as human for Black men, Black women, and Black queer and trans people. This demand for gender recognition as a method of human recog-nition spans from Sojourner Truth's 'Ain't I a Woman' speech to young Black men in Ferguson and Baltimore protesting their own murders by wearing placards stating 'I AM A MAN'.

The gendered dimension of racism continues in the so-called colorblind age. Colorblind racism operates using symbolic, coded language which hides racism while allowing the racist subject the ideological high ground of being morally opposed to racism. Post-racial racism operates through the language of law and order rather than open hatred or chauvinism. A good example of post-racial racism is the phenomenon of neighborhood surveillance networks, where vigilante property owners warn one another of suspicious characters: Black men and boys are automatically cat-egorized as suspicious.[45] Meanwhile, law enforcement is extending a new sort of negative gender equality to Black women and girls by treating them with similar brutality. What can this be other than the same old nineteenth-century racism that insisted that Black women were 'biologically tougher' (i.e. less feminine) than white women and therefore could be treated more roughly? Still, this does not mean that femininity is some sort of natural right desired by all women. The political meaning of femininity is historically and socially specific. In the mid-twentieth century, the expectation of femininity was a source of violence against white women just as the social denial of femininity was a source of violence against Black women. Eradicating gender expression or finding new empowering ways of expressing gender is not the basis of political liberation; it is the right to gender expression in light of historically specific strictures that is emancipatory.

Historically, the de-gendering of Black men has always been contradictory. The racist emasculation and desexualizing of Black men into 'boys' is the flip side of the fantasy of Black male hyper-masculinity; similarly, Black women are treated as both sexless and hypersexual. This de-gendering and re-gendering is a method of and precursor to intense social violence, an excuse for refusing to recognize that Black lives matter. On the one hand, it is a dismissal of the systemic sexual violence against Black women, and, on the other, a fear of justified retribution for the violence committed. The fact that the Black family has been a site of struggle and a refuge from racist violence makes gender non-conformity particularly difficult political terrain for Black queer and trans people.[46] The intersection of Black oppression, queer oppression, and women's oppression is not the experience of all three oppressions in three separate moments, but is the very historically conditioned concrete experience of Black queer and trans oppression.

Davis also outlines the particular incongruence of the historical experiences of Black and white women regarding reproductive freedom and motherhood, and the effect these histories have had on reproductive rights reform movements. While freedom from unwanted pregnancies is a concern for all women, Black women have also wanted the freedom to be mothers, the freedom *not* to be pressured to abort due to poverty, or, historically speaking, the freedom not to be pressured to bear a human commodity for slavers. The criminalization of Black male lives has had an enormous effect on Black mothers, who, as mothers, want the political agency to protect their sons from state violence. The legacy of forced sterilization also looms large in Davis's analysis of Black women's oppression. The numbers of mid-century sterilizations performed on Black women read like a strategy of extermination. During the Nazi regime, 250,000 sterilizations were carried out under the Hereditary Health Law. In the United States, up to 200,000 sterilizations were performed on Black women *in 1972 alone* (Davis 1983: 218). This history of reproductive violence has put Black women at odds with the white and middle-class feminist movement's demand against waiting periods for abortions. While waiting periods absolutely present hardships for poor women of color – transportation logistics, hotel bills, childcare concerns, and days off without pay to name a few – the legacy of sterilization has left women suspicious about being rushed into medical situations: many Black women (and other women of color) have walked into clinics for abortion care and left permanently sterilized.

The sterilization of Black women in mid-century America is not politically unique. There is an ongoing sterilization campaign in India based on the neo-Malthusian paranoid belief that too many brown people are a global ecological crisis.[47] Forced sterilization of people in groups relegated to serving as capitalism's surplus populations have occurred regularly throughout the twentieth century: in Namibia, Peru, and Uzbekistan, and against the Roma in Eastern Europe as well. Forced sterilizations do not emerge from existential racial hatreds of certain peoples. All that is necessary is the adoption of a rational-sounding analysis tied to ecological or other material crises, in the same way that post-racial rhetoric uses a rational-sounding 'tough on crime' framework. After all, who wants ecological crisis? Who wants to be pro-criminal? This language is not antiracist or race neutral; it is a not-so-new white supremacist logic of domination.

But why would a system that thrives off Black labor want to sterilize Black women? The violence against Black women has curious contradictions that only make sense when looking at racism in the context of the entirety of economic social relations. Under slavery, Black women were forced to have children: their labor produced commodity-children who could be sold on the open market. Under capitalism, Black women's children serve in both the active 'free' labor force *and* the reserve army of labor, as the surplus population capitalism uses to drive down labor costs. Since wages are based on the cost of the reproduction of the labor force – generally measured by debates around the cost of what commodities the working class needs to reproduce itself – the base value of labor power is always at the market's assessment of the least amount of wages it can get away with paying. This has a two-fold effect on the unemployed. First, the economic system names particular workers as having or being identified with particular numerical values. The unemployed are assigned the numerical value of zero, and value to the system is equivalent to human value. Second, the amount of wages circulating among the working class is generally close to subsistence level, which means that the class as a whole does not have the money to support capitalism's surplus population. If capitalists themselves or the states who enforce their interests are not pressured politically to pay to maintain the unremunerated workforce capitalists need in order to keep profits high, then the moral pressure to financially support the unwaged section of the working class falls to the waged section of the working class. This creates a rift in the working class itself because the waged are the only ones facing the burden of paying for the people that the system abandons.

From the perspective of working people, however, there is no reason for the surplus population to remain unemployed. If everyone worked, there would be a slower and shorter working day for each person. Of course, it does not serve capital to admit that the system requires structural unemployment to keep wages down. The system benefits from the psychological severance of the waged working class from its unwaged others. Structural unemployment can be obscured through moral ideology: it is not capital, but the unemployed themselves who are the reason why full employment is impossible. The unemployed are lazy, they want handouts, they are greedy, parasitic, and criminal. A more recent neoliberal theme is that state interventions on behalf of the surplus population (won through the struggle for reforms) impedes employers' ability to create jobs. Yet structural unemployment is a necessary feature of the free market system. The ability to discipline the labor force is necessary to extract profit from it. The concepts of familial duty and personal responsibility form the moral orthodoxy that keeps the system afloat. Familial duty puts the onus on the labor force to provide for their own individual children regardless of how low wages fall. Children are property and legacy. Paternity operates as a form of social status. We are squarely in the territory of Engels' *The Origin of the Family, Private Property, and the State*. But family legacy is entirely different for the bourgeoisie (bankers and industrialists), the traditional petit bourgeoisie (i.e. shopkeepers), and landed peasants than it is for the working classes struggling to give their children a stable present, let alone a future. It is this notion of family that queer opponents of marriage equality have in mind: the bourgeois family of means clinging to their private belongings and the moral and ideological pressure the upper classes instill in working-class people and the poor using the family form. But there is a difference between the politically motivated ideological image of the family generated by capital and actually existing people arranged into genetic or affective kinship groups. And as we have seen above, striving to dismantle the family under capitalism does not threaten capitalism in the least. Fighting for reforms that help people socially reproduce themselves – whether in families, non-traditional groupings, or as individuals – this is where push-back against capital *begins*.

An additional aspect of moralizing attached to capitalist produc-tion is the sense that a worker's value is tied to their production of things valuable to capitalism (note how the word 'value' here has a double meaning). Having a job affirms that one creates value; being returned a piece of that value reaffirms personal worth; the fact that one can support oneself with wages suggests that one has social value. The fact that the economic system requires an enor-mous underclass supports the supposition that a certain cluster of behaviors, a certain way of genuflecting at the system, is how one achieves the financial stability one desires. The random status to which one is born, of course, has nothing to do with it. In this way, tenuously placed waged workers can adopt and internalize the language of personal responsibility. What would be mere moments of personal abandonment in the middle and upper classes – drug experimentation, unprotected sex, dropping out of school – can easily devastate a working person's life. This reinforces the rhetoric of the necessity of moral fitness. The rite of passage for the rich is the moral failing of the poor.

But it is not only the working classes who turn their frustration towards the unemployed. If workers attempt to create distinctions between themselves and the unemployed, the middle classes often act as if the distinctions are inborn. As Davis cites, the reason why doctors sterilize Black women is the presumption that their offspring are automatic surplus: for example, the only obstetri-cian in Aiken, South Carolina required that recipients of public assistance involuntarily submit to sterilization if they wanted him to deliver their babies. The doctor claimed that he was 'tired of people running around having babies and paying for them with my taxes'. Ironically, Davis shows, he received $60,000 in tax money to perform the sterilizations (see Davis 1983: 217).[48] No one wants to pay for the structurally unemployed. The racialization of capitalism's labor surplus and the legacies of slavery shape Black women's sexuality and gender, the social meaning of Black motherhood, and white anxiety about Black masculinity. The economic precursors to the creation of race also shape gender expression. The systemic dehumanization of Black people in the United States simultaneously involves de-gendering, un-gendering, and sexualizing. Black queer and trans people are not immune to this phenomenon.

The white dominant queer counterculture, like the overwhelmingly white cultural feminism that preceded it, often unwittingly promotes racist arguments about surplus populations, even though queer people themselves are more likely to fall into the surplus population.[49] Like the feminist movement that, as Davis puts it, made abortion a choice for white middle-class women and a duty for poor Black women, queer counterculture – particularly American middle-class queer liberal and 'lifestyle anarchist' counterculture – often reinforces racist tropes through neo-Malthusian populationism. The Slow Food movement hawks individual, moralistic solutions to the pollution of the food supply, but the crux of the fast food problem is that: 1) capitalism accelerates production, which in turn accelerates culture, whereas slow food takes time and labor – the exact things that capital takes from workers in the first place; and 2) in addition to trying to attract buyers with scientifically produced addictive combinations, cheap food lowers the cost of maintaining the working class, which helps keep wages low and surplus value high even when the rate of overall profit decreases due to intensifying mechanization.

Poor and working-class queer people are right to challenge Western assertions of 'queer supremacy' based on countercultural eclecticism. When queer subculture is raised to the level of political principle, it becomes an elitism that ultimately can be inhabited only by those financially independent enough to break their ties with the working classes and by those who do not have to worry about racist, anti-immigrant violence. Concurring with populationists that 'breeding' is ecologically toxic and that childcare is synonymous with capitalist values bolsters the racist ideology that forms the basis of attacks on poor people's reproductive freedom. No matter how radical the phraseology, a movement that disdains the majority of existing humans cannot be anti-capitalist. This is a strange reversal of the rich Western gays[50] who rent the wombs of South Asian women to start their families. Here, the surrogate is literally reduced to becoming a breeder, reduced to a set of servicing organs.

Of course, most queer and trans people in the West are neither rich nor preoccupied with populationist and anti-consumerist ethics. There is also a cross-section of people who suffer such intense abuse and discrimination that interpersonal gender violence has trumped other concerns for survival, including class solidarities. *When solidarity fails, it is not a failure of queer and trans people seeking refuge, but a failure of labor and socialist organizations to sufficiently challenge the conservatism within the straight sections of the working class.* However, the failure may not be in the policies or habits of unions and organizations, but in the fact that labor and socialist organizations themselves have declining influence on the working class under neoliberalism. Ironically, working-class queer and trans people can transform working-class politics by strengthening the deteriorating structures of working-class power.

The environmental movement must also distance itself from racist, populationist philosophies, such as *deep ecology* and ahistorical theories of the 'Anthropocene' as the origin of environmental distress.[51] Instead, the movement must turn its attention towards the processes endemic to capitalism: crises of overproduction, profit-driven reliance on oil and coal, profit-driven monoculture. The thesis of 'too many people' has a clear enemy: poor people.

The Black Lives Matter slogan – although, of course, its rhetorical specificity that it is *Black* lives that matter is critical – also has an unspoken economic demand: *no one is surplus*.

X. Marxism and the second wave

Part of the New Left's critique of the Old Left was a critique of Marxist economics, or at least of those nations and parties who claimed to represent Marx's legacy. The Soviet experiment's failure to enshrine workers' power was, in part, the occasion for renewed criticism. But at the same time, the working class's position at the revolutionary center was also challenged by Maoists, who saw the working classes as complicit with national imperialism; working-class centrality was additionally challenged by Western Marxist philosophers. Where Western Marxists such as Herbert Marcuse saw racial and gender minorities as new agents for social change, Maoists mobilized poor peasants and surplus populations as the moral agents of revolution; the latter were considered revolutionary not due to their structural position in the system – their capacity to shut down the production of surplus value (profit) – but because of their capacity to defend national territories through guerrilla warfare against imperialist states. This had the advantage of awakening anti-capitalist movements but it also assumed an international rift: the pro-imperialist nationalism of exploited laborers in the First World was implicit. The view of First World workers as a conservative population complicit in the domination of the Third World shifted the locus of liberation to peasant insurgence and oppressed populations whose voices would be amplified by white Western academics. With national liberation movements, bourgeois and rich peasants of colonized nations could even be revolutionary subjects (see Fanon 1963b: 97–144). This move towards nation over class among middle-class academics dovetailed nicely with what would later be called the 'cultural turn' in the academic world – where theories of culture and ideology supplanted economic reasoning. Such ideas would later be narrowed and made ethereal by poststructuralism's 'linguistic turn', whereby language structures and the subversion of those structures defined the whole of politics.

The critique of Marxist attitudes towards gender and sex was not without merit, and the legacy of the Soviet Union – despite debates about whether or not it in any way reflected Marxist economic theory – did not see an advance in the fight against gender oppression, despite the promise of the early Russian Revolution. Stalin's New Soviet Family and his preoccupation with building Socialism in One Country led to the outlawing of abortion and the return of the double day for women. According to Kon, this process of Soviet re-gendering occurred alongside a level of desexualization that unwittingly turned towards idealist philosophy – *literally* idealist: mid-century Soviet philosophy turned to Plato, Aquinas, and Leibniz. The development of a sort of sexless sexism in the USSR was a response to its political opposite: women's equality was considered a fait accompli after full social and legal equality was formalized by the fruits of the October Revolution. Truly idealist, no one bothered to examine what this 'equality' might mean in the real world. Formal law, economic proclamations of socialism, and ideological purity were enough. Soviet life underwent an extreme sort of disembodiment – the body was disavowed. The language of sexuality, where it existed, emerged in crude, functionally descriptive pornographic jokes and in scientific language. The average person under Soviet life had almost no vocabulary to communicate sexual desires or gendered experience (Kon 1995: 137–8).

Despite its overt commitment to fighting traditional sexism, Soviet life was simultaneously gender neutral and oppositionally sexist. There was also a particular disdain for femininity, which was synonymous with decadence, artifice, and weakness. The necessity of uniforms during the poverty of the October Revolution left a legacy connecting genderlessness with revolutionary spirit. Yet anything that smacked of 'cross-dressing' was forbidden. Women in suits and men with long hair were not permitted, Kon argues, perhaps more from the Soviet aversion to flamboyance than from a distaste for gender-bending. But, as Kon notes, the prohibitions on sexual and gender expression, paired with strident insistence that equality had been achieved, actually left biological essentialism intact. Most people thought little was said about gender and sex because little needed to be said: men were men and women were women and that was that (ibid.: 141).

In China, women saw considerable gains during the revolution of 1925–27. Foot binding was banned. Women moved from being homebound non-entities to taking roles as labor organizers and guerrilla fighters. Left nationalist movements in Latin America also showed solid gains for women, with a women leadership emerging, despite the consistent problem of machismo (see Kampwirth 2004). Women could be more than mothers and wives; they could be comrades.

Despite early decriminalization of gender non-conformity and homosexual relationships in Russia, the restoration of homophobia began with the medicalization of queerness under Stalin. In 1934, consensual sodomy became a criminal offense that carried a five-year prison sentence. In January 1936, the People's Commissar for Justice 'announced that homosexuality was a product of the decadence of the exploiting classes' and was 'directly tied to counterrevolution and ... the moral decadence of the bourgeoisie' (Kon 1995: Chapter 2). Kon remarks that this shift 'reiterate[d] verbatim the arguments of the German fascists'. The image of queerness as bourgeois moral decadence carried over to China, resulting in violence towards gays during the Cultural Revolution, and to Cuba, where men convicted of homosexuality were sent to labor camps. The rhetoric of 'bourgeois decadence' was translated into 'white' or 'Western decadence' within Third World nationalist movements. Today, free-market Christian organizations in the United States connect queerness to wealth and decadence. Clearly, it is not queerness that is counter-revolutionary but homophobia, sexphobia, and oppositional sexism when it is employed as an ideological wedge between poor or working queers and financially struggling heterosexual families. Gender and sexual diversity is global. Identifying gender and sexually diverse people as counter-revolutionaries or decadent Westerners does not harm the West in the least, only local queers.

While Soviet cultural feminists braved the KGB, and Latin American feminism emerged from anti-imperialist struggle, in the United States the feminist second wave emerged from educated white women from the middle classes. The term 'middle class' is often used imprecisely and, in the US, is often interchangeable with whiteness; sometimes it includes all people who do not live in abject poverty or light cigars with hundred-dollar bills. But the term 'middle-class feminism' is an appropriate term for discussing the origins of second-wave feminism in the United States since academia was its political territory, and academia did not start drawing in substantial numbers of students from working-class backgrounds until the late 1960s and 1970s.

Despite their location in the middle class, second-wave feminists came to political consciousness in a period of ascendant radicalization, and, for this reason, second-wave feminism took Marxism seriously, if only as an interlocutor. Marxist-feminist thought was prominent in the movement. Juliet Mitchell's 1966 critique of the socialist classics entitled *Women: The Longest Revolution* (Mitchell 1984) argued that the work of Marx, Engels, Bebel, and Lenin treated women's liberation as an ideal separate from the nuts and bolts of socialist revolution, and that while women's liberation was supported, it was never rigorously integrated into the socialist program.

Mitchell names four structural aspects of women's oppression that she claims must be separated out before they can be conceptually reintegrated: production, reproduction, socialization, and sexuality. She argues that there is a dialectical relationship between two equally problematic approaches: reformist demands on the one hand and voluntarism on the other. The latter term might be better described as outraged, maximalist sloganeering, while the reformist approach demands social changes without any fundamental examination of the real contradictions of women's position in society. Voluntarism upbraids everyone through leftist speechifying: calls for abolition of the family and total sexual freedom. Such calls are divorced from concrete, real-world demands. Behind the radical language, Mitchell reveals the conservative stagnation. Later Marxist-feminists would critique Mitchell for problems in her own formula. Separating women's oppression into four 'structural aspects' is a schematic exercise – if not an exercise in futility. Production, reproduction, socialization, and sexuality are integrated, mutually constituting factors, not parts of a sandwich that can be removed and reassembled. Furthermore, as with so many structural analyses, Mitchell presents 'women' as an ahistoric entity.

Margaret Benston's 1969 article 'The Political Economy of Women's Liberation' (Benston 1989) reacted to Mitchell's article and in doing so inaugurated what came to be known as the domestic labor debates. Benston considered domestic production to be the primary source of women's oppression within capitalism. Her argument was that women's primary job producing household objects for immediate consumption positioned women in a pre-capitalist mode of production, a mode of production that non-capitalistically produces the working class itself. In Benston's formulation, when the products of household labor are socialized or made public, then women's oppression will disappear. However, how exactly the production of use values in the home becomes subsumed into capitalist production remains unexplained.

The domestic labor debates continued throughout the 1970s without finding a satisfactory explanation of the economic function of women's work in the household within a capitalist society. Some feminists, irritated by the impasse, turned from Marxist ideas towards a new definition of politics. In 1970, both Shulamith Firestone in *Dialectic of Sex* and Kate Millett in *Sexual Politics* (Firestone 2003; Millett 2000), argued that, while Marxist economics had been a reasonable jumping-off point, a feminist analysis separate from Marxism was required if we were ever going to figure out what was necessary to achieve women's liberation. Firestone's argument – that the root causes of all oppressions, including racism, imperialism, and economic discrimination, are all based in the biological distinction between the sexes and the sexual division of labor necessitated by this biological difference – made radical feminism a tool for economic theory. The word 'radical' here does not mean militantly feminist; it means root or originary point, not intensity. Radical feminists, such as Firestone, argue that women's oppression is at the root of all oppression. In fact, despite the disavowal of rigid sexual dimorphism, what some queer theory and some radical trans analyses retain from radical feminism is the privileging of sex categorization and discrimination as the ultimate foundation of all political ills. Kate Millett's *Sexual Politics*, another radical feminist voice, claimed that Engels' work was a critical starting point for examining women's oppression, but Millett argued that it paid insufficient attention to the problem of ideology. In order to understand women's domination in full, Millett argued, it is necessary to embrace patriarchy as an explanatory framework.

In 1979, Heidi Hartmann wrote an influential essay suggesting that feminism should divorce itself from Marxist theory: 'The Unhappy Marriage of Marxism to Feminism: Towards a More Progressive Union' (Hartmann 1979). Hartmann's analogy was that feminism was to Marxism what the wife is to her husband. Feminism was always in the shadow of Marxism, playing second fiddle, eschewing its own needs to advance the needs of its spouse. Hartmann suggests that the terms of the divorce be that the two theories should part ways amicably and accept one another's distinct needs. In fact, capitalism and patriarchy might be separate to the point where the two need not even intersect. Although dual-systems theory (the premise that women's oppression has two origins: capitalism and patriarchy) was not new, Hartmann's essay threw down the dual-systems gauntlet. Hartmann also claimed to reconcile economic theory with patriarchy theory by tracing what she called patriarchy's 'laws of motion'. If Hartmann's laws of motion could intersect with material reality in a meaningful way, it would resolve considerable problems within dual-systems analyses. A volume of essays responded to Hartmann's challenge: *Women and Revolution: A Discussion of the Unhappy Marriage of Feminism and Marxism* (Sargent 1981). The essays in the book largely critiqued dual-systems theory, but also found the traditional Marxist position on sex-based oppression to be wanting.

In one essay, the book's editor, Lydia Sargent, discusses the very practical problems of sexism in everyday organizing inside Marxist parties, anarchist groups, and labor movements. Sargent had a number of complaints with the behavior of men on the left: women's leadership was generally confined to 'women's issues', women's role in public was to be the emcee introducing lists of all male speakers, women who carried out the male leadership's wishes would be chosen to chair meetings, and women were used by men to interject unpopular ideas because they could do so more gently. While speakers were carefully timed to ensure that blowhards and ramblers wouldn't hog the floor, men talked over women when they spoke or used their comments as downtime to compose their own ideas. Sargent also raised the issue of 'horizontal recruitment' – using political debate as a pretext for sexual relations – as well as male comrades' dismissive attitude towards collective cleaning duties. Sargent's down-to-earth analysis exposed the distance yet to be traveled. While male comrades were praised for not harassing or catcalling feminist comrades, much of the socialist movement was still hostile towards feminist theory, considering it to be a bourgeois formula reducible to either liberal feminism or rigid radical feminist analysis of biological male domination.

Iris Young's critique of dual-systems theory clarified the many conceptual problems of understanding women's oppression as the product of two distinct systems. Much of the work on dual-systems theory before Hartmann had treated the two systems as a sort of Cartesian body and soul. Patriarchy theory was the 'mind' driving the psychology of men to oppress, while Marxist economics still explained the movement of the real world. This way of thinking makes patriarchy an ahistorical ideology, a sort of universal world spirit. Young argues that this approach to 'dual systems' does not really describe two systems at all, but rather one economic system and a political problem external to it; unfortunately, such a description is exactly the problem that dual-systems theory was created to solve. Dual-systems theory had so far only accomplished begging the question. Hartmann, to her credit, tried to move beyond that contradiction. She argued that patriarchy itself had a material base because men controlled women's labor power by withholding accesses to key resources. While most dual-systems theory had been based in the concept of 'separate spheres of labor' – in other words, women's confinement to household production – Hartmann argued that patriarchy was an economic system of its own even in labor relations outside the home. Young remarks that if this is the case, then it seems unlikely that the economics of patriarchy could ever be separated from the economics of capitalist reproduction. In light of these incongruities, Young calls for a unitary theory of women's oppression. Vogel, unsatisfied with Young's argument that the division of labor is more important to social production than class, attempts to develop such a unitary theory based on a close reading of *Capital*.

Before venturing back into Vogel's work, let's examine a fuller account of how the equivocal term 'patriarchy' becomes problematic within radical feminist thought. Women have suffered mistreatment throughout history. But does one ahistorical structure explain the realities of mothers living in patrilocal communities in India, de-gendered Soviet women with formal political equality, young college women in Kabul, Black slaves in the American South, their white slaveholding mistresses, white transgendered women who are also corporate lawyers, their secretaries, trans and cis women who sell sex to make ends meet, migrants and the wives and lovers of those living in migrant camps, and teenage girls standing silent for fourteen hours a day on assembly lines in Shanghai factories? Aren't these gendered positions shaped not only by sexual anatomy but also by the economic use of anatomy? Aren't some of these gendered relationships divorced from anatomical thinking altogether? A system of oppression based on male dominance and female penetrability seems to explain very little. This is not to say, of course, that (cis) male chauvinism isn't real or that Marxist theory did a bang-up job of explaining it.

Sharon Smith and Abigail Bakan, for example, have addressed the shortcomings of their training in the US and Canadian sections of the Trotskyist International Socialist tradition. Smith details the unfortunate argument made by Chris Harman in a 1984 article where he stated that the benefits men received from their wives' domestic service was marginal, not more than one or two hours of extra work a day. This, of course, only served as proof for many feminists that Marxists did not take women's issues seriously. Considering the labor movement's struggle for an eight-hour working day, dismissing just 'one or two hours of extra work a day' as marginally important seemed absurd and profoundly anti-Marxist. Smith cites the work of Marxist-feminist Martha Gimenez, who points out that tying women's oppression to capitalism is not mere economic reductionism but the historical analysis of 'macro-level effects' on gendered relations (Gimenez 2005). Saying that women are in a disadvantaged position within the household structure is not the same as saying that solidarity between working-class men and women is impossible.

Vogel's book, published in 1983 at the onset of neoliberalism, entered the debate in a political vacuum. The early 1980s marked the start of a thirty-year decline in leftist activity and a rise in both reactionary ideology and anti-labor policy. As communism crumbled beneath the weight of its errors (not to mention its very un-communist reliance on the world market) and the Western welfare state was no longer necessary for the political stabilization of the capitalist system, neoliberalism brought about massive de-industrialization of the US and other parts of the West, and a rise in both reactionary ideology and reactionary policy. Capitalism had entered the age of *TINA*: There Is No Alternative. Economic analysis from a labor perspective declined in the academic world even as academia was newly opened to the working classes – the neoliberal economy in post-industrial nations would require an increase in what Zetkin had called 'proletarian brain workers'. Economic debate in universities was crushed under the weight of linguistic and cultural analyses. In the US, the massive shift in the tuition burden from the state to the individual working-class student, skyrocketing tuition fees on account of government deals with banking institutions, and hyper-reliance on student loans as a form of funding all served to curtail political activity within the university. Student patience was taxed by anything that didn't neatly result in job placement. Discussions of race, gender, and sexuality – although controversial in their own right – did not wholly lead away from the job market: social work, education, non-profit management, political punditry, and public service were still on the table. But analyzing the problems of capitalism led one nowhere in the job market. Because capitalism is accepted as the final stage of history, criticizing it seems like a purely theoretical exercise devoid of politics. Of course, 'professional revolutionary' has never exactly been a job description, but after the collapse of the Soviet Union and Eastern Europe, the economic liberalization of China, the decline in American union membership, and the pronouncement of the 'death of Marxism' everywhere, the study of Marxist economic theory was easily disappeared from curricula on a global scale.

By default, the themes of the New Left – sexual liberation, cultural diversity, mind expansion, the flourishing of the individual, the fight against conformity, discipline, and 'normativity' – were the only progressive concepts remaining in the wake of neoliberalism. Of course, there have always been fits and starts of anti-capitalist rage: solidarity with the Zapatista uprisings in 1994, the Seattle protests of 1999, the Occupy Movement of 2011, even an expansion of strike activity in China. There is never a hard split between historical moments because the seeds of the future are buried in the graves of the past. But, truth be told, feminism finally resolved its dispute with Marxism due to the fact that Marxist economics was no longer taken seriously. Unitary theory was similarly gauche: unitary theories, universalisms, appeals to the existence of an 'everybody', and big ideas had been replaced with modest, small narratives, tiny bits of empirical research that might or might not help paint a larger picture. This was especially true in the humanities, where poststructuralist, radically specific, always 'problematized' analysis was reassuring to upper management precisely because analysis could never arrive at an actionable solution. The goal was, in large part, to recognize the human condition as one of infinitely deferred meaning. The point was the journey, not the destination. The effect was to sensuously relish the world in little bits and pieces instead of confronting the terrifying whole.

But one upshot of the cultural turn in sex and gender theory is that the incoherence of patriarchy theory became clearer, particularly for queer and trans people. Why were the gendered experiences of working-class lesbians utterly alien to middle-class lesbians in the mid-twentieth century? Why has gender expression been different across space and time if all gender expression is a form of patriarchal oppression? If patriarchy is anatomical or biological, why do matrilineal and matrilocal societies even exist? If patriarchy is based on physical superiority, how can one account for the continuance of sex oppression in the digital age?

Lise Vogel's feminist analysis of *Capital* has important implications for queer and trans politics. Dual-systems theorists argued that economics and patriarchy were distinct modes of social control. Iris Young argued against this, maintaining that the gendered division of labor was the key to the production of both women's identities and women's role in social relations. Vogel agreed with Young's instinct to criticize dual-systems theory, but she argued that the origin of women's oppression was not the gendered division of labor. The gendered division of labor had not produced inequality at earlier points in human history and there was no theoretical reason why it should do so now. Vogel centers her theory of women's oppression on the general biological situation that, under capitalism, pregnant (cisgendered) working-class women require a larger share of the social product, which means that a working-class pregnant woman is not only unavailable as a worker (unavailable to produce profit for the capitalist) but she requires the capitalist to return to her the surplus he has extracted from the other workers so that she can survive during the period when she cannot work.

A good chunk of sexist ideology can be directly traced to this economic reality. For example, the 'deadbeat' dad is a fantasy born from the desire for someone other than the capitalist class to provide for low-wage women during pregnancy and the early years of child development for their future workers. Capitalists do not allocate a portion of the surplus they have extracted from the working class to be returned to working-class women; so, the burden for financial support becomes a moral requirement for working and unemployed men. In this way, the maintenance of those who are designated as members of capitalism's surplus populations is sexually moralized. Instead of realizing that surplus population status is arbitrary and historical, it is imagined as being a logical consequence of 'certain people' being hypersexual and/or excessively fertile. This sexual denigration of the poor is one dynamic aspect of the cheapening of working people's life and labor. This scenario is rooted in Smithian, Protestant fantasies of the poor as having decided to trade financial luxury for laziness and sexual pleasure.

Of course, capitalists strive to compensate wage-earning men only to the extent required for them to drag their bodies to work the next day. How much extra any worker has for others – if any – is determined by the level of class struggle of a given society. If it is very low, then he will not earn enough to support the women and children the system tasks him with supporting due to his 'innate strength and superiority'. While upper-class men want to control who their wives sleep with so that they do not pass their property on to another man's child, working-class men need to know whether or not they are responsible for a child because it is a matter of whether they are socially obligated to support their partner until she can return to the workforce. A woman is socially 'good' if her sexuality is tied either to one capitalist who will pass his wealth to the heir she produces or to a man who isn't a capitalist but who somehow has the means to support her without demanding money in the form of extra wages if he impregnates her. (It is no wonder that liberal society eventually began to welcome high-earning professional and capitalist lesbians who could afford to support their children without demanding money from other capitalists.) A woman is socially 'bad' if: 1) she bears a child for a capitalist and that child is obviously not his biological material; or 2) she becomes pregnant without enough money to support herself during pregnancy – the situation of almost all wage-earning women during low levels of class struggle – and, in addition, she cannot name a definite father to be legally responsible for supporting her. In the first case, the non-monogamous woman is an embarrassment to the ruling class, or perhaps considered reckless. In the second, the woman is considered irresponsible and bourgeois morality says that the capitalist class should not have to pay for her mistakes and her partner's financial failure. If she has no partner at all, the woman is considered morally repulsive because her (assumed) pleasure has burdened the system. If a poor trans man were to become pregnant, he would be treated no better.

But let's return to why she (or he, in the case of a trans man) is a 'burden' on the system: she simply did not earn enough money to support herself through pregnancy and childbirth. Why didn't she earn enough? Because her wage is too low. Why is her wage too low? Because the level of class struggle is low and the capitalist class has expropriated so much from her labor that she cannot survive. So, capitalists want to avoid having to provide for the biological reproduction of the next generation of workers because that means returning what has been expropriated. One sneaky way to avoid having to give back some of what they have taken is regressive taxation: if the rich avoid taxes, then the working and middle classes shoulder the burden. In such a situation, when labor fights for childcare and support for pregnancy from the (capitalist) state, it is the working and middle classes who pay, not necessarily those who profit from pregnant people's waged labor. This reinforces the ideology of the need to control all poor and working women's sexuality.

Of course, these ideas are hardly 'natural' to human existence. In fact, the unnaturalness of this situation manifests itself in all sorts of wild contradictions. Capitalism uses sexuality to sell commodities, so the world is papered with advertisements featuring highly sexualized women. While wealthy women are child-bearing trophies for wealthy men, there are entire industries that cater to providing wealthy men with the bodies of poor women (and poor men and poor children). Working-class men, meanwhile, are (quite cruelly) sold the idea that they *could be* in the position of having their every desire catered to but, sadly, they are beneath the men who can make such claims. Women's bodies must be available to men, but they must only become pregnant by wealthy men who desire for them to be pregnant so that they can pass on their legacy. Trans women and cis women who cannot bear children are useful only for propertied men's sexual pleasure (or for cheap or free reproductive labor).[52] Working-class women who get pregnant are the responsibility of working-class men, who are socially punished through humiliation and attacks on their masculinity: masculinity here being their ability to fulfill the invented responsibilities of their social gender.

So, to summarize: working-class women sell their labor power in exchange for a wage that covers the expenses of the commodities necessary for them to return to work the next day. Everything they produce beyond this exchange is a surplus for capitalists. Working-class (cisgendered, heterosexual) women who become pregnant often cannot work for a period of time during and immediately after pregnancy, and during childbirth, which means that they require support while their wages are suspended.[53] The capitalist class does not wish to return any of the surplus obtained from working women's labor – or anyone else's, for that matter. Therefore, they require that men 'take responsibility' for women during pregnancy and for their children. At earlier points of capitalist development there was a family wage, whereby the capitalists begrudgingly calculated a bit more of the surplus into male workers' wages to care for women and children who were not supposed to work, but who often did anyway.[54] The family wage was a benefit and a curse. It gave families a bit more money, but forced women to be dependent on men or else face a harsh existence that included disciplinary sexual degradation. And, of course, the family wage provided significant material support for oppositional sexism.

But working men's wages are, in truth, generally not intended to reproduce more than their ability to get themselves back to work. This puts the emphasis on paternity, which means that men and the state are socially entitled to monitor women's sexual activity. When working-class women who have multiple poor or working-class sex partners become pregnant, it is a crisis for capitalism because there is no specific man to take up the burden for the capitalist class. If there is no specific man to take the burden, then politically aware working-class women could make demands on their employers (or the employer class as a whole) that the wealth expropriated from them – or, for that matter, the wealth expropriated from their lovers or any other working-class people in solidarity with them – ought to be returned to them so that they can support themselves. Instead, the capitalist class does everything it can to limit its social contribution to the capitalist state (for this and many other reasons) and instead shifts the burden to workers and the middle classes, who, as shown numerous times throughout this book, have difficulty meeting their own material needs. This transforms the working and middle classes into a disciplinary force over women's sexuality and it transforms children into property that adults have the responsibility to maintain: I don't want to pay for *your* child, *your* birth control, *your* abortion. Of course, these beleaguered taxpayers would be shocked if there were no one to repair their car or stock their groceries – tasks completed by workers who were at one time very likely the child of someone struggling to pay the bills. Many of these complainers also sexually desire the very women to whom they deny reproductive freedom, and they would be horrified to have to pay for *her* child, *her* birth control, or *her* abortion.

The disciplining of working women's sexuality reinforces the disciplining of working men whose social gender is denigrated if they are not able to provide financially. Working men would not experience gender-based ridicule based on their ability to provide for dependents if what they produced was not expropriated from them. Their love for their children would not be judged by their financial ability but by actual love and real participation in their children's lives, and in the lives of others in the community. It would be unnecessary to infantilize women because women would be able to provide for themselves and their children with or without a partner. Of course, all of this would be solved if the capitalist class returned the wealth extracted from the working class to it – including provisions for the reserve army of the unemployed that it depends upon. *Women's sexual liberation is directly tied to class struggle.* But class struggle depends on working people's awareness of capital flows, awareness of their own place within the totality of social relations. Individualist ideology strives to interrupt this awareness by stroking egos and reminding people that they 'own themselves'. This is a very flattering proposition, especially for people whose employers own the majority of their time. Working people own everything about their lives! Well, except for much of the time required for this 'life' to take place. When the capitalist needs you, you must be a team player; when you need something, you're suddenly an individual who must own yourself and 'accept personal responsibility'. But no one is self-made. Everyone is raised.

So what does any of this have to do with queer people? The above explanation is largely heteronormative. And that's precisely the point. Economics is the origin of the 'normativity' in hetero-normativity: not intolerance of difference or the other, not a pure desire for power or an abstract need to control, not a lack of sexual creativity or dullness, not a Eurocentric racial spirit. It is the fact that the generational replacement of the labor force requires sexu-ally active people with certain body parts to go through extended periods of non-activity. The capitalist class benefits from this generational replacement, but it does not want to make conces-sions to the people who make it happen. Social gender and the management of sexuality under capitalism are shaped according to the struggle over who pays for what is necessary to socially reproduce the working class. A normative ethos is created to regulate the sexuality of those who produce children for the ruling class, a category called 'woman' (which is also normative). Another category also bearing the title 'woman' has a separate normative ethos that regulates the sexuality of working-class women. These normative categories are not empirical categories populated with actual ontological beings called women. The categories are filled with all sorts of people: heterosexual cisgendered women, lesbians, bisexual genderqueers, gay trans men, people who consider themselves to be third sexes or agender, intersex people, surrogates for wealthy gay men, colonized people, and people living in imperialist nations. Genderqueer, two-spirit, third-sex people, and trans men are emerging political subjects who have been forced into these categories. Solidarity between working-class people in the category called 'woman' – including the men lumped into it – is critical for the fight for all people's bodily freedom.

There are a number of enormous obstacles to solidarity. Men and genderqueer people are fighting to escape the normative category called 'woman' while still having body characteristics that leave them vulnerable to the same economic and social forces as working-class women. Women who are currently excluded are fighting to be accepted *into* the category, despite the fact that their body characteristics lead to different consequences in terms of social reproduction and sexual health. All of the above – those in the category and those fighting to get into it – share a common situation in that they are all limited by misogyny and the sexualization of working-class women. Another obstacle is that some whose lives and personalities correlate with the normative expectations imposed upon the category survive the systemic violence of misogyny by strongly identifying with the normative ethos assigned to them: they gain strength from their mothering ability, social acceptability through sexual fidelity and modesty, and affirmation of value through beauty. The fact that some gain strength – and are socially permitted to gain strength – by internalizing the normative ethos of the 'woman' category creates tension within the whole. Slut-shaming, opposition to the veil, oppositional sexism, anti-queer attitudes, and transphobia are easy to exploit ideologically to disunify the class. To be clear, it is not debates and criticisms within the working class that disunify. Tensions between working-class people are easy to exploit.[55] Debate and constructive criticism are the solution, not the problem.

But what about those other people called 'woman' and the normative ethos assigned to them? Engels' theory of property relations in *The Origin of the Family, Private Property, and the State* correctly explains the source of oppression for women of the propertied classes. Women in the upper classes are required to make themselves sexually available to their wealthy husbands and bear the husband's children so that property can be retained for their kinship line (and, if the woman becomes pregnant by another man, the lover's physical features should at least be close enough to those of her husband that she can pass the child off as belonging to him). Wealthy wives are a commodity that depreciates with age – unless they themselves were born into wealth. For low-income women, children are a symbol of low status. Poor women's sexuality is always immoral.[56] In the highest echelons of capitalist accumulators, women are paid for childbirth and for their children's achievements. Children are a symbol of high status (Martin 2015). Wealthy women's sexuality is moral. The social meaning of motherhood is entirely shaped by class.

But once again, the normative ethos differs from the actual, empirical, really-existing people inside the group. There are, of course, transgendered people, queer people, and intersex people in this group as well. In the West, gays and lesbians have fought with varying degrees of success for their property rights, inheritance rights, and rights to have their children recognized. The ruling-class structure is changing. Space has been made for wealthy lesbian women, especially those who have children, ensuring some continuance of the property line. The same is true for gay men who hire poor women as surrogates to carry their genetic offspring. Celebrities such as Caitlyn Jenner – trans and openly right-wing – facilitate the negotiation of trans acceptance in the ruling class. Gender itself is different in the ruling class. Physical masculinity is for show, not for survival. Where lower-class men have always been pressured to bulk up in order to protect their partners, sisters, and daughters, wealthy men have no such need. Teams of lawyers protect the ruling class, regardless of sex (of course, not from one another, which does leave young upper-class women vulnerable to rape by their privileged peers). Aspects of femininity are also for show within the ruling class. There is no reason to develop maternal gentleness when other women raise your children.

So, economic social relations are critical to understanding both oppositional and traditional sexism. The generational replacement of workers is a permanent point of struggle between workers and bosses, between poor pregnant people and the upper classes. Bebel was partially correct in his analysis that women's dependency was a key factor in women's oppression. However, getting women out of the private sphere and into the public arena is no solution. The fact that people who bear children also work for a wage only leads to the double working day. The misogyny produced by the situation means that solving this particular economic problem is key for lesbians, genderqueer, and trans people along with all cisgendered, heterosexual women. Queering gender won't solve the problem. Opening masculine-gendered occupations to non-masculine gendered people won't solve the problem. Railing against normativity and the normative family won't solve the problem. Class struggle surrounding the problem of social reproduction is not a political panacea for working queer and trans people. However, without class struggle, misogyny will continue and no real justice will be possible.

Some have already begun to tie queer and trans political struggle to a new, twenty-first-century approach that thinks through queer and trans oppression from an economic perspective. This new approach is called *queer Marxism*, and it is where we will now turn our attention.

CHAPTER 3

From queer nationalism to queer Marxism

I. The vector model of oppression

Towards the early middle of the twentieth century, new European political theories emerged after the failures of Enlightenment rationalism and German Romanticism. The West was tasked with grasping the unthinkable (the Holocaust) and the unthinking (the mass adoption of fascism). Theorists wanted to go beyond the surface logic of political operations in order to investigate the mass psychological and emotional traits that concretized political ideology. While in the United States politics became yoked to positivist analyses of data sets, in Europe issues of consciousness, ideology, and the power of language and imagery drove academic inquiry: could structural a priori formations in the unconscious account for human behavior and desires? Is the subtext of rational communication its actual message? How is technology transforming not just the delivery but the ideological content of material? At

best, Marxian historical materialism was thought to be epistemo-
logically weak, incapable of grasping the total picture. The notion
of history seemed to operate as a logical imposition on quasi-
logical and radically contingent causal chains; analyses of language
and meaning began to replace inquiries into actual economic
processes. This phenomenon in continental thinking came to be
known as 'the linguistic turn' in Western thought (see 'Philosophy
and the Marxian roots of queer political thought' in Chapter 1).
Unimpressed with continental philosophy's goal of grasping the
ineffable, philosophers in the US turned towards analytic philosophy, which endeavored to tame existential chaos through absolute
precision in language.

In other words, while they differed over methods and areas of
inquiry, both varieties of philosophical thinking maintained that
the best way to assess the anarchy of life under capitalism was to
get a better grasp on language and meaning. Despite Louis Althusser's attempt to build a philosophical anti-humanism opposed to
Enlightenment Man ('the spoiled brat of history') as the origin and
agent of all meaning, the mid-century focus on language generated an obsession with human thought patterns. With the advent
of Jacques Derrida's deconstructive method, language became
the Platonic overlord of puny human attempts at thought. Text
preceded speech. *Language itself made meaning*, while humans were
left mouthing words that never quite described their intentions.
People were not masters of language; language was the master of
people. The possibility of freedom and agency would be located
in moments of radical indeterminacy. The philosopher Martin
Heidegger described this as beings being thrown into a world
of language, into language systems that precede the existence of
individual beings (see Heidegger 1971). As a result, continental
academic writing began to sound a bit like religious incantations,
impenetrable to the uninitiated. Where Anglophone philosophy
saw European pretensions in continental language – a bunch of

meaningless babble masquerading as profundity – the continental European tradition saw analytic attempts at clarity as at best pedantic, and at worst another kind of pretension, one grounded in an American need to dominate reality as a whole, to capture the ineffable within a system of command and control.

From a Marxist perspective, attempts to solve the riddles of life through mental gymnastics are the fetishistic product of alienation. Workers experience the commodities they themselves produce as fetish objects that emanate an almost mystical power. Working people's world is full of trains and devices and apples and skyscrapers that all appear as if by magic. The solution to the mystification of everyday life is an understanding of how social relations produce the world. It makes sense that philosophers and writers – faced with the proliferation of books, journals, lectures, blog posts, newscasts, and political speeches – would come to see language as a mystical power that descends from the heavens to dominate life as we know it. The impasses and anxieties philosophers faced when trying to move beyond the reductiveness of attributing modern thought to capitalism were themselves, in the end, a product of capitalism. The philosopher may work in a teaching factory instead of a sausage factory, but they too are alienated from their labor.[1] Of course, Marx was no stranger to the weirdness of material life under capitalism. In Volume I of *Capital*, he depicts a world where nothing is as it seems, a world dominated by social relations expressed in commodities laden with 'metaphysical subtleties and theological niceties'. Far from presenting a flat, reductive vision of the world, Marx's economic analysis portrays a constantly revolutionizing economic system with tentacles that both reach and disappear into every aspect of human existence.

The linguistic skepticism of twentieth- and twenty-first-century Western thought reflects the alienation of capitalist modernity, but it is also an expression of the public's general cynicism towards the sense of emptiness produced by the contradictions of capitalist commodity exchange, the Soviet Union and China's failure to change the world, and the limited successes and eventual decline of the New Left student movements. The 'Old Left' movements turned out to be largely blind to the complexity of gender oppression in advanced capitalism; the post-Stalinist 'liberation-by-tank' method of socialist progress mirrored the imperialism it purported to defy. Trapped within this contradiction, colonized populations attempted to address imperialism and racial oppression through a new idiom; those in the United States and Europe found the maxims of deconstruction appealing. Meanwhile, women and queer people developed new strategies for survival and resistance that had little to do with revolution. As the Western academy began to detach from Marxist thought, poststructuralist analyses were applied to the struggle against patriarchal mores, oppositional sexism, and ethnic cleansing. But what the Western academy liked to call 'economic determinism' wasn't replaced with rich complex analyses of emergent phenomena; it was replaced by linguistic and cultural determinism in which discursive complexity often sufficed as a stand-in for knowledge. This new Western cultural politics retreated into the academy, a most proper place for the development of a middle-class, language-based cultural politics. Queer theory, third-wave feminism, and postcolonialism developed inside the academy to explain new types of struggles for self-determination in the classroom, as well as in the streets.

Identity politics might be better understood as a form of schematic politics where the development of theories of oppression is detached from theories of exploitation. Race, class, nation, gender, sexuality, and disability are understood as wholly different vectors capable of intersecting. From this perspective, Marxists supposedly distort the math by identifying class as the most important and worst oppression, and the subjects of class are those who, subtextually, have no other oppressions: straight, white, cis, heterosexual men. So, according to this model, attention to class is a covert method of oppressing women, queer, trans, and colonized people by putting class at the top of the oppression hierarchy, thereby reinforcing the trauma of all other vectors. In this model, class becomes so marked by whiteness and maleness that it must become a secondary consideration, only meaningful when another oppression already exists. What distinguishes identity politics from Marxist politics is how it detaches oppression from exploitation and separates each oppression from every other.

Oppression is thought to emerge from an abstract lust for domination and therefore has a life separate from the economy. Although social problems might *intersect* – like two lines from nowhere that suddenly crash into one another at angles – they have wholly different points of origin and they jet out towards the individual, transparent, blank-slate subjects to cut through them. For those situated on the dominant plane – wealthy, European, white, cis, male, able-bodied, heterosexual, non-immigrant people from imperialist nations – the vectors are privileges that pass through their bodies like beams of healing white light. For those situated on subjugated planes – poor, Black or brown, trans, female, intersex, disabled, queer, and colonized – these vectors cut through the body like lasers. Each new line of oppression uncovered (having experienced sexual abuse, having a multiple personality, age bias, lookism) helps better explain the total force field of human suffering. This model of understanding suffering has some positive aspects. It is humane and attentive to the experience of marginalized people. Those who have experienced subjugation can build new languages to express their suffering. In its own way, this 'vector model of oppression' attempts to build a unitary theory of oppressions through the figure of the individual body, the body that experiences the oppressions and privileges that pass through it. By the continuing discovery of new vectors that shape experience, the human condition becomes concrete.

Of course, the above model is inspired by Foucault and the source of these vectors is 'Power'. While poststructuralism has a cynical disdain for terms such as 'Truth with a capital T' and 'Knowledge with a capital K', the entire edifice depends upon a mysterious 'Power with a capital P'. The subject is always an individual experiencing the pleasures or pains that come from a privilege or oppression that constitutes them. With individual bodies experiencing the vectors of privilege and oppression flowing through them, the individual becomes social through its status as a conduit for Power. To continue the metaphor, privilege acts like a mirrored ball so that the red laser sights of Power can be redirected towards other, more vulnerable bodies. The grounding principle of sociality in this model is self-preservation. One saves oneself by refracting Power onto other bodies. Ethics and the interpersonal become the horizon of politics, where recognizing one's privilege is the first step towards blackening the mirror so that Power will be absorbed and not violently projected onto others. For those outside the vectors of privilege, the trick is to twist the pain of disciplinary power into strength and self-empowerment, to let Power know that you, although powerless, will resist.

But there are downsides to this model of oppression. The first is that it is an interpersonal model of politics grounded in individual experience. The rational man of the Enlightenment may not be at the center of the universe in this model, but the individual is still the focus. What ultimately determines political meaning and interaction is the pleasure and/or mortification of the individual body arranged in a transactional, market-like configuration where disciplinary power is refracted through the masses by the masses. The model's individualism produces other problems. A history that is the sum of individual responses to and refractions of Power is no more of a history of human existence than a relay of blinking lights is a history of light. Such a schema is not a history, but a situation, a meaningless existential crisis in which one is positioned arbitrarily.

This schematic, space-driven focus on the individual experience of oppression rejects the notion of History as metaphysically suspect, but requires a strange and godlike field called Power[2] to ground the meaning of existence. Is it possible to see this mysterious force called Power? All we can see is Power as it is refracted through the other. We can see only the traces it leaves behind.

So what kind of political solutions are generated by this model? First of all, individual behavior is the limit of political power. One can limit the effects of Power, but Power itself is an eternal force. Capitalism is not an arrangement that produces certain types of social violence; it is an effect of Power. The best one can do is care for the self and attend to one's language, language itself being the symbol of human interaction. To punch, strangle or rape someone is a discursive activity that conveys the message of Power to the body of the other. Violent speech is another discursive activity disseminating Power. To misrecognize or mis-categorize the being of the other through intention or ignorance is another form of asserting Power. Sarcasm is the form of discursive blasphemy that tames the power of Power. Finally, the care of the self can extend to an awareness of others and attentiveness towards them.

What kind of politics is this? It is left (neo)liberal politics promoted by the academy as a critique of neoliberalism: awareness campaigns, 'dismantling the system' by putting aware individuals in positions of power so that they can better extinguish power, commitment to ethical living, locating one's privileges and renouncing them by not acting upon them or extending them. Thinking deeply about Power leads to a recognition that capitalism is but one of Power's effects. However, just because subjects are not capable of stopping capitalism does not mean that they are not ethically bound to resist it as they would any other vector of Power: ethical consumption is therefore paramount – buying local, reusing and recycling, promoting 'fair' trade, and eating organic are all little ways of resisting Power. If reflecting violence onto another is micro-aggression, small ethical acts micro-heal the world. Despite the rejection of Aristotle's essentialism, his virtue ethics are foundational to this configuration of radical resistance. In many ways this mode of political activity is a distortion of Gramsci's idea of the war of position. Here, the war of position does not lead to or complement the war of maneuver; it supplants it.[3]

It is difficult to reconcile the vector model of oppression with Marxist models of social relations, not because Marxist models are hostile to theories of oppression, but because the vector model cannot account for economic and historical development. While poststructuralists chide Marxists for failing to be radically specific, the vector model relies on vague, permanent categories that too easily slide into symbolism and imagery – which makes sense for a worldview where the boundaries between language and reality are porous: that is, when 'Reality with a capital R' is even considered to exist.

Classical Marxists and Marxist movements, *as empirical phenomena*, have often failed to develop and implement workable methods for challenging oppression in the here and now. Tracing the history of an oppression and the resistance to it is no substitute for an analysis of what is to be done about it. However, this does not mean that Marxism fails as a theoretical model for understanding oppression. It just means that Marxists still have work to do. Oppression that results from an identity, understood as a position within the system, is not beyond the explanatory power of Marxist theory; however, models of intersecting vectors of oppression are completely incompatible with Marxist theory. Indeed, where many 'really existing Marxists' have failed is that they see oppression as a mere epiphenomenon of capitalist development. For example, if one wants to learn about the situation of Greek or Egyptian or Indonesian or Canadian women, one usually must read about the political economy of Greece or Egypt or Indonesia or Canada – which is presented as gender-blind – and then later read about the conditions of Greek and Egyptian and Indonesian and Canadian women, which may only glance at general political economy. The failures of Marxists to think in an integrated way is not equal to the failure of the model itself.

Some Marxists have embraced the term *intersectionality* not as an abandonment of dialectics, or as a way of opposing a unitary framework, but as an expression of the Marxist commitment to understand the ways in which bodies construct and are constructed by political economy. Because Marxism does not focus its politics on the individual embodied subject, it does not see oppression as vectors passing through an individual subject – not even if the schema is made materialist by reimagining Power as Capitalism or The Economy. This is because the vector model separates and reifies oppressions instead of viewing them as the outcome of material social relations. Race, gender, religion, and nation are not 'things that happen to individuals': they are social relations conditioned by capitalism *and conditioned by one another*. Each relation is defined by all other relations with which it always interacts. The experience of maleness is always conditioned by race, class, and ability, and the concept of race is always inflected by gender and sexuality. This is because what happens in the world happens all at once. Just as the vector theory seeks to tease out the radical specificity of each oppression in order to separate each oppression from all others, the understanding generated by Marxist analysis is only as rich as the tensions and conflicts incorporated into analyses of historical change: because the history of the world *is* the motion of those tensions and conflicts. This is the universalism of Marxism. It is not the reduction of human experience to a model but the acknowledgement that we all exist in one world – not a river flowing into a sea of meaning and final truths, but a river folding and unfolding from its own internal dynamism. This is a metaphor of immanence, but it is not mystical. Oppressions cannot be pinned to the wall like so many dead butterflies. They do not come at us like bolts from distinct and unrelated points.

II. Racecraft and ideological repetition

Barbara Fields' analysis of the ideology of race is an excellent example of the use of dialectical reasoning in which categorical and schematic understandings of historical cause and effect are revealed to produce tautologies. Fields exposes that not only is race not a separable vector of oppression emanating from a power field, it is not a 'thing' at all. Race, Fields shows, is an ongoing ideological effect of the conflict between the doctrines of liberty and the fact of enslavement in the American colonies during the seventeenth century. Race is produced by racism, not the other way around. She shows that there is no way to prove that race is an entity with causal powers. Any attempt to do so collapses into circular reasoning. To invent collections of characteristics that define race and then to find those characteristics in the world is to find only what you set out to find. If I assign the name 'rightiferous' to trees that bend to the right, and I take a walk through the woods and discover trees that bend to the right, I have made no discovery at all. Fields points out that because race is a historical creation and not biological, it cannot cause itself any more than an entity called 'lamp' can produce lamps. And if the *form* of race does not cause race, then racism cannot be caused by race either. Next, she criticizes the circular logic necessary to prove that racism is the product of Europeans' innate sense of superiority. For example, when race scholars reach conclusions such as 'it may be more useful to see Anglo-American racism as a necessary precondition for a system of slavery based on ancestry and pigmentation' (Vaughan 1989: 97, quoted in Fields 1990), Fields remarks that this is nothing more than saying 'Anglo-American racism is a necessary precondition for Anglo-American racism' (Fields 1990: 100).

Fields considers the idea that race could take on a life of its own as tantamount to conceptual Lamarckianism. Race is an ideology born and maintained through history itself. Race is impossible to understand ahistorically. Fields explains, and it is worth quoting in full:

Race is not an element of human biology …; nor is it even an idea … that can be plausibly imagined to live an external life of its own. Race is not an idea but an ideology … So much ideology is. Here is what it is not. It is not a material entity, a thing of any sort, that you can hand down like an old garment, pass on like a germ, spread like a rumour, or impose like a code of dress or etiquette. Nor is it a collection of disassociated beliefs – 'attitudes' is the favoured jargon among American social scientists and the historians they have mesmerized. (ibid.: 111)

Nor, Fields continues, can ideology be explained away as propaganda or dogma. So what is ideology? Ideology is a 'distillation of experience' that continues through and is normalized by the repetition of the day-to-day experience of social relations. Fields gives the example of stopping at a traffic light. One hesitates to run a traffic light in the middle of an abandoned intersection on an open prairie because the commonsense of obeying traffic lights is impressed upon us from a lifetime of accepting a cause-and-effect relationship between stopping for red lights and human survival.

So, the ideology of race did not spring from the minds of the British living in the American colonies because culturally buried within them was a deep-seated desire to invent white supremacy. People had enslaved members of their own communities for millennia. Race-based slavery was a specific invention used to preserve property rights in the midst of new ideas in British politics along with the decline in the numbers of indentured servants coming from England. The question was: what is the best way to maintain an endless supply of cheap labor that can be worked to death to generate cotton and tobacco in a nation founding itself on republican ideals like natural right, liberty, and equality? The answer was to establish a social category of subhumans to whom natural right, liberty, and equality did not apply: Black slaves. Ideology developed from the repetition of the day-to-day subjugation of Africans in the newly minted United States. And that repetition continued because of the profits derived from a slave-based agricultural economy.

Racism was not passed down through generations 'like a germ'; race is still crafted[4] through capitalism's need to devalue labor and leverage surplus populations. It is not only a process endemic to the United States. Racecraft is a global phenomenon working against immigrant populations who are in desperate situations and who have features that can distinguish them from natives (including cultural and religious dress). The normalization of the treatment of certain groups as surplus and the impulse of other precariously positioned groups to reassure themselves that they are not surplus are the foundations of racist paranoia. Economic value becomes social value. Ending racism entails ending surplus populations and the devaluation of labor.

III. Sexcraft and ideological repetition

If race is not a self-contained vector of oppression crashing through the body, neither is gender or its so-called biological effect: sex. While feminists since Simone de Beauvoir have argued that gender is a socially constructed psychological supplement to real biological sex rather than an innate expression of sex categories, Butler's *Gender Trouble* exploded the debate between essentialism and social construction by troubling the category of sex itself. While, unlike race, there is a predictable set of physical characteristics that enact a biological function called reproduction, the reduction of sex to biological function is simply not the way human gendering works. First and foremost, we cannot predict biological capacity by visually sorting people without the development of coded gendered behavior: *social gender* (see Stryker 2008b). Second, the ideological attributes of social gender extend far beyond moments of biological reproduction. If you meet an androgen-insensitive woman with XY chromosomes and undescended testes, you will likely recognize her as a woman regardless of her genetics and regardless of her capacity to reproduce. Monique Wittig's declaration that lesbians are not women (Wittig 1992: 32) – which seemed absurd to some – makes perfect sense in this context. If women are distinguished by the use of certain reproductive organs, wouldn't women who don't use those organs trouble the category? Butler's argument is that gender is established by performance, not understood as a socially intentional act (which she clarifies in the second edition of her book) but as an iteration, a repetition of the body that becomes normalized. Far from being incompatible with materialist analysis, Butler's intervention meshes nicely with Fields' conception of ideology as a repetition of actions originating in social relations, but actions that continue to be normalized through habit, experience, and the organizational logic of a given society.

One of the most maddening aspects of analyses of gender is that they are usually maintained by the same circular logic as Fields observes in the ideology of race: that is, delicateness should be cultivated in those we categorize as women because it is a feminine characteristic as evidenced by the delicateness of those we categorize as women. Of course, class divisions undermine the notion of natural gender because it is not necessarily financially advantageous to consider working-class women physically delicate – not to the worker selling her labor nor to her boss. So, the gendering of women becomes a biological judgment about racialized and classed bodies and since such biological judgments are attributed to nature, it appears as if there could be a biological component segregating women by race and class. The need for race, class, and gender to appear as natural sets of innate biological characteristics rather than as historically situated positions is perhaps more obvious when we look at the search for a third sex in England, where scientists considered the possibility that prostitutes weren't really women after all.[5]

A merger between Butler's explanation of gender as grounded through iterability and Fields' explanation of ideology as repetition is distinct from Pierre Bourdieu's idea of *habitus* (defined as the dispositions created by a subject engaging with a particular field). What Fields is getting at is not how people learn to play different games within their social milieu, ending in different affects and values. Fields is not approaching epistemology from the perspective of class culture, but as a conceptual and social process developing out of material and economic processes. For this reason, Bourdieu's post-Marxist equivocal concept of 'cultural capital' falls flat. It transforms the term 'capital' into a synonym for wealth or riches; however, capital is a point in a process, a particular use of profits to yield more profit. One cannot invest one's cultural capital (education, for example) on the market in the hope of doubling one's cultural capital, but then instead lose all your cultural capital in a bearish cultural market.[6]

Although we may repeatedly perform our assigned social gender until it feels like nature (if we are not trans) or until every moment of our life's performance reminds us that our assigned gender is completely at odds with who we are (if we are trans), the fact that we are disciplined into a social gender is no more the origin of gender oppression than the sexual division of labor is the origin of misogyny. Vogel's explanation shows that we are disciplined into a social gender according to the mode of production under which we live; its expectations of who we are are based on its best guesses about what our bodies can do for it. Working women, queer people, trans people, and intersex people have conflicting use values for the ruling classes under the current mode of production. What they demand of us is a knot of contradictions and impossibilities. Therefore, the political goal cannot be to resist being the way they want us to be. The political goal must be to take back what has been materially taken from us so that we can build the lives we choose.

IV. Class is not a moral category

Class is the category that is most difficult to reconcile within the vector system for a number of reasons. First of all, in American culture – the real birthplace of the vector system – class is not and has never been anything resembling caste; it is not fixed, it is something one can fall in and out of. Workers can win the lottery; small capitalists can 'lose it all' through poor investments. Because of the slipperiness of class as conceived by American academic models of oppression, class appears as more of a temporary bad situation than a real oppression. This way of thinking is covertly shaped by ideology: where there are no other oppressions, a person is poor because they aren't as smart or hardworking – in short, not as good – as their more successful counterparts. While Black and brown people are held back through discrimination, and all women are held back through sexism and some by the burden of childrearing, and disabled people are held back by their exclusion from the world's expectations and its architecture, if straight white cisgendered men are poor it is because they are of limited talent, intelligence, and moral character. Equating the exploitation of straight white working-class cisgendered men with the violence levied against trans women or immigrants sounds about as misguided as comparing discrimination against hippies with Jim Crow segregation. This tendency to be suspicious about class reveals the liberal inflection of the vector model. When neoliberalism is invoked, it is generally spoken about as if it were a mechanism by which all First World consumers perpetuate violence against all Third World peoples. The majority of the world proletariat may be outside the wealthy regions of the global North; still, the vast majority of people even in the global North own no means of production and have nothing to trade for survival but their own labor.

In capitalism, race, class, and gender are mutually conditioning components of an ideology produced by material social relations. But the vector model cannot accommodate economic analyses that go beyond specific intersecting points, and in this way the vector model is the concretization of the poststructuralist rejection of grand narratives. So, without economics, what can class be? Class becomes *classism* or discrimination based on class. Class oppression is reduced to having to endure the snobbishness of the upper classes. It does not explain how upper and lower classes are maintained. The only thing one can take away is that poor people are poor because the upper classes do not graciously accept them into their sphere. Once again, the culprit of all social ills is power, privilege, and othering. The material relations of social production never enter the picture. In fact, classism could even be stretched to accommodate how wealthy individuals can have their feelings hurt when working people make them feel guilty for being rich. However, it is the belief that feelings alone indicate oppression that takes us into a bizarre world in which wealthy white people, men, cisgendered heterosexuals, and colonizers see the political struggles of poor people, Black and brown people, women, transgendered people, queers, and colonized people as evidence of reverse racism, reverse classism, reverse sexism, and discrimination against traditional values. Indeed, recent research has shown that American whites in the late twentieth and early twenty-first centuries believe that they experience *more* racial discrimination than Blacks (Norton and Sommers 2011: 215).

But when Marxists talk about class, they are not appealing to the American sociological and cultural definition of the working class, nor do they want to convince those operating on the vector model that it is important to be considerate of working people's pain. Marxist materialism has an entirely different model for understanding exploitation and oppression. Under capitalism, the mechanisms for reproducing life – land, infrastructure, large-scale technology – are concentrated in private hands. The vast majority of people must either sell their labor power to survive or beg or hunt for scraps to sustain themselves. When working people become pregnant, their wages are too low to properly care for themselves or their future children. The gendering and racializing of bodies on the labor market assigns roles and values to those bodies in new ways. Disability is understood in terms of the inability to compete on the labor market, the inability to support oneself, and the 'demand' that employers make accommodations. Sexual orientation is a problem for capital insofar as it disrupts the oppositional sexism that helps regulate the labor force at work and at home. Intolerance is a mixed bag in the workplace – fights on the shop floor have the potential to disrupt efficiency, but also the potential to prevent solidarity and strike activity. So what is the politics of class? It starts with understanding that the world is organized in such a way that a subset of people extract a surplus from others, that they purchase influence from the state with that surplus, that they devise fictitious investment schemes and own and maintain systems of social control to maintain their dominance, and then they create a situation of dependence upon the goods and services they hire other people to develop. The centrality of class in the struggle against capitalism does not mean that the working class suffers more than peasants, or that class position is more of a barrier to individual achievement than color or gender or trans status or nationality. It is simply political activity based on the idea that serious challenges to capital are contingent upon collaboration between the diverse people who produce and maintain the profitable circulation of goods.

V. The rise of queer politics

Queer theory, born from a mixture of Foucauldian analysis and conflicts within second-wave feminism, rightly challenged the mythologies of heterosexual universalism. Scholars in diverse disciplines sought to challenge oppositional sexism in research, trouble static conceptions of sex and human bodies, and confront the assumption that heterosexuality is the human default. Heterosexism is based on the implicit demand that all persons project heterosexuality. This is achieved through heteronormativity, or social pressure and legal obligations to mimic heterosexual social forms. Queer studies has done a good job in outlining the extent of heteronormativity as well as historical instances of rebellion against it. It has done a less thorough job in explaining why heteronormativity exists in the first place. Vogel's analysis, however, gives us a solid foundation for understanding the reasons why the capitalist mode of production pressures capitalists and workers (although for separate reasons) to publicly perform certain social genders and sexual expectations. Heteronormativity is not the same in all periods of history; it is not even uniform within capitalism, as different nations have different histories and cultural customs that pressure people in different ways.

Gender and sexual diversity seem to have always been with us on all parts of the planet. However, homosexuality is a political-medical concept constructed in nineteenth-century Europe: the construction of heterosexuality followed shortly thereafter. Gay political identity was not established in the United States until the mid-twentieth century. Mass industrialization allowed individuals to escape from the strictures of rural communities, and then the massive expansion of the military during World War II created a division of labor that separated men and women onto different continents (see D'Emilio 1983). Facing similar conditions, Europe's earlier industrialization during World War I led to the rise of gay rights in Germany, with Second International era socialists such as Bebel and (later) Hirschfeld being major proponents of the movement. Before the development of a gay political identity, the first form of queer sexual politics was behavior-based. Both the French Revolution and the Russian Revolution overturned sodomy laws as part of their political platforms. European colonization, on the other hand, produced a reactionary sexual politics of enforced heterosexuality; European colonial forces eradicated queer cultural norms in the Middle East and Africa just as they had erased the sexual and gender diversity from indigenous peoples in the Americas during the earliest phases of capitalist development.[7] But while the European military leadership went about its project of eradicating same-sex desire from Middle Eastern and north African social life, the troops stationed there participated en masse not just in homosexuality but also in same-sex relationships (see Aldrich 2003).

A political pattern emerged within early capitalist modernity: the struggle for sexual freedoms arose within the development of a general emancipatory politics. This continued to be the case during the rise of New Left social movements in the West. The modern gay and trans liberation movements emerged at the high-water mark of mid-century left politics inspired by May 1968 and the protests against the war in Vietnam (and later protests against Pinochet in Chile),[8] as well as the struggle for Black rights, Puerto Rican rights, and women's rights. This mid-century political upheaval was, as the saying goes, not a dinner party. Quite literally. In 1966, trans women made history by fighting police at Compton's Cafeteria in the Tenderloin district of San Francisco. During the Stonewall Riots, gay and trans youth led a battle against police that lasted for six days – many of the protesters were queer people of color, with Yippies and Black Panthers playing a (very) minor role in the struggle (see Carter 2004). Inspired by the ethnic pride parades common to New York City, the gay and lesbian pride parade was established in 1973 by the newly formed Gay Liberation Front.

It is often lamented – and certainly true – that the radicalism of the gay and lesbian liberation movements succumbed to 'Gay Inc.': the politics of inclusion, market consumption, corporate identity, and assimilationist demands such as marriage and military service. Earlier movements had always been attached to radical demands for broader social transformation. These demands were never reformist, but sought to end oppression in all its forms. The Gay Liberation Front (GLF), Street Transvestite Action Revolutionaries (STAR), and Radicalesbians were not seeking inclusion into the heterosexual world or citizenship by way of marriage and military service; rather, they openly challenged those institutions as repressive, in the case of the former, and oppressive in the case of the latter.

Indeed, there has been a retrenchment in the political militancy of queer activism in the United States over the past half-century. The radical politics of GLF and STAR quickly began to attenuate, in part due to their failure to build a solid united front with movements such as the Young Lords and the Black Panthers.[9] By the end of the 1970s, the gay movement was less militant, but it had expanded to build bridges with labor. Interaction between the labor movement and queer radicalism did not move in a smooth forward march, along the lines of the progressive narrative of social change, where generation after generation would become more tolerant as society matured naturally.[10] The relationship between labor and LGBT rights over the years was more complicated than a simple teleological unfolding towards a more just society. By the 1950s, even the most radical elements of the union movement had drifted far from their counterparts in the National Union of Marine Cooks and Stewards, who in the 1930s, operated under the slogan 'If you let them red-bait, they'll race-bait, and if you let them race-bait, they'll queen-bait. These are all connected. That's why we have to stick together' (Bérubé 2011: 310). Then McCarthyism took its toll. The overall trend of gay and lesbian politics was a movement away from radicalism towards a more modest homophilia. Emblematic of this shift, a patriotic, law-and-order tendency within the homosexual political group the Mattachine Society ousted the union-aligned communists who had founded the organization.

In the years immediately following the McCarthy era, individual gay icons began to emerge within the Black civil rights movements, such as Bayard Rustin, who simultaneously struggled for Black, gay, and labor rights. The Stonewall Riots took place in June 1969, rather late in the political history of the New Left. As gay politics was in its ascendency, the New Left itself slid into the quietude of the mid-1970s. After the decline of the more militant sections of the gay liberation movement, the 1970s at least saw a return to labor activism. Activists worked with teachers' unions to fight the Briggs Initiative which threatened a ban on gay teachers. Harvey Milk famously organized support for the Coors boycott alongside the Teamsters in support of workers forced to take lie detector tests to prove they weren't queer. Pushing for the rights of gay workers within the larger labor movement had less radical panache than rioting, but combining New Left demands of social and sexual equality with an Old Left militant labor lineage had its benefits. The merger of gay liberationists and striking miners in the UK might be considered 'assimilationist' by today's standards, but having wave after wave of small-town Welsh miners and their families at the head of the gay pride march in London in 1985 reflected bonds of solidarity and political possibilities that earlier movements had failed to achieve.[11]

Then the AIDS virus transformed the gay political landscape. The old Stonewall-style struggle for liberation of the late 1960s and the labor alliances of the 1970s were replaced by a new type of struggle that was more attuned to the realities of late twentieth-century gay life. Political energies were redirected towards community initiatives such as the Gay Men's Health Crisis. Eventually, the more radical AIDS Coalition to Unleash Power (ACT-UP) used direct action tactics to demand funding for AIDS research, to support the development of needle exchange programs, and to condemn the Catholic Church for opposing condom distribution; ACT-UP protested against the first Gulf War with the slogan 'Money for AIDS not for war'.

The realities of the spread of HIV and the political tactics adopted by AIDS activists pushed queer politics into a number of directions at once. The first was the reinstitution of militant cultural queerness; however, by the 1990s, neoliberalism was in full force. Computing power allowed American manufacturing to lower wages through offshoring, labor was in crisis, and public infrastructure was becoming privatized. Militant right-wing Christian ideology was employed to redirect the public's anger towards the poor and disenfranchised. Religious fundamentalist organizations developed moral panics around the AIDS crisis and Black women's sexuality to galvanize political hegemony. It wasn't neoliberalism causing the decline in living standards; it was Black 'welfare queens' spending everyone's money and queers spreading disease and immorality. Instead of being wedded to larger movements on the left – movements that were in decline – queer activists felt vulnerable and abandoned, entrenched in a desperate fight for immediate reforms surrounding affordable access to medication. AIDS activism became a global social justice movement focused on reforms that would benefit HIV-positive people and serve to eradicate the virus: affordable healthcare, the promotion of safer sex, and access to AIDS medication for the African continent.

The fall of the Berlin Wall, and later the Soviet Union, produced a retreat in Marxist movements. Marxism was dead. Capitalism was the final and highest point in history. The popularization of the internet combined with the millenarian sensibilities around the coming of the new millennium produced a new era of capitalist chic in the United States; de-industrialization was softened by a frenzy of optimism surrounding petit-bourgeois start-ups. Now, former steelworkers could try their hand at day trading or web design. But, in addition to the wild spread of fictitious capital, the new irrational exuberance promised crises of overproduction. The offshoring of jobs had brought about a continual decline of union membership during the 1980s and 1990s. Manufacturing jobs, once plentiful in urban areas, moved overseas, leaving behind a suburban service economy that was inaccessible to Black men in particular. Where direct discrimination failed to block Black male employment, lack of access to automobiles was the final blow. The Black community faced unemployment, the distribution of crack cocaine into Black communities, and a disproportionate rate of HIV infection and AIDS (Alexander 2012: 1–58).

The American labor movement wasn't faring any better. For all the inadequacies of American business unions, it would have required a strong international labor movement to challenge neoliberalism. If a union made demands, the factory would threaten to flee the country. This contradiction left unions in the position of either making more militant (i.e. international) demands – without the infrastructure and networks in place to do so – or agreeing to concessions so extreme that union membership had little financial benefit. The business sector pushed the idea that it was union demands for higher wages that had forced them to move overseas in order to cash in on a cheaper labor supply. Not only was it now easier to paint labor in an unflattering light, the wave of deregulation following the free-market expansion of the 1980s made it easier for the capitalist class to get their message onto the airwaves in the US. Before the 1990s, the Fairness Doctrine required news outlets to provide a balanced perspective. Stations were less eager to hire talk-show hosts and newscasters with extremist views. After the Fairness Doctrine was repealed in 1987, and after the Telecommunications Act of 1996 allowed corporations to expand their media holdings, a nationwide campaign of conservative talk radio developed that fostered hostility towards labor unions, immigrants, Blacks, queers, and feminists. Neoliberal capitalism had become the only alternative. The North American Free Trade Agreement (NAFTA) facilitated the overproduction of American corn, flooding the Mexican corn market and destroying farms – and, given the genetic tampering pushed by Monsanto, it can be argued that the flood of cheap corn destroyed the corn as well. The Mexican government permitted the privatization of the communal *ejidos* often held by indigenous populations in Mexico, leading to the Zapatista uprisings in 1994. The occupation of indigenous land in Mexico pushed indigenous people into the cities in the hope of finding work. With the destruction of the Mexican corn industry, marijuana became a new cash crop, accelerating the drug war and forcing even more workers to flee Mexico to the United States, where they could become a cheap supply of labor under 'Juan Crow' laws (Casey and Watkins 2014: 146–83). The carefully groomed hysteria over crack cocaine would mature into the War on Drugs, which brought about the militarization of police forces across the United States and a wave of mass incarceration, especially of young Black men, for drug offenses, even though the selling and use of drugs among Black teens are equal to or lesser than the selling and use of drugs by white teens (Alexander 2012: 99). Along with the vicissitudes of advanced capitalism, the politics of the 1990s proved the motto of the National Union of Marine Cooks and Stewards to be prophetic: race-baiting, red-baiting, and queer-baiting were indeed undermining working-class power.

Queer nationalism developed within this political climate. With the logics of material production well obscured, the ties between political communities loosened. Each individual group would pursue its own survival. Not only was solidarity eroding, even coalition politics had become strained.[12] Queer Nation, one of the most visible and militant formations of American queer politics, marched under the slogan 'We're here, we're queer, get used to it'. But another slogan within the group was 'I hate straights'. The decades-long debate about whether lesbians belonged in the feminist camp or the gay camp seemed to have come to an end: the gay camp would have to be queered by feminism in the name of queer nationhood. Those at the intersection of the Venn diagram of cultural politics – Black queers, immigrant queers, working-class queers – were pressured to take a side, or, to put it less succinctly but more bluntly, to choose between the lived aspects of their oppression – like choosing the lemons over the water in your glass of lemonade. Essays in Michael Warner's *Fear of a Queer Planet* show that this problem did not go unmentioned, even though it was never solved (see Seidman 1993: 105–42). However, in Warner's inaugural collective of queer nationalist theory, solutions from the Marxist camp are absolutely unwelcome. In the opening section, dedicated to undoing 'heterotheory', Marx is the first theorist undone. In fact, he is accused of all but inventing heteronormativity itself.[13]

The paradox of this militant retreat into self-care and safe spaces at once individualized struggle and created a clear inner–outer protective barrier between the oppressed and their oppressors. These oppressors were now also individualized as people who did not share the defining experience of the group, or, if outsiders were welcome, those who did not take the time to educate themselves about the group's specific oppression. Socialists and labor organizers arguing for reforms or, worse, suggesting that oppressed people wait until 'after the revolution' were marked as absolute enemies. By the late 1990s, even radical queer street politics had gone into retreat. AIDS activism was now the terrain of non-governmental organizations (NGOs) and specialists, not militant queers holding fluorescent placards.

If safe spaces were protected environments that excluded the ignorant masses, then there was no better place for the queer movement (and other movements based on identity) to retreat to than the university. In fact, with the erasure of public space in cities, universities were often one of the few venues still available in the United States. In addition to being a protected, public space where groups and individuals could educate themselves, the university also had a solid pedigree of activist history: the students who braved the massacre in Mexico City, the May 1968 movement in

France, and the antiwar movement in the United States all spoke to the possibilities for student activism. However, the queering of the university did not so much start a revolution as create a network of support groups and an opportunity for self-reflection. The death of street activism and gay liberation is sometimes blamed on the rise of postmodernism, with its celebration of fragments and its obsession with the particulate and the incommensurable over the connected and relational. But working-class queer people didn't just abandon the streets because of what some academics were saying. Neoliberal pressures, the privatization of space, the privatization of the media, and targeted ideological offensives against working-class solidarity are more likely factors in the relative decline of organized queer street politics.

VI. Marxist critiques of queer theory

The first intervention against the postmodern turn in queer politics was the publication of *The Material Queer*, edited by Donald Morton. The title must have been a concession, or ironic, because Morton's polemical introduction to each chapter bristles with outrage at the political move from gay and lesbian identity to the mucky concept *queer*. The book itself is a political response to the publication of Warner's *Fear of a Queer Planet*, which had eviscerated Marx's theory of emancipation – or, more accurately, a straw version of it. Morton's diatribe against the rise of queer (anti-)politics is a fascinating snapshot of a moment in intellectual history – the height of the clash between Marxist class-consciousness and the new politics of queer nationalism. Indeed, Morton's work was so vehemently polemical, he was unable to obtain the rights to reprint many works he wished to review. Morton is particularly outraged at the 1990s penchant for connecting queerness to the new non-hierarchical mode of online communication and its fascination for techno-libertarian and transhumanist visions, which accompanied the rise of the petit-bourgeois obsession with triumphant tinkerers. For Morton, this turn towards the techno-queer smacked of a hatred of the working class, who, outside the rose-colored windows of the IT entrepreneur's corner office, were still suffering under the weight of capital. Morton describes the new concept of queer as part of the nihilistic punk ethos of Dennis Cooper – a queer writer who openly despised the generation of gay men before him. But Morton's polemical take on queerness cements him into an unhelpful rigidity. Most telling, he reacts with horror to the way in which the fight for the rights of gays and lesbians, with the interference of middle-class academia, had turned into an 'unthoughtful celebration of transvestism' (Morton 1996: 14).[14] Instead of revealing the fallaciousness of Warner and company's anti-Marxist arguments, the book creates an (often equally fallacious) counter-polemic against queer theory's 'atmosphere of sexual "deregulation"', insinuating that the deconstruction of identities in queer theory mirrors corporate deregulation. Unfortunately, despite the linguistic nearness of the implied terms (corporal deregulation and corporate deregulation), neither bodies nor sexuality itself are equivalent to corporations or the organization of corporations inside the capitalist state. Deregulating corporations intensifies the exploitation of workers. Troubling gender categories does not. Overall, the book argues that capitalism undermines identity in service of a 'have it your way burger' society where consumers are encouraged to create themselves through commodities and commodified relations on the market. In a nutshell, eclectic postmodern visions of the self mirror the politics of liberal pluralism. However, this provokes the question: if capitalism undermines identity, and the celebration of the destruction of identity is a celebration of capitalism, then does anti-capitalism imply a return to stable identities? And, if so, why do the twentieth-century Marxist opponents of queer theory also denounce identity politics? There is actually nothing new about this problematic. Clara Zetkin promoted conservatism in the proletarian movement with her idea that working-class women's desire was a return to peasant housewifery and motherhood. Populists such as Christopher Lasch argued that 'The Family [is] a Haven in a Heartless World' (Lasch 1976). Both arguments reflect the nineteenth-century political theorist Ferdinand Tönnies' idea of the gap between *gemeinschaft* (the village with its old-fashioned communal warmth) and *gesellschaft* (the cold, self-centered and impersonal world of modern capitalism) (Tönnies and Loomis 1957; Cahnman and Heberle 1971). The rejection of the anti-identitarian world of *gesellschaft* and the return to the deep connectedness of the *gemeinschaft* is the opposite of the progressive position: it is, in fact, a reactionary impulse. Clearly, the return to *gemeinschaft* is not a line of thought that Marxists should pursue. In the end, the censuring of queer anti-identity in favor of a gay and lesbian identity was not a Marxist refutation of queer theory, but the criticism of one (anti-)identity in favor of another.

The contributors to Morton's reader are clearly put off by early queer theorists' faith in the world-transforming power of liberated Eros.[15] Teresa Ebert calls this postmodern turn *ludic feminism* – the feminism of play.[16] Like Morton, Ebert is concerned with the rejection of materialism in favor of what she dubs a form of idealism called 'matterism' – the 'matter' of the body, the 'matter' of sexuality, the 'matter' of race, the 'matter' of media, and, above all, the 'matter' of language (Zavarzadeh et al. 1995). Indeed, the rethinking of materialism as 'matters of this or that' is clear equivocation, a sleight of hand that redefines the material world as an idea. Ebert argues that anti-realism is the logical conclusion of post-Marxist queer thought. Where others see revolution, she sees a pseudo-radical politics of pleasure in linguistic idealism. For Ebert, poststructuralism is a form of discursive avant-gardism that is little more than a reflection and reaffirmation of capitalist individualism. Poststructuralism has a class character: 'Ludic feminism is, in effect, a theory for property holders' (Ebert 1995).[17]

Queer theory's emergence in academia created another clash that would have consequences for the scattered remains of Marxist-feminist theory. Debate raged on whether *women*'s studies should become *gender* studies. The tension between woman-centered politics and gender politics is unresolved. The charge against queer theory and the field of gender studies is, first, that it ignores heterosexual cisgendered women's issues including abortion, housework, and childcare. Using Lise Vogel's work, we see how divorcing cisgendered heterosexual women's economically driven political issues from queer issues impoverishes queer and trans struggles against oppositional sexism (Chapter 2). The second charge against it is that it erases the category 'woman', and that it is women, specifically, who are targeted by political conservatives.[18] Turning the discussion from women to the gendered oppression of gay men, Black men, and trans people has been a particular sticking point. Academic cisgendered men have also come forward to defend the purity of the political idea of Woman against trans inclusion. This rush to the defense of women, *which is always also its paternalistic inverse*, is patronizing and pathologizing; and despite their protestations, these noble knights are clearly arguing that trans women are actually not women at all. Since cis men rarely feel empowered to enter the fray when women are fighting amongst themselves, what is it about the interactions between trans and cisgendered women that makes middle-class academic men feel that they have the right to intervene to protect womanhood as they understand it? While the dominant classes want to control the bodies and reproductive capacities of cis women and trans men, attacks on cis women are only one moment in the cycle of oppression undergirded by processes of reproduction under capital. The political establishment does not simply want access to women's bodies, it wants the maintenance of order through traditional and oppositional sexism. All

Black bodies, all trans bodies, all queer bodies, all immigrant bodies, and all women's bodies are determined by the social stability oppositional sexism provides.

However, it is true that in its zeal for uncovering the complex relation between social gender, sexual pleasure, and physical embodiment, the material processes of social reproduction within global capitalist production have been neglected – and this means that cisgendered, heterosexual women around the world have been largely abandoned by the dominant queer narrative. Queer and trans political thought has not shown much concern for commercial surrogacy in India; it has not overtly connected femicide in Mexico with violence against trans women of color; it has not defended women globally against sterilization campaigns in the name of the environment. The privilege politics model becomes both counterproductive and skewed when it develops conceptual hierarchies of oppression. Is a cis woman still more privileged than a trans woman if she is the victim of femicide or a child bride or financially forced into commercial surrogacy? In the real world, a dialectical model that understands oppressions as manufactured and reinforced by social relations is more valuable than taxonomies of oppression; solidarity, defined as a willingness to fight militantly for others, builds support between the bearers of variegated oppressions instead of undermining the strength and courage of those who experience different sets of tribulations.

Since Ebert and Morton, queer theory has been appraised throughout the Marxist canon. Max Kirsch in *Queer Theory and Social Change* (Kirsch 2000) covers much ground and in a far less polemical tone than earlier queer Marxist analysis. Kirsch, like many other progressive academics, faults the contemporary queer world for consumerism and tries to fathom how the movements for military and marriage came to be reforms that were demanded. (I would argue – and will argue later – however, that these demands hardly seem to be coming from queer theorists or their students.)

Kirsch criticizes queer theory for being an academic field that puts itself beyond criticism. He shows that analyses of sex and gender construction and oppositional sexism were happening already without queer theory. (My question here, though, is to what extent?) The last portion of the book urges the queer movement to align itself with social movements and political movements that extend beyond the politics of sex and gender. It has a particularly interesting and innovative chapter on the idea of energy and how it is expended and conserved within movements and political practices.

James Penney's *After Queer Theory* is a twenty-first-century lament about queer thought's infatuation with instability, its avant-garde posturing, and the abysmally thin multicultural politics of difference that intellectually sustains it. Indeed, Penney takes up right where Morton leaves off and even adds some gusto to the polemic. To emphasize the bourgeois character of the intellectual movement, Penney characterizes queer theorists with more than a bit of hyperbole – he imagines queer theorists sipping organic tea while doing yoga poses in their corner offices; later, he accuses them of being millionaire libertarian pornographers (Penney 2013). Penney's project involves a critique of the idea that liberation from homonormativity is valuable – one of the rare instances of such a critique. He certainly does not celebrate the marriage equality movement – but it makes sense to him as a materialist. What distinguishes Penney from most other critics is that, although Penney has definite Marxist commitments, his first allegiance is to Lacanian psychoanalysis. In addition to his polemic against queer theory's middle-class character, its complete divorce from economics, and the fact that it can often be self-indulgent and even paranoiac, Penney is most convinced that Lacan makes queer theory irrelevant in the first place. For Lacan, no one achieves gender wholeness: such an achievement is not possible. Everyone fails at being a man or a woman. And everyone is polymorphously perverse. Queer people aren't special – queer people aren't even particularly a legitimate category. I would argue, however, that while it is true that it is part of the human condition to fail to live up to idealized forms, and while, empirically, it is also true that queer people are no more perverse or 'non-normative' than heterosexuals, actual material conditions determine the consequences of what it means to fail to live up to gender expectations. There is a distinct difference between the consequences of a CEO having low self-esteem deep down because he does not feel 'man enough' and a trans woman being assaulted for not 'passing' as a woman; and while heterosexuals are as perverse as anyone else, their perverted relationships take on the veneer of respectability in the eyes of the state due to their assumed ability to reproduce laborers (or heirs).

It is true that the linguistic turn moved analysis into the realm of empty jargon: *discursivity* (first, poststructuralists reduce everything to a text and then discuss its discursivity – which begins to sound a lot like 'this thing is very thingy'),[19] answers are *problematized* (instead of problems being answeritized), and *phallogocentrism* (which is a polite, poststructuralist way of saying that someone is being an argumentative dick). However, it seems to me that Marxist criticism concedes too much to poststructuralism by playing on its terrain. Irritation with poststructuralist lingo aside, blaming 'postmodernism' for the move from gay liberation to queer consumerism overemphasizes theory. As Christoph Henning argues in *Philosophy After Marx*, society is not a separate thing layered on top of economics. While elements of queer theory may reflect and even strengthen bourgeois political consciousness, we can say without reduction that consciousness flows from life itself. The breakdown of gay liberation into market individualism, self-care, and small reforms was not generated by postmodern theory. The retreat into communal safe spaces and self-care was a response to the dismantling of the welfare state, privatization, and the outsourcing of caring responsibilities. The move towards reforms after Stonewall reflects lessons learned from the AIDS crisis. Although its style was radical,

ACT-UP did not bring about queer liberation. In fact, the group never even demanded liberation. The goal of such radical direct action campaigns was the implementation of basic reforms meant to make life under advanced capitalism not just tolerable but survivable for queer people in a violently heteronormative world. On the other hand, mundane issues such as paperwork, contracts, and power of attorney determined whether or not one's partner would be evicted from their home, or whether or not a person was able to spend their last days with their loved ones or instead spent them with estranged blood relations who had suddenly been empowered by the state. The reason why gay liberation has declined and gay and lesbian people have been 'colonized' by the neoliberal attitude is not on account of postmodern ideas. It is because the United States has been mired in a thirty-five-year period of reaction and political retreat, and there has been a global trend towards political retreat since the 1990s. There is no reason to suggest that gay politics should be the outlier, keeping the militancy of the late 1960s alive against the grain of history as if it were a political phenomenon distinct from the whole of that history. But the queer West often sees itself, and is often seen by others, as a consciously self-constructed political entity that should be by its very subaltern nature a subversive, anti-capitalist, aesthetically radical formation.

This is where the now decades-old Marxist criticism of queer theory as ludic eclecticism and contemporary queer anti-capitalist critique part ways. Morton, Ebert, and Zavarzadeh argue that poststructuralist thought is a pre-millennial expression of bourgeois ideology. From this point of view, queer identity is a murky anti-identity that helped turn a militant movement for gay and lesbian rights into a market-like quest for self-expression and self-development. The petit bourgeoisification of the movement – or 'Gay Inc.', as it is called – is then a real expression of this conceptual malaise. But a new model of thinking through queer collusions with capitalism has developed over recent decades, and this model contains some of the earlier critiques of gay consumerism. Certainly, the gay pride parade – now an *actual corporation* – has turned a political march into a procession of corporate sponsors vying for the so-called gay dollar. Corporate employees are encouraged to march and wave at the crowd. These participants are not a section of class-conscious workers, but waged ambassadors of their employers' good will towards a market segment. Your parents might have disowned you, your neighbors might vote against your interests, but Apple supports you, Coors supports you (at least post-boycott Coors), and the local car dealership supports you. This cynical display of corporate affection exists in a gap where genuine solidarity could be: the labor unions support you, the Black power movements support you, the immigrants' rights groups support you, reproductive rights groups support you, the revolutionary Marxists support you. But this would require progressive political groups to actually support one another – an uncommon and sometimes even unpopular position since the neoliberal turn.

Some groups have formed as an attempt to organize parallel marches to corporate pride. QueerBomb in Austin, Texas is one example. After an Austin Gay and Lesbian Pride Foundation official remarked that the pride march was for gays and lesbians, and that if bisexuals and trans people wanted to march they should form their own damn march, queer and trans people who did not fit squarely into gay and lesbian identities went ahead and did just that. While the march started with anti-capitalist planks embedded in its manifesto, those planks were quickly discarded. This was partly because the parade was never anti-capitalist – it was merely anti-corporate and anti-consumerist. The new march was quickly supported by eclectic local businesses and restaurants. So now there are two marches: a big bourgeois march and a petit bourgeois march. This 'battle of the parades' appears to uphold the Morton–Ebert–Zavarzadeh thesis that queerness is bourgeois eclecticism. But their thesis does not explain why the gay and lesbian pride march isn't *more radical* than the queer one. It also does not explain why identity politics is valuable to a materialist worldview when it comes to gay and lesbian struggles, but eye-roll-provoking political idealism in all other struggles.

In an anti-capitalism that understands itself only in terms of critiques of consumer culture and – when at its rare best – critiques of Western military aggression, gay and lesbian populations are treated as a sort of ruling class by their younger queer and trans counterparts. The radical queer argument is the reverse of the early Marxist critique of queer theory. It is now the gays and lesbians with their stable and solid identities who are the market-oriented capitalist dupes, and queers who are synonymous with subversive possibility. Gay and lesbian identity is equated with wealth and middle-class assimilation. Just as earlier Marxist critiques upheld queerness as a form of market logic, queers have begun to see the gay and lesbian capacity to self-categorize as a capacity to collude with market forces. But more recently, trans activists, particularly trans women, have attacked queerness as a form of cissexism that *enforces* fluidity as a norm, thereby undermining trans people whose political demand is recognition as men and women. However, trans critiques of queer theory, unlike queer critiques of gay and lesbian identity, do not muddy their claims with the conflation of cisgendered existence and economic position. So the past decade has seen a reversal of the 'queer eclecticism is bourgeois' argument. Now, non-queered homosexual expression, or *homonormativity*, is the bourgeois kernel undermining queer radicalism. This version of queer anti-capitalism suggests that a stable gay political identity depends on a Western construct of homosexuality, one that is assimilationist in its demand for reforms, in its determination to be recognized by heteronormative culture. Here, it is precisely the poststructuralist, Deleuzean 'assemblage'[20] that is imagined to be inherently more radical than Marxist-humanist hopes of organizing a clear political subject.

Classical Marxism, held back by its usual knee-jerk suspicion of cultural politics, failed to keep up with much of the argument. Long into the twenty-first century, the term 'queer' was still emblematic of postmodern contamination. Ironically, for all the Marxist complaints about the corrosive elements of identity politics, it was *precisely* an identity politics that early critics of Marxist queer theory were demanding. The identity of not having an identity was not readily seen as a possible opening towards a genuine internationalism, nor was it viewed as a struggle between all those unnamed by the current system and those who wished to categorize them for their own benefit. Much of the classical Marxist tradition constructed a false choice between three political modalities: reactionary protection of the family from erosion by capitalism, liberal pluralism, and a vision of liberation connected to the good old days of yesteryear's material conditions. Thankfully, a new generation of queer and trans Marxists are beginning to think through gender within the current challenges posed by the neoliberal age.

VII. Beyond homonormativity and homonationalism

Emblematic of the acceptance of the radical potential of queerness is the influential queer postcolonial critique of twenty-first-century gay and lesbian social movements levied by Jasbir Puar. Her groundbreaking book *Terrorist Assemblages: Homonationalism in Queer Times* (Puar 2007) undermined nostalgia for pre-postmodern gay militancy in two ways: first, such a political subject would need a stable gay political identity, which, she noted, depends on a Western construct of homosexuality and gay liberation, one attached to the Christian confessional 'coming out' narrative; second, against Morton's and Ebert's critique of the queer as an expression of late capitalist bricolage, Puar queered the concept of terrorism through the poststructuralist notion of assemblages. Puar raises concerns about the Eurocentrism of the

Western gay and lesbian movement, with its focus on marriage, military service, and the language of citizenship. While gays ride under the cover of assumed progressivism, gay rights have cynically been used as a wedge by conservative politicians against Muslims. Pinkwashing – the use of LGBT rights to obscure political violence – has been used to justify Israeli occupation, and – after exploiting homophobia for their benefit in the 2004 elections – American conservatives had the audacity to use gay rights in their fight against allowing a mosque to be built in the vicinity of the Twin Towers. Acceptance of gays and lesbians has now become a litmus test to show whether Muslims can 'belong' in a Western democracy. The mainstreaming of gay culture has even prompted portions of the American right into accepting gay marriage as part and parcel of family values. Pinkwashing has become such a boon when fanning the flames of racism and anti-Muslim hatred in France that even ultranationalist Marine Le Pen briefly resorted to championing gay rights.

This is not simple right-wing hypocrisy; it is a strategy to dominate the political field. Conservatives can leverage the use of gay rights for racist propaganda at the same time as they fund the extermination of gays in Uganda and promote anti-gay violence in Eastern Europe and South America, while ignoring and minimizing the seriousness of forced feminization of detainees at Guantanamo Bay. Such feminization is a weaponization of queerness against those perceived to be queer, and detainees are perceived to be queer because they have been feminized by violence, because victimhood belongs to women. Puar is right to note the complexity at work, how homophobia, misogyny, racism, and imperialism don't just intersect but blend into a grotesque malevolence.

In the face of such madness, the American gay and lesbian movement has not had much to say. Puar points out that the gay and lesbian rights movement is skewed towards reforms that will benefit wealthy, white, cisgendered gays and lesbians of the global North. While some queers disdain marriage equality as an affront to the supposed radicalism of queer sexual ethics, Puar, along with Lisa Duggan and the Against Equality movement, argues that the funds going to secure equal marriage would be better spent fighting the immiseration of people who fall along the trans spectrum, who face enormous obstacles in securing work, housing, bathroom access, and basic healthcare, and who face suicide and violence at astronomical rates. In the United States, trans people of color, especially Black and Latina trans women, face violence from police, courts, and the prison system. Ending such violence and granting basic needs is grossly underfunded, while the securing of property rights for wealthy white couples seems to garner all the attention of mainstream gay and lesbian organizations. Puar and Duggan note that reforms such as same-sex marriage will do little to help poor women of color, who would lose state benefits if they married.

This focus on marriage and integration into mainstream white, heterosexual Euro-American life is what Lisa Duggan calls homonormativity (Duggan 2002: 175–94). Homonormativity refers to the pressure to conform to heterosexist society or to provide a narrative of the self that will be recognizable to the heterosexual world. The concept has now been extended into transnormativity – the pressure put upon trans people to conform to traditional, oppositional sexist understandings of gender. Whereas homonormativity tends to explain the pressures gay people put on one another, Puar's idea of homonationalism extends its reach from the domestic to the international. Blending into 'mainstream society' is not only color-coded white, it is coded in terms of citizenship and nationalism as well as imperialism and empire building. As Puar and others have noted, homosexuality is not always a political identity within nations of the Middle East, Africa, and South Asia; rather, it is considered a behavior or practice. 'Coming out' is not a relevant political experience in this context. Moreover, the goal of marriage (as others have noted) is not in tune with the less couple-centered and more communally focused childrearing practices developed by African American women.

Opposition to homonationalism means that goals of marriage and military service in American and European nations cannot be divorced from the ongoing legacy of imperialism. When gays and lesbians demand the right to be included in military service, they are demanding the right to participate in the destruction of Iraq, Afghanistan, and Yemen, the right to partake in racist, ethnic-cleansing. More than just marriage and military service, when gay rights discourse centers on the language of citizenship, it is automatically a homonationalist appeal to the state for acceptance and legitimation. The demand for naturalization rights for gay and lesbian immigrant couples also reinforces such appeals, as does accepting 'legitimate' appeals from immigrants fleeing violence and discrimination in the Middle East, which is then easily used as racist interventionist propaganda.

Similarly, gay culture has been commodified into a market, and gay politics has become a form of advertisement. Corporations cynically brand themselves as advocates of certain political demographics in order to pose as concerned corporate members of the community. Social values become the ruse of surplus value. The fast-food chain Chick-fil-A markets itself to the anti-gay demographic; Apple uses its support of gay rights as part of its brand experience, appealing to an urban progressive demographic. In this way, Apple isn't just a company that extracts profit from factory workers in China who are so unhappy with labor conditions that they resort to suicide as a protest tactic; no, Apple is a champion of human rights. Beyond the corporate infiltration of gay and lesbian culture, same-sex marriage has been celebrated for its capacity to generate revenue for the petit bourgeoisie: just think of the expansion of bridal boutiques, florists, and banquet halls. Moreover, as we know from *The Origin of the Family, Private Property, and the State*, marriage involves the passage of property, and a good number of queer people have no property to transmit.

But the concepts of homonormativity and homonationalism should not pass without criticism. Puar herself has criticized the way in which her work has been used. In her essay 'Rethinking Homonationalism', Puar argues:

> Homonationalism ... is not another identity politics, not another way of distinguishing good queers from bad queers, not an accusation, and not a position. It is rather a facet of modernity and a historical shift marked by the entrance of (some) homosexual bodies as worthy of protection by nation-states, a constitutive and fundamental reorientation of the relationship between the state, capitalism, and sexuality. (Puar 2013)

Lisa Duggan and Dean Spade also attribute the rise of the focus on marriage equality to the rise of neoliberalism, because marriage models the neoliberal demand that social care be privatized into the family. The writers repeatedly underscore the material basis of their analyses, reasserting that homonationalism and homonormativity are systematically deployed in Euro-American political culture.

But given the erosion of class and economic analyses, opposition to homonormativity and homonationalism becomes more of a moral position than a political one. Discussion of homonormativity generally produces little more political activity than complaining about 'homonormative gays', who are less real people than caricatures of that segment of the petit bourgeoisie who live in gentrified white 'gayborhoods' where they own local shops and restaurants, and where they donate to causes that promote the mainstreaming of gay culture such as marriage initiatives and the development of international gay and lesbian film festivals.

Yet for all the talk of the homonormativizing influence of neoliberalism, Duggan's contention is usually understood to imply that same-sex marriages in themselves are political anathema because same-sex married couples collaborate with and amplify the neoliberal policy of privatization. This is true in the smallest sense possible, in the same way that each heterosexual family amplifies privatization. Of course, as an ideological practice in the sense used by Barbara Fields, of ideology as repetition, engaging in or supporting same-sex marriage concretizes and normalizes the project. However, these repetitive gestures are not born from a desire to abandon world-changing radicalness in order to win pats on the head from heterosexuals or an elite club of gays. This field of activities and ideas is conditioned by the socio-material situations of ordinary people. Worrying about whether or not individuals desire assimilation swaps a concern about normative affects with actual anti-capitalist struggle. It assumes that queer people maintain dignity by communal separation. But separation from whom?

The concept of heteronormativity is concrete. Dress code laws and/or expectations require certain persons with certain physical characteristics to wear certain articles of clothing or else face state and interpersonal violence. Indeed, a presumption of heterosexuality is still culturally ingrained. Lesbians, even after repeat visits to the same doctor, may be asked if it is possible that tests will show that they are pregnant without their knowledge. It is still uncommon in most of the world to say to young children: 'When you grow up, you may or may not fall in love with someone somewhere along the gender spectrum ...' On-screen romantic dramas are generally heterosexual unless a movie is trying to make a heavy-handed sociopolitical point. When the working class is invoked, or the Black family, or refugee crises, or an international conflagration, it is generally imagined as a crisis of heterosexual people or a movement of heterosexual people. Gay people exist within the bubble of the gay problematic. They do not suffer economic crises, play video games, care for aging parents, or fight for the rights of fellow immigrants. Heterosexuality is the false generic.

So what then is *homonormativity*? Is homonormativity a matter of being aligned with non-queer people? Is it the demand for access to certain activities made popular by the straight middle class? Is there a systematic, state-sponsored oppression of Kinsey fours by Kinsey sixes? Does this mean, then, that the oppression of gays in Iran could be characterized as *transnormative* because homosexuality is imagined as latent transsexuality? One example of homonormativity commonly discussed is the attempt of older, white, wealthy gays in Greenwich Village to expel poor and working-class Black queer and trans youth congregating near their property – even naming their community patrol after a drugstore product that removes lice. But I find it difficult to imagine that these upper-class gays and the gay city officials who support them would be less likely to push Black youth off their property if their presentation conformed to gender norms. I see no evidence that this is a case of a gay elite patrolling queer identity. Instead, I see business owners expelling non-customers. I see landlords concerned with property value. I see the racist assumption that Black youth are dangerous. Part of the shock at the behavior of these propertied gays is based on a prior assumption of community harmony. Certainly, wouldn't the white, propertied gays be supportive of queer youth of color? We're all in one community, aren't we? From a Marxist perspective, it would have been clear from the beginning that a cabal of property owners worried about the bottom line would conspire against the poor regardless of gender presentation. To be intelligible to the logic of queer nationalism, *class dynamics are rewritten as a problem of affect* resulting in intra-community betrayal.

The content of homonormativity is an aggregate of assumptions about how gay people live according to its most vocal (which generally means most wealthy) figures: lobbying organizations such as the Human Rights Campaign (HRC) and National Gay and Lesbian Task Force, images of white professional gay characters on television. Radical queer criticism bristles with disdain for lesbian soccer moms with their babies in tow and gay men who own tastefully decorated houses. But the real inequality here is not the pressure of the normative on free spirits. This is just business as usual. The wealthy and professional classes are expressing themselves and assuming that the rest of the world aspires to be like them. These expressions are a melding of their interests: being worthy of receiving their inheritance, the right to pursue a high-level career, the desire to see reflections of themselves on television. Just as it is a cultural effect of capital that *bourgeois* heterosexuals dominate screen dramas (working-class and poor heterosexuals are always comic or tragic), it is also an effect of capital that screens reflect *bourgeois* gays. The prevailing ideas are generally the ideas of the ruling class. The people who own the means of production create the world in their own image.

Recasting class as normativity is unhelpful in a number of ways. The most basic is that railing against normativity in itself is, frankly, bizarre. The human capacity to share and reflect one another's behavior is the basis of culture. The expectation that a subjugated nation conform to the language and customs of a colonizer is not a pressure to be normal; it is a pressure to forget one's own history. It is an outright act of political and material domination to prevent insurgency, not an attempt to mold a group of people to an abstract norm. What is a fight against normativity if not a fight for the Enlightenment individual's self-expression or the creation of an isolated, elitist subculture? Even anti-homonormative, self-styled radical communities in the West are also constructed by norms: consensus voting, veganism, sharing music, norms of 'subversive' dress. The rejection of normativity has little to do with rejecting capitalism or even ending generalized social pressure; it is a demand that one be allowed to participate in a subculture that rejects the lifestyle of the professional or capitalist classes (but a subculture that also admits individuals from the professional and capitalist classes who wish to live more creatively). However, as discussed in Chapter 2, sometimes normativity is as much a form of protest against capitalist or racist domination as it is a concession to it. Moreover, replacing class with normativity is not a class-neutral activity. Not only does it put self-expression and symbolic resistance above the solidarity that would be necessary to abolish the capitalist mode of production, it gives upper-class queers a way to frame themselves as more radical and anti-capitalist than the working classes: if oppression and resistance are ranked according to normativity, then the banker's child who resists homonormativity is more anti-capitalist than a working-class lesbian mother who shops at a big box store could ever be. It makes the urban queer more *politically* anti-capitalist than the small-town 'basic' gay by virtue of lifestyle alone.[21]

The fight against normativity is not an opposition to neoliberalism but its mirror inverse: the product of a generally (upper) middle-class and ruling class movement of academics and students from elite universities who are angry at the pressure to conform and (very rightfully) angry at the violence of imperialism and the racist violence against Black and brown queers in the West. This is not to say that oppositional sexism and transmisogyny does not affect queer people in the ruling class. Nor is it to say that queer people of color and working-class queers are necessarily normative. It is only to say that swapping economic analysis for categorizing people by affect can be an effective sleight of hand that directs attention away from the issues of working-class and poor gender-diverse and sexually diverse people. Normativity expresses the problem of economic and social injustice in the declassed language of academics.

VIII. The spinning compass of American queer politics

The problem of marriage and family

For queer academics, homonormativity is now the defining political problem of the movement. The term helps make sense of modern queer politics' aimlessness amid the palpable misery of the neo-liberal period. Whereas the twentieth-century gay rights movement struggled against the fact that the modern world was structured to accept only heterosexual coupling (heteronormativity), the new movement is concerned with the disciplinary pressures people impose on one another inside the movement itself (homonormativity and transnormativity).[22] The question, then, is what does queer politics demand today? Is it about militant visibility and expressing that we are different from cisgendered heterosexuals? Is it about creating concentric circles of safe space for intersectionally marginalized queers? Is it about fighting for broad social justice reforms alongside the heteronormal masses? Or is it about fighting for such reforms but at a skeptical distance from the mainstream? Are individual queer people within movements representatives of queer politics, or does the presence of queer politics necessitate an identifiable queer contingent within the whole? Or, is queer politics simply an internal critique of the failures of the gay rights move-ment – in other words, are gay rights themselves the antagonist for political queers? I would argue that queer politics is amorphous enough to be any or even none of these things. It makes sense that a sexual politics based on the idea of fluidity would resist pinning itself down to a particular task. The movement's creativity and spontaneity are why many gravitate towards it. However, the flip side of fluidity is conceptual nebulousness: a lack of clarity and a lack of precision. And it is a short distance from lacking precision to completely lacking *a point*.[23]

Queer political identity started as a Western phenomenon. Let me be absolutely clear: queerness, same-sex desire, being trans, two-spirit, and intersex are not phenomena specific to or origi-nating in the West. Industrialization transformed queer identities and queer bodies into reified, politicized objects, but sex and gender diversity is a fact of life that predates capitalism. However, the reification of queer politics in the West provokes questions about gender and internationalism. Does queer politics need to go global under neoliberalism, and, if so, how could a global queer politics be possible without distorting gender and sexual diversity through the lens of the West and the global North? Is it only possible as a cross-class movement, or is a working people's queer internationalism possible? This question is not mere rhetorical pondering. Western conservatives are already globally politicizing *heterosexual* identity by actively fomenting violence against gender and sexual minorities in Eastern Europe and Africa.[24] This right-wing radicalization is contributing to the murder and imprisonment of gender and sexual minorities in these regions, and its continued expansion threatens the ability of the global working class to self-organize. Anti-queer violence is a working-class issue on a global scale.

In addition to the question of how queer politics should be situated within international struggle, its relation to anti-capitalism has also been unclear. The murky relationship between anti-capitalism and queer politics is often attributed to the hegemonic power of gay middle-class politics and its focus on marriage and the military – that is, homonormativity. But I would argue that queer politics in the West is unclear about its relationship to anti-capitalism because the term anti-capitalism is itself so unclear that it becomes difficult to make inferences about what constitutes productive political activity. In the US, anti-capitalist thought is usually limited to anti-consumerism and – at its best – anti-imperialism. Relations of production do not usually enter the discussion. This is reflective of what Christoph Henning called 'the primacy of politics', which substitutes ethics for economics.

Of course, American queers have not been silent about poverty. But the analyses are largely sociological and descriptive in nature, commissioned by large non-profit organizations compiling statistics to make queer people who fall outside the middle class more visible. In other words, there is an ongoing awareness campaign about economic injustice but few analyses that explain how capitalist production engenders it. The most visible organizations directly addressing queer poverty and labor rights in the United States have been the labor organization Pride at Work (a member of the American Federation of Labor and Congress of Industrial Organizations or AFL-CIO) and the grassroots organization Queers for Economic Justice (QEJ) in New York City. Pride at Work is a mainstream labor alliance in favor of marriage rights and non-discrimination acts and other reforms that the radical queer world is either skeptical of or openly opposed to, while QEJ was largely a local initiative with a direct-action approach to politics. QEJ advocated for homeless trans youth and adults in the New York City shelter system, worked with labor to advocate for employment rights, struggled against propertied gays' and lesbians' attempts to remove queer youth of color from their neighborhoods, and mounted a visible campaign against the pinkwashing of Israel. The organization maintained, unlike most queer organizations, that class was a queer issue.

Leaders of the radical queer left had long argued – with bitter exasperation – that the marriage equality movement was diverting funds from the most struggling members of the queer community to bolster the property rights of wealthy queer couples. This argument clearly echoes Engels' analysis of the cross-class family in *The Origin of Family, Private Property, and the State*: monogamy came into existence to control women's bodies so that men could transfer property rights to their offspring. Organizations such as Against Equality – and nearly all radical left academics in the US – argued that there was nothing progressive about the demand for marriage. Marriage was a patriarchal tool of propertied men. Moreover, it allowed the state to control and monitor relationships. Gone were the days of free love and revolution. In their place were the neoliberal years of corporate pride and the politics of respectability. Dean Spade, one of QEJ's founders, has argued that the marriage equality movement mirrored the Reagan-era economic idea that benefits for the rich would trickle down to the poor. Spade argued for the reverse – that *trickle up* platforms were necessary: when the most marginalized members of the queer community made progress, upper-class queers would eventually reap the rewards too. But the anti-marriage movement was a political failure in the United States. And despite the organization's important work, QEJ closed its doors in 2013, in part due to a lack of charitable funding.

QEJ fought under the slogan that class was a queer issue – which is, of course, absolutely true. But the good work of the radical queer left is beset by three problems in its understanding of class: 1) despite Marxist language, it relies on a sociological definition of class that does not factor in the effects of capitalism as a *mode of production* or the pressures this mode of production places on the social reproduction of the working class; 2) as a consequence of the first problem, it does not grasp the fundamental aspect of class struggle – that it is a *struggle* between classes, which means that the queer rich will never be reliable allies of the queer poor; and 3) lastly, this line of thought suffers from the problem that Clara Zetkin attributed to Engels' analysis: the origin of the bourgeois family is indeed the passage of property, *but the working-class family does not exist for the same reason.*[25] In other words, when equal marriage passes, queer working-class people probably opt to get married for the same reason heterosexual working-class people do.

The concept of queer nationalism still grounds the logic of radical queer politics. It assumes that LGBTQQIAA people are a genuine community based on a common experience of marginalization due to sexual orientation and gender identity: the Queer Nation transcends class. That the queer rich would fund social justice programs for the queer poor suggests that the queer mind is immune to free-market ideology. In this way, queer nationalism reflects the ideas of liberal pluralism – it ignores the economic grounds of hegemony and instead imagines a marketplace of ideas, an agonistic sphere where interests compete for attention. Charity is based on pity, and while the rich may have pity for the sick and the suffering, for the discriminated against and the abused, this does not extend to something as abstract as economic *justice*. Should we be surprised that the queer rich have failed to fund social justice foundations for the queer poor and instead use their money to selfishly advance their own propertied interests? Take out the word queer and we find the status quo. The argument that marriage equality has hurt queer poor people by diverting the community's much-needed funds to the rich assumes that these funds are community funds rather than rich people's money expro-priated from poor people's labor.[26] Spade's argument for trickle-up reforms skirts class antagonism. We wouldn't say that the political benefits of labor struggles *trickle up* to the rich. The problems of poor queer people is that too much has trickled up already.[27] So, if the queer rich are not the allies of poor and working-class queer and trans people, who are? My answer is: non-queer and non-trans poor and working-class people. The contradiction here is that queer and trans people usually suffer violence and discrimination within their own class. But struggling for queer and trans-positive hegemony inside the working class – in fact, boldly demanding acceptance within the working class – is still a much better tactic. Although QEJ closed its doors, FIERCE, the militant organization of queer youth of color in New York City, is thriving, advocating for queer and trans homeless youth and organizing a copwatch to stop police brutality during pride events. There is such a thing as radical integration with non-queers just as there is such a thing as reactionary acts of defiance.

The argument that marriage equality organizations hurt queer poor people because they stopped rich people from funding other initiatives is weak. It is completely possible that they would not have donated to anything at all. Another common argument is that marriage is assimilationist and regressive on principle, and that those who prop up the family are doing nothing less than propping up capitalism itself. It is true that the economic mode of production shapes people's sex lives and gendered behavior. But the reverse – that people's sex lives and gendered behaviors shape the economic mode of production – lacks evidence. In fact, as mentioned in Chapter 2, there have been many challenges to the nuclear family throughout capitalism's history: Black slavery in the American South, sex-segregated migrant labor camps around the world, factory dormitories, and the prison-industrial complex to name but a few. Capitalism has done quite well using these anti-family methods of social reproduction. There is a dimension of wishful thinking at work here, a hope that queer sexuality itself could be a material force capable of challenging capitalism. This is the latent subtext of all queer radical arguments in which radical queer is a conceptual parallel to radical feminism (i.e. hetero-patriarchy is the origin of all injustice). But there is never a specific explanation of how queer sexuality undermines capitalist hege-mony. I suggest that perhaps it doesn't. Owning one's sexuality may be an important aspect of personal empowerment, but a queer sex party is no more likely to disrupt capitalist production than a heteronormative grandmothers' knitting circle.

As Lise Vogel's work shows, working-class families do not exist to pass property on to offspring (see Chapter 2); they exist to pool resources for survival in the present. The marriage equality move-ment in the United States did not suggest that the state strong-arm a population with little investment in coupling and children into assimilationist, heteronormative families. It demanded the state *recognize* bonds between people that already existed. Marriage equality did not just demand a positive freedom to participate in the state and family life; it simultaneously was demanding freedom *from* interference by the state. There is no opting in or opting out of the capitalist state (you might not wish to stare into the abyss, but the abyss stares into you). Radical queers may have opposed marriage equality on the grounds that economic justice is a more important cause for poor queers and queer people of color; however, when asked, LGBT people of color in the United States listed marriage equality among their top goals *along with* fighting economic injustice. Perhaps this is because 46.7 percent and 41.5 percent of female-identifying Black and Latina queer couples respectively are raising children and marriage recognition is an imperfect tool for helping parents protect their children under current circumstances. Children of color are more likely to be raised by LGBT parents than white children.[28] It is true that many populations are unable to participate in marriage equality: some families on public assistance will not fare as well depending on their partner's income; nor would it be advantageous to a couple if one partner has extensive student loan debt; and, of course, polyamorous relationships have gained nothing. But reforms under capitalism, by nature, are partial. The tension between the limitations inherent in reform and the possibilities of revolutionary change can only be examined in context. Given these statistics, perhaps communities of color – particularly the Black community – were angry with the marriage equality movement not because marriage is a bourgeois heteronormative construct, but because the mainstream LGBTQ organizations led by whites unjustly blamed the Black community for the passage of anti-gay legislation in California and consistently ignored all other concerns of working and poor queer and trans people of color.

There is another curious contradiction in the marriage equality debate. Most left opponents of marriage equality are queers in cosmopolitan cities where no one but the very wealthiest own property. But for those living outside the queer meccas – and the largest portion of American queers with children live in the South (Krivickas and Lofquist 2011) – 'property' may mean a single-wide trailer or an old car with a broken taillight. The reason why small-town queers are more supportive of same-sex marriage may not be because they champion heteropatriarchal norms but because they simply have different needs to those of urban gays due to rural poverty.[29]

The problem of queer imperialism

The other reform that plagued the conscience of the queer left was the rescinding of the military policy 'Don't Ask, Don't Tell' (DADT), under which speaking of one's homosexuality was criminalized. Challenging the repeal of DADT contained a contradiction for the queer left. How does one support queer rights when the right demanded is military service inside an imperialist nation? The answer for most of the left was quite simple: you don't.

Puar is correct in noting that gays and lesbians have become weapons in the cultural arsenal against Muslims immigrating to the West, just as feminism as 'universal sisterhood' was cynically employed as a progressive cover for the wars against Afghanistan and Iraq. Now that it has passed, we can safely say that repealing DADT was a political concession made to transform gays and lesbians into literal weapons within the US military. But state concessions to minority populations in exchange for doing the dirty work that keeps the system afloat is nothing new. The *hijra* in India and Pakistan, a third-gender community culturally present since the Mughal empire, have recently achieved such 'vassal' gains. Pakistan has taken steps towards integrating *hijra* into society through the issuance of national identity cards and the formalization of third-gender recognition. But the impetus behind the change was not a sudden warming to sex and gender diversity within the Pakistani state; it was a concession made so that the state could hire them as tax collectors to increase revenue. The move was not to alleviate discrimination towards *hijra*, but to use the discrimination that already exists to benefit the state: the *hijra* were hired to humiliate business owners through their very presence. The Russian Women's Battalion of Death served a similar function for the provisional government. The willingness of women to fight was meant to humiliate men into enlisting. African American troops in the United States were desegregated in 1948, six years before the desegregation of the school system. Unlike the situation of the *hijra*, gains made by gays and lesbians through the repeal of DADT did confer some quantity of social integration. However, the ending of Don't Ask, Don't Tell in the United States was not the unconditional mark of collaborationist queers passing into state acceptance but rather a political concession levied with the hope of boosting enlistment to alleviate a backdoor draft.

Viewed from the great moral heights of academia and middle-class comfort, the progressive position on the repeal of DADT is clear. To support the repeal is to support the pinkwashing of the US military machine; it is yet more evidence that queer political consciousness has declined, that queers have moved from a propensity towards liberation to a propensity towards colluding with state violence and assimilation into patriarchal norms. A depressing state of affairs indeed. But viewed from up close, the situation is much more complex. First, queer enrollment in the US military is nothing new. Military service has always been a way to run away from a violent home life. San Francisco's gay history is in large part formed by the fact that soldiers would return to the States through the city when stationed in the Pacific. It is also worth underscoring the fact that the military operates through a poverty draft. It doesn't just employ the jingoistic sections of the middle class; it largely hoovers up surplus populations. The reserve army of the unemployed in the US is a *literal army*.

One might be surprised that the repeal of DADT generated excitement among heterosexual troops organizing against the war. The fight for the DADT repeal was a way to stick it to the military, to force the will of the people onto a rigid bureaucracy. But there were also important, invisible gains inside the reform that were rarely acknowledged. DADT was being used as a form of black-mail to silence sexual violence against women – a practice called *lesbian baiting*. Regardless of sexual orientation, the law was used to prevent women from reporting sexual assaults and sometimes even employed to force enlisted women into sexual servitude. The policy was also perceived by soldiers as a form of wage theft. Knowing all along that a soldier was queer, this information would suddenly become relevant around the time of the soldier's discharge. Dishonorable discharge for being queer is not a mere tarnishing of a person's reputation. Dishonorable discharge is the military equivalent of a felony conviction: no right to unemployment benefits, the loss of all accrued military benefits, including the GI bill to pursue a college education, loss of the right to vote, the right of banks to discriminate throughout one's life, and discrimination in housing. In other words, DADT was a queer-to-prison or queer-to-homeless pipeline. And, once again, this disenfranchisement disproportionately affected women of color, who had a higher rate of discharge under DADT than white women (Stalsburg 2010).

But one could still take a utilitarian position that the suffering of oppressed populations inside the US military cannot be compared with the mass devastation levied against Iraq and Afghanistan; the death of millions – including many on the queer spectrum – cannot be compared with the suffering of a few American servicewomen (and men) who volunteered to join the armed forces and participate in campaigns of shock and awe. This is true. If suffering were quantifiable, as with Jeremy Bentham's felicific calculus, the lion's share of pain would fall at the feet of Iraq and Afghanistan and the cause of that pain would in large part be located in the US armed forces. However, I would wager that these sorts of comparisons are not political questions at all, but can be more properly understood as moral questions: who is a morally worthy victim and who has caused their own suffering, or whose actions have been so morally reprehensible that their suffering is beneath consideration?

Yet there is another layer. What counts as participation? Of course, many in the military are support staff. Does a woman whose job is filling vending machines on a navy warship far from battle have any more moral responsibility for American imperialism than a teacher – myself, for instance – who trains veterans using their GI bill between deployments? Given that so many humanities departments in the US have been accused of being 'progressive cover' for the military research conducted in physics departments, are anti-DADT-repeal queer theory professors also guilty in some sense for academic pinkwashing? On the one hand, the New Left 'no one is innocent' claim is true. On the other, when no one is innocent, no one can really be held accountable. Once again, such questions are *ethical*, not political. They concern the ethical behavior of the individual, their culpability, their innocence. So what might a *political* question be? I would argue that the main political question is: what kind of force is necessary to stop imperialist expansion? Following this, who are allies and who are opponents to developing these political forces? What sort of material limitations check the development of such forces? What is the balance of forces? In the case of DADT, does the repeal of DADT hinder or help the antiwar effort? How does queer left skepticism or even outright hostility to initiatives such as the repeal of DADT serve the political questions raised by anti-imperialist organizing?

The question as to whether the fight for the repeal of DADT hindered or helped the antiwar movement is not an abstract one: it implies an assessment of concrete conditions. The first condition to assess would be the state of the antiwar movement in the United States. Essentially, at the time of the DADT repeal, there wasn't one. The election of Barack Obama had quelled unrest. What had been so morally intolerable to progressives under George W. Bush went unnoticed under Obama. Only the Marxist, anarchist, and (right-wing) libertarian movements – remarkably weak forces – continued to protest. So it cannot be said that DADT reform 'sucked the life out of the movement', or had any negative impact at all on antiwar organizing. The election of Obama trumped all. If anything, DADT organizing served as a small reminder that America was at war. It is true that DADT repeal groups were silent on state-sponsored violence, but opportunism is a general staple of reformist politics – abortion rights groups have been silent on the denigration of Black motherhood and the police murders of young Black men; immigrants' rights organizations have marginalized the issues of trans immigrants. What's more, as with the failure of the queer left to build a positive countermovement for universal healthcare rights to protest the limitations of spousal benefits, radical queers did not mount an antiwar campaign of their own. In fact, moral outrage at soldiers, if anything, *hampered* the antiwar movement's ability to support the efforts of war resisters.[30]

I would wager that radical queer opposition to the war was founded on cultural grounds informed by a separatist ethos. This separatism was fueled by specific conceptions of what it means to be political, by what it means to resist. In a society where the awareness campaign is the limit of political participation, outrage and righteous disgust become the measure of investment. Queer antiwar practice has not been to mix with heterosexuals coming to political consciousness but to morally resist state disciplinary power in the abstract through affect, sexual transgression, and challenging cultural norms. This response also reflects the rigid, identitarian, two-party American political psychology: no one on *our side* would join the military in the first place. There are enormous class implications of such a position. The US military is the largest single employer in the United States and, while some troops are true believers, many are working-class and poor people, including large numbers of Black and Latino/a troops, who want to travel, need a job, and/or hope to go to college on the GI bill. To provide some anecdotal evidence for this thesis, the response to war resistance at Fort Hood reflected the weak ideological pull of military service. When Victor Agosto[31] protested in front of his platoon, the other troops were either indifferent or quietly supportive, but he faced no hostility. Shortly after his protest, a sergeant in his battalion became a conscientious objector. When Agosto went to jail for resisting, his protest was popular and respected among the other inmates. This cynicism towards the war was not isolated to troops in Texas. When reporter Anand Gopal was embedded with US troops in Afghanistan, he held a secret straw poll about the perceived validity of the war among two dozen troops. Not one person supported the war.[32]

To return to the political questions posed earlier: how can we calculate the political activity of the American queer left? The main tactic of radical queer politics seems to be opposing normativity through disentangling itself from American life to culturally reinvent the nation on more ethical grounds by staging defiance through art and affect. Allies are those who participate in the development of such counterculture; the political opposition would be, beyond the obvious answer of 'straight' nationalists and traditionalists, queers seeking integration. It is through an assessment of the balance of forces that cracks in the logic of cultural politics are revealed most clearly. Not only is the radical queer community tiny in comparison to the immense power of the United States military-industrial-prison complex, as a counterculture it must always remain small and entrenched by definition. Once counterculture goes mainstream, it's the new normativity.

As to the question of whether or not queer activity in or abstention from the fight to repeal DADT helped or hindered the war effort, I would argue that the answer is they did neither. Protections afforded to gay and lesbian troops (the trans ban remains) neither hindered nor helped the war. In terms of homonationalism, it is true, gays and lesbians are becoming integrated into American society, which is warlike and nationalistic. But the opposite of citizenship is not becoming a free-roaming champion of the global community. The opposite of citizenship is social repression from the particular capitalist state whose borders you are stuck inside.

In this vein, let us return to the same-sex marriage debate in radical queer circles. Indeed, the rhetoric of marriage *equality* is problematic because equality is conditioned by class and race. There can be no equal marriage in an unequal society. This is the crux of the more nuanced argument of organized radical queer movements (including Against Equality, Beyond Equality, and QEJ); however, the emblem of this movement, a *greater-than* symbol, reflects the subtext beneath the fight against reforms – that there is something about queerness that is inherently transgressive, and if we agitate this transgressive spirit out of its commodity-culture slumber then the kernel of radical potential would burst from its neoliberal shell. But, so far, this has not happened. The Queer Nation has not yet reached radical consciousness. It has not been able to return to its energetic high water mark of the Compton's Cafeteria riot and the Stonewall rebellion. Instead, it is mired in conservatism and conformism. In other words, American queer liberation is a reflection of the larger sociopolitical picture stuck between imperial war, the war on terror, the war on drugs, the decline of the labor movement, the end of the social safety net, the immobility of the working classes within global capital, and the rise of ultranationalist movements, along with the rise of Islamophobia in Europe and the global immigration crisis born out of the destruction of civil society in Syria and Iraq. Without a larger movement, queer liberation is the dream of decades past lived in the present through a series of meager attempts at reform and cultural isolation; it is the dream of our past dreams, our political nostalgia. Like religious suffering, it is 'at one and the same time, the *expression* of real suffering and a *protest* against real suffering' (Marx 1982: 127). And queer communality and culture are our safe spaces – 'the heart of a heartless world, and the soul of soulless conditions'. We remember days of protests past as neoliberalism weighs 'like a nightmare on the brains of the living' (Marx, *Eighteenth Brumaire of Louis Bonaparte* in Marx and Engels 1979: 103).

The cohesiveness of queer nationalism depends on the minimization of class conflict and the minimization of the need for outside solidarities. But it is those outside solidarities that are necessary to achieve both reforms and revolution; without integration into the world beyond the 'safe spaces', there is no hope of ending neoliberalism. A subculture cannot end global injustice. The everybody cannot be ignored.

IX. The world is a very queer place

Since the rise of queer theory correlates with a decline of debates in the West surrounding Marxist economics, there is a dearth of scholarship on how capitalist production shapes the lives of gender and sexually diverse people; nor is there a wealth of scholarship on when and where capitalism requires heteronormativity to function and when and where it intentionally disrupts heteronormative gender expectations to serve its goals. Such a historical project could never be a universal economic history about a universal people; it would always be particular: regional economic policy, customs, traditions, colonization and decolonial struggles, war, natural resources, and the level and character of class struggle would all factor into the way in which capitalism locally effects gender and sexual diversity. Only then would we begin to understand the complex effects of modern production arrangements on the production of social gender. Two examples of this sort of careful materialist attention to queer politics are John D'Emilio's (D'Emilio 1998) trailblazing materialist history of the development of gay politics in mid-century America and Kevin Floyd's (Floyd 2009) inaugural queer Marxist analysis of how Fordist capitalism reified men's desire into homosexual and heterosexual identities in the same period. Interjecting Marxian economic analysis into the historical examination of modern gender and sexual diversity is clearly possible.

As discussed above, queerness (and transness) as a political identity originally emerged in urban contexts within an industrial framework. The Stonewall rebellion in Greenwich Village was inspired by trans women standing up to police harassment at

Cooper's Donuts in Los Angeles in 1959, a sit-in of Black gay and trans youth in 1965 at Dewey's Lunch Counter in Philadelphia, and Compton's Cafeteria riot in 1966 (see Stryker 2008a). The development of queer political subjectivity in the United States was molded by the lessons of Black civil rights. It is this *specific* political sequence that shaped American queer politics. Of course, queer and trans politics around the world have not developed and will not develop in the exact same way. But as we saw with the reciprocal support between the political revolution in Tahrir Square and the Occupy Movement, international solidarity strengthens movements. We also know that sexual and gender diversity predates capitalism around the globe.

The history and meaning of sexual diversity in many parts of the world are conditioned by the spread of Christianity and Islam, the class divisions and kinship structures in pre-capitalist societies, and the combined and uneven development in the growth of the world market. *Hijra* in South Asian, *kathoeys* in Thailand, *kinaidi* and *tribades* in Ancient Greece, *hassas* in Morocco, and *khanith* in Oman (see Murray and Roscoe 1998; also see references in Drucker 2015) cannot be reconciled into modern Western gay and lesbian or even queer or trans identities. Attitudes towards same-sex behavior and transgender identities shift throughout history; norms change with changes in the mode of production. Peter Drucker's *Warped: Gay Normality and Queer Anti-Capitalism* provides a materialist basis for the development of a queer Marxism. Drucker outlines the changes in the reception of sexual diversity during various phases of pre-capitalist and capitalist development, from antiquity to neo-liberalism. His approach to understanding the relationship between queer internationalism and queer materialist history marks a new point in queer Marxist analysis. Queer and trans existence tends to be debated along two poles: the first, an ahistorical universalism which suggests that queer and trans people are a biologically based single group moving through history; the second, a poststructuralist view that every phenomenon is incommensurable with every other. Drucker's Marxist approach allows us to see broad historical relations independent of stable biological categories and it enables us to compare similarities without reducing phenomena to the historical qualities being compared. Placing broader materialist analyses such as Drucker's alongside more specific, geographically bounded analyses (Kevin Floyd's work, for example) allows us to understand our present historical and political ground – and solid theoretical foundations can help us make sense of the nebulousness of contemporary queer politics.

But a broad approach that bears international solidarity in mind will not sit comfortably with some on the left. The reason for this is, in part, that queer theory has absorbed a number of criticisms from postcolonialism. To make a case for transnational queer anti-capitalism, it is necessary to review the Marxist critique of postcolonialism.

X. The queer Marxist critique of postcolonialism

Of all the lines in the vector model, the oppression of nations is – outside class – the least coherent fit. This is because colonialism and imperialism do not merely intersect the individual body, they interrupt a collective body; they are not reflections of an abstract power, but forces set into motion by the dynamics of capitalist development. The problem of colonialism and imperialism, and now transnational capitalism, requires attention to capital flows and the relations between corporations, states, and people. It provokes questions about the boundaries between globalization and community, between the everybody and the us/them. Just as Marxist methods were replaced by poststructuralism in gender theory, postcolonial theory replaced Marxist approaches to colonialism, imperialism, and international relations in the Western academy.

First: what is postcolonial theory? Postcolonialism is a late twentieth-century form of literary and social theory with (much like queer theory) strong poststructuralist commitments. Its object is the literature and history of 'Third World' nations and the thought arising from territories where the colonized struggle against their colonizers. The original goal of the field was to interrupt the Western canon by including the voices of those who suffered under European colonization, the subaltern, people who may have been outside a working-class *identity* yet who still suffered under Western hegemony. This would include unemployed slum dwellers and colonized and postcolonial surplus populations as well as middle-class populations in diaspora, particularly middle-class academics and artists challenging European cultural hegemony and its amnesia about its colonial projects, including its refusal to admit cultural works from colonized people into the Western canon. One of the most prominent postcolonial projects was to put an end to what Edward Said called *orientalism*: that is, how the Western imagination dehumanizes the East by making it seem romantic, exotic, and feminine, by attributing to it an otherworldliness that is at once charming and inferior.

Inspired by poststructuralist theory, postcolonial theory exposed what it understood as Eurocentric thought. The European colonizer was an Enlightenment rationalist, a teleological (linear) thinker who subsumed everyone into his own way of thinking. Universalism and totality were code words for Western hegemony and control. But not only was the colonizer a linear thinker, linear thinking itself motivated the colonization process. The political answer – which will be familiar to us now in light of the overview of queer theory – is to eschew linear thinking and adopt non-linear thought that is local, specific, and unique. By embracing non-linear, non-Western thought, postcolonial subjects could 'decolonize the mind' by rejecting Enlightenment values, the expansion of the sciences, and, hence, the rational use and abuse of others. Marxist economic theory was decidedly *not* the answer. It too was a Eurocentric, rationalist, teleological, grand narrative. Marxism was just a sneakier form of colonial thought, and Marx himself was exposed as harboring orientalist sentiments in his youth.[33] People from postcolonial territories who adhered to Marxist thought were now considered to have had their minds 'colonized', similar to the accusations of false consciousness levied from some sectors of the feminist and Marxist camps.

But thinkers living in the so-called Third World were not necessarily convinced that postcolonial theory was a meaningful or useful cultural advance. South Asian literary scholar Aijaz Ahmad wrote an incisive critique of its project and the accommodations given to it by 'First World' academics. Ultimately, Ahmad sees postcolonial theory as a specific ideological project led by immigrant professionals living in European and Anglophone centers of culture. What counts as postcolonial is decided by professors and publishing houses in the West. Postcolonial theory is not indigenous to the areas of the world it claims to represent. South Asian, African, Caribbean, and Latin American people do not see themselves as being on the periphery. People living in former colonies are, like everyone else, at the center of their own world. Ahmad traces the ideological origin of the theory to what he calls the 'redoubled vacuum' (Ahmad 2008: 34–5). The vacuum redoubled here is a political one. Originally, socialism was supposed to be the final challenge against colonial power. But after the political trajectory established by Stalinism, not only did socialism fail in this respect, the Soviet Union itself went about liberating many colonized nations by tank and setting up shop. To many on the Left (including feminists), this felt like just another method of imperialism – 'Marxist' imperialism. Third World nationalism promised another way. But, as Ahmad notes, after the high water mark of the anti-imperialist struggle in Algeria and Vietnam, the conservative co-optation of the Iranian Revolution dashed the possibility of nationalism as a necessarily liberating force. So what remained?

Third Worldism had shifted the revolutionary subject from the (inter)national proletariat to the bourgeoisies of the (former) Third World. As Neil Larsen puts it, the national bourgeoisie is 'vouchsafed by "three worlds" theory as the revolutionary opposition to imperialism' (Larsen 1995).

But at the end of the Third World nationalist movement, opposition to imperialism no longer had a political subject. However, the anticolonial upper classes saw no reason to cede being the political subject of revolutionary change. The diaspora of petit bourgeois intellectuals would be the ones to fill the vacuum. But how? Ahmad shows how Said's work ambivalently uses the language of non-identity as a new way to support nationalism. Radical intelligentsia would be the '"bridge" between cultural nationalism and poststructuralist antinationalism' (ibid.: 3).[34] This postcolonial ambiguous, anti-identitarian subject appears to possess the same strategic ambiguity as the fluid subject of queer theory.

Larsen expands Ahmad's argument to show exactly how postcolonial literary theory operates. The traumatic point of colonization is marked when the colonizer forces his text on the colonized population. The colonized respond by creating a hybrid of the original work, by appropriating the text for their own purposes. The very hybridity of the colonized subject undermines the dominant colonial narrative. When the radical intelligentsia deconstruct the hybrid text, they reveal the colonizer's original intent of supplanting real history with their supposedly universal narrative. This revelation opens up the possibility of changing the 'coercive reality' of colonization (Bhabha 1994).[35] Larsen argues that the theory rests on two premises. One, it suggests that colonizer and colonized make up a 'primitive disunity', an originating *incommensurability* which is itself the prior condition of identity relations (Larsen 1995: 6). The second premise is that the political is comprised of 'speaking truth to power'. The colonized become a political subject when they reveal the primitive disunity that the colonizer tries to hide, usually through his universalism. Here, Larsen simply points to the Marxist critique of idealism. When has revealing coercion ever liberated anyone from it? Politics is reduced to a simple awareness campaign and it is the radical intelligentsia who reveal to the rest of the colonized how the colonizer works.

Sociologist Vivek Chibber took a scalpel to the ideological heart of the postcolonial project (Chibber 2013). It was not the literary aspect of postcolonial theory that interested Chibber, but the expansion of its vision to the social sciences through the Subaltern Studies project.[36] The goal of the latter is to attribute the historical failures of Marxist groups in the East to Marx's failure to predict that capitalism would develop under different principles there; in other words, the development of capitalism in different locations is radically specific and incommensurable. The following are the postcolonial arguments Chibber addresses:

1. *The European bourgeoisie was special.* Postcolonial theorists argue that the bourgeoisie in Europe was a progressive class capable of representing the interests of the masses against those of the feudal lords. The bourgeoisie indigenous to India, by contrast, collaborated with feudal lords and colonizers; this is because India remained tied to traditional religions and local cultures, unlike Europe, which developed into politically unified modern nations that embraced individual human rights (Guha 1998).
2. *Capitalists in colonized regions used direct violence.* According to Marx, in the feudal age, lords used direct violence whereas capitalism disciplines the workforce through economic measures. But Marx failed to grasp that old power dynamics aren't suddenly transformed just because a new economic system emerges. In India, the capitalist class is different because it is violent towards its workers (Chakrabarty 2000).
3. *Labor is not homogeneous.* Marx's *Capital* describes a homogeneous workforce. But workers are 'neither abstract labor nor

The Politics of Everybody

abstract citizens' (Lowe 1996: 27). Marx never took into account how workers use their culture to resist the homogenizing force of capitalist modernity. For example, in India, workers pray to the machines at the start of the workday.

4. *People of the East are not self-interested European individuals.* Europeans act out of individual interest, whereas in India (and presumably in other traditional cultures) community is the ultimate motivating force (Chatterjee 1993: 165–8).

5. *Marxism is both teleological and deterministic by design.* Such determinism is ultimately reductionist; it ignores the radical contingency of possible political paths and social futures and, by extension, limits imaginative possibilities for collective action.

We have already seen some of these criticisms in earlier overviews of feminist theory and poststructuralist analysis. But I think, since we are looking at a specifically anti-capitalist and internationalist approach to the intersectional project – how anti-capitalism handles the problem of 'everybody' – it is worth looking at Chibber's response at length. *Postcolonial Theory and the Specter of Capital* picks apart the arguments, one at a time, unraveling them by uncovering the ambiguity, inconsistency, and inaccuracy of their assertions. Perhaps more damning, Chibber argues that insisting that people in the East are incommensurable to those in the West is relentlessly orientalist in its own right. Subalternist arguments about the intransigent backwardness of the global South match neoconservative arguments that 'cultural poverty' is the cause of material poverty in less developed regions. Chibber's rebuttal to postcolonial theory's specific claims are as follows:

1. *European capitalists were not progressive.* This assumption rests on a failure to understand the histories of the English and French revolutions. In the former, the revolution marked a split between two factions in the ruling class, both motivated by

capitalist investment; in the latter, the progressive 'bourgeoisie' were not actual capitalists but relatively impoverished lawyers and intelligentsia. When faced with the radicalizing masses, most of the European bourgeois revolutionaries reversed course and adopted reactionary positions.

2. *Capitalism does not require that capitalists renounce violence.* For something to be produced capitalistically only requires that the primary motivation for 'free' labor entering the workforce is economic need. Feudal lords resorted to overt violence *outside the hours of required labor* because they had to pressure serfs, who had access to resources, into working the land to their benefit. If a capitalist abuses workers in the workplace, it does not signify feudalism. If a worker endures on-the-job violence, it is precisely because they need wages to survive.

3. *Abstract labor does not refer to homogeneity.* This is perhaps Chibber's most important refutation for a queer Marxist analysis, because of queer theory's proclivity to slide between terms such as normativity, homogeneity, and abstraction. Abstract labor, Chibber notes, has nothing to do with capitalism requiring a culturally homogeneous workforce. As mentioned in Chapter 2, abstract labor is not a description of workers; it is an economic term for the calculations capitalists use to compare the economic output of their own workforce with that of their competition. What the capitalist sees as an abstraction is always, for Marx, *a concrete condition.* The term 'abstract labor' simply has nothing to do with ignoring cultural diversity. At times, capital prefers a homogeneous workforce; at other times, it thrives on diversity. Either is fine so long as production of surplus value is at maximum capacity. The goal of capitalism is not the homogenization of workers but the extraction of profit by any means necessary. If workers pray to machines and those prayers do nothing to stop the production of surplus value, then praying is not a tactic that disrupts capitalism. This also

applies to queer theoretical approaches to politics: in contrast to what both Butler and Foucault argue, rebellious bodies are not revolutionary in themselves; as meaningful and empowering as self-expression might be, expression itself does not mount a challenge against capital. Survival is the precondition of any revolutionary act, but it does not produce revolutionary change on its own.

4. *If individuals in traditional cultures are not self-interested, then why are they self-interested?* Next, Chibber then dismantles the chimera of self-interest. Partha Chatterjee argues that poor peasants in the East did not rebel when the wealthier peasants took their land because tradition and community are more important to Indians than crude European notions of 'individual interest'. Chibber's response is simply this: if Indian peasants are so immune to self-interest, then why did the wealthier peasants take the land from their neighbors in the first place? If self-interest is an imported concept, then how did some Indians become capitalists in the first place? There is a difference between making minimal claims that human interest exists as a political factor and claiming that people *only ever* act out of ruthless self-interest. Regardless of their culture, all humans would rather not suffer pointlessly if given the option. Atrocities are atrocious everywhere.

5. *It is racist to assume that non-Europeans are innately irrational.* Chibber shows that Marx's depiction of history is not teleological – there is no essence of history unfolding itself towards a final destination. Teasing out historical repetitions in search of patterns is not teleological in itself. (In fact, Foucauldian genealogy depends on it.) One does not need to be a determinist to notice that some historical activities and material facts close off some possibilities and generate others. Finally, Chibber argues that referring to logic and science as born from a European mindset is irredeemably racist, not to mention historically

inaccurate. In addition to consigning the vast majority of the planet to unreason, it is also a distorted vision of the West. Despite the decline of religion in Europe after the wars of the twentieth century, religious fundamentalism and anti-science movements have been a constant presence in the United States. There is no malevolent European (or male, for that matter) spirit of rationality that transcends history.

So what can those of us working towards a queer internationalism take from the work of Ahmad, Larsen, and Chibber? First, we can accept that the capitalist mode of production produces certain results wherever it goes. When a factory worker dies from machine malfunction, be it in Birmingham or Baku, the goal of the factory owner – queer or not – will be to get everyone back to work as soon as possible, and the hope of the machinists – queer or not – will be that they don't want to die. Second, there are grounds for solidarity across borders. Grounds for solidarity do not require homogeneity, disembodied abstract selves, acultural, ahistorical, or asexual selves. The world does not translate perfectly from one language to another, from one perspective to the next, but we do have methods of communication that, while imperfect, are *possible*.

Orientalist fantasies of Africa, Eastern Europe, the Middle East, South and East Asia, and the Americas are not politically harmless. Insisting that the world beyond Europe is incommensurably different – different meaning hyper-religious, mystical, antirational, and pre-Enlightenment – echoes imperialists who argue for interventionist policies under a humanitarian guise. Postcolonial orientalism falls into the same political problematic as cultural feminisms that celebrate women's cultural and intellectual 'difference', their circularity of thought, their preference for emotion over reason. Queer feminist communal thought also, at times, embraces orientalist trappings: one prominent example is the prevalent suspicion of Western medicine – not suspicion of medicine developed

within a market economy with pharmaceutical interests comman-
deering policy and care, but a suspicion that Western medicine is
bad for health because it is Western, and therefore patriarchal (even
when it is globally practiced and women are its practitioners, and
even though men practice Eastern medicine).

I would like to submit that we *can* know one another, and that
it is politically important that we *do* know one another. Sometimes
objectively. Sometimes subjectively. But epistemology need not be
a zero-sum game. One need not consider objective knowledge to
be the sinister product of a philosophical chess move in a political
game in order to assert that subjective knowledge has social value.
Part of that objective knowledge is understanding the material
bases for our interactions. We should not be required to oppose
rational thought to legitimate our struggle against economic
conquest, which is not merely a Western phenomenon.[37] Particular, localized Marxist analyses can (and do) help us understand
how the reproduction of modes of production shapes gender and
sexuality in particular regions and communities around the globe.
Such concrete analyses by people reporting objective conditions –
and even their own experiences – when translated and shared could
become a transnational collaboration of people interested in both
system change and ending traditional and oppositional sexism.

A queer Marxism could go a long way towards developing a
more accurate and sincere analysis of how the global economy (and
global economic history) affects every dimension of our present
social relations: gendered relations, sexual relations, relations
between ethnic groups, racial groups, castes, and religions. Or, put
another way, how it affects everybody.

CHAPTER 4

Conclusions

I. Solidarity means taking sides

This book has outlined three attitudes towards the problem of everybody: the segregationist 'essential nationalisms',[1] the inclusive internationalisms, and the denial or skepticism of wholeness or meaningful sustained aggregates common to radical empiricists, poststructuralists, and free-market ideologists. The Marxist disposition is squarely grounded in an inclusive internationalist[2] vision, where the whole is assessed and the parts are not reduced into taxonomies (races, sexes, and so on) that pre-exist material and historical interactions. This inclusive attitude towards the politics of everybody is akin to Alain Badiou's idea that universality and alterity can be conceptually integrated:[3] solidarity is not a condition that results from mature humans learning to accept diversity; it is a political recognition that our futures are tied together.

257

This model of commitment to inclusion, of acknowledging universal alterity, is opposed to, for example, Richard Rorty's model of liberal pluralist solidarity based on non-aggression (see Rorty 1989). Rorty sees the road to a better world as one paved with self-doubt, particularly about one's own use of language. Solidarity is grounded in a willingness to listen to others. We can say with no economic reductionism that Rorty's argument in favor of intellectual humility is a consummate example of a thoughtful person responding from within the specific social relations that define their existence. The field of philosophy in general, and American philosophy in particular, is almost defined as a milieu where middle- and upper-class men make a business of being confident in their opinions. The intellectual humility of the ironist is the adoption of the sort of practices inculcated in those raised as or living as women. A working-class or poor woman who discovers philosophy doesn't have to work to become an ironist, to come to terms with the fact that other ways of making meaning might have intellectual merit. The big hurdle for most young women and gender non-conforming people is coming to believe that their own way of making meaning has intellectual merit. Based on a willingness to listen, solidarity is imagined as a situation where the problem of 'us and them' is resolved through mutual patience and understanding. Rorty imagines that the barriers to human togetherness are mental. What he misses entirely is that social relations are not just affected by coherent logics and worldviews but that the development of thought itself is grounded in material reality. Solidarity is presented here as if the secret of peaceful coexistence is understanding. But liberal society is founded on substantive inequality maintained through violence. Perspectives are a result of larger battles for hegemony and one's position in relation to the productive and reproductive arrangements that sort the planet.

To see this at work, we do not need to take on the history of religious intolerance. We can look at one of the possibly most superficial and ridiculous hostilities that ever was: the American 'Disco Wars' of the 1970s. Was the hatred of disco by the partisans of rock music just an instance of intolerance? A rigid inability to accept that the pleasures of others are distinct from one's own? A dislike of those who consume different sorts of commodities? A random need to define a sense of self in a homogenizing world? What, then, should we make of the fact that the partisans of rock were white, heterosexuals (mostly men and boys) from the laboring classes doing routinized physical labor and working in factories, and that the world of disco represented to them Blackness, homosexuality, and fantasies of glittery nightclubs? These identities are not 'mere consumer preferences' but are representative of the racist paranoia induced in the American white, heterosexual working class of yesteryear that Blacks and gays are off somewhere experiencing forbidden pleasures while they themselves are forced to submit to drudgery. The Disco Wars were wedded to the propaganda that hard work and sacrifice are rewarded under capitalism, and that enjoyment experienced by the poor is in fact the cause of their poverty.

Solidarity is not a matter of pluralist, multicultural unity and harmony. The latter is not a vision of solidarity; it is a vision of the Kingdom of Heaven. Solidarity implies antagonism, the taking of sides; it implies commitment to support for one's comrades. Solidarity is not the end of schism; it is the recognition of schism, hence the old union slogan: *Which side are you on?* The violence of liberal pluralism lies precisely in its denial of the formation of solidarities, requiring instead that one mutter banal catechisms about the unity of mankind. This is perfectly reflected by the liberal/conservative desire to 'correct' the hashtag #blacklivesmatter into the hashtag #alllivesmatter. In the aftermath of a procession of police murders of Black people, *only* the phrase 'Black lives matter' can possibly reflect the sentiment that 'all lives matter' because Black lives are precisely the lives that are being treated as if they do not matter.

The #bluelivesmatter campaign, by contrast, is much more honest. It knows what side it is on, as proved by the 'I *can* breathe' shirts worn by supporters of the NYPD, which poked fun at the last words of Eric Garner, who died after being asphyxiated in a police choke hold for selling loose cigarettes. There are only two sides: the Black side and the blue side. However, the fight is ultimately not just between two groups. The politics of the fight is not reducible to identities: it is about taking a side and being faithful to it, and being faithful means developing solidarity with one side or the other. You are committing to the project of acknowledging that Black people are being killed by the police and the racist vigilantes who emulate them; you denounce the idea that the dead are responsible for their own deaths. Alternatively, you are committed to the project of asserting the possibility that Black people are in some way, however large or small, responsible for their deaths: wearing hoodies, sagging pants, drawing attention to themselves, lurking in the shadows (i.e. not drawing enough attention to themselves), therefore inherently possessing some reasonable likelihood of cop killing. There is no bridging the gap.

Black police are in a curious bind, but this does not imply that a 'third way' exists, only the imposition of an internal conflict on the individual. The situation of Black police has interesting implications for Fields' argument that race is produced by racism, that it is not a thing that exists prior to racism. As a consequence, fighting racism does not entail pre-existing groups engaging in 'race relations' any more than people accused of witchcraft can have 'witch-based relations' with those who persecute them.[4] In other words, race is presented paradoxically: as a physio-cultural thing, something you cannot escape yet also something capable of being renounced. Whiteness is presented in the same double way in liberal pluralist variants of privilege politics. In this account, racism is a property emanating from white minds; thus, ending racism means eradicating this mental tendency. In other words, in the liberal pluralist view, ending racism is not a struggle aided by awareness, it is the awareness campaign itself.

Of course, the development of consciousness is not meaningless to struggle; but the development of consciousness is not the struggle itself. Post-Marxists who appeal to Gramsci's 'war of position' to confront liberal hegemony forget that the whole point of the 'war of position' is that it will facilitate a 'war of maneuver'. One isn't really fighting for a position if one never intends to take it. Solidarity, in the political sense, is not an end in itself; it is *a process that seeks to achieve the decisive resolution of a political antagonism through allied forces*. The resolution is not based on establishing pluralist social harmony; it is based on resolving injustice and material devastation. It is ending the expropriation of labor, economic invasion, theft of the commons, and it is ending the violence necessary to maintain those injustices. The maintenance of a surplus population is a systemic requirement, as is the cheap reproduction of labor. Misogyny and oppositional sexism, along with racism, help dissolve political solidarities. But misogyny and oppositional sexism are not mere instruments used to divide, they are also ideologies that develop through repetition, and through repetition they are naturalized. The source of this repetition is not mere indoctrination; repetition occurs during the navigation of material social relations. Disrupting ideologies can produce a sense of world collapse, particularly for those who are positioned precariously. Ideologies can be, all at once, expressions of real suffering, protests of real suffering, and the conditions of real suffering (Marx 1982). Moreover, one can be emotionally and morally opposed to a specific ideological effect – racism, anti-immigrant sentiment, Islamophobia, oppositional or traditional sexism – and still unwittingly support the social relations that produce the effect. The goal must be to politically challenge the social relations that produce injustice. However, if a subject politically challenges social relations without examining how they themselves have been ideologically shaped, they are unlikely to develop the capacity for solidarity necessary to be politically effective. An effective political subject must be vigilant against their own cultivated ignorance.[5]

So building solidarities (i.e. collectively addressing antagonisms from inside the antagonism) within a politics that acknowledges everybody requires having a political goal and requires that the partisans become *solid*. When the political goal is the eradication of oppression, becoming solid means that those who are not under siege 'have the backs of' those who are. Whenever possible, 'having the backs of' means that those under siege must be their own vanguard, must be self-determining. However, no matter how much solidarity is developed in the fight against particular oppressions, oppressions will be reproduced systemically until exploitation and expropriation are ended. Racism, misogyny, and oppositional sexism are produced from repetition based on conditions and contingencies of the organization of production and reproduction under capitalism.

Critical race theory has characterized this as an 'instrumentalist' view of racism, as little more than the argument that racism is a rich man's tool used on the mutable minds of the docile poor. This characterization, detached from economic theory, makes ideology appear as a sort of conspiracy theory that requires the ruling class to operate like an omnipotent god with evil intent. But the ruling ideas of the ruling class would predominate in any situation because they are the ones with the power to structure the world according to their interests, and how they structure the world shapes the experience of those who are not in control of the organization of resources. This is not to say that racism is never overtly instrumentalized – Michelle Alexander's analysis of the new Jim Crow shows how anti-Black racism is used as a cudgel to win elections, fracture possible unities among ordinary people, funnel federal funding into local governments, and enrich police departments by giving them a pretext to seize property. But this doesn't explain why others *believe* the propaganda, why it is effective. It doesn't explain why implicit-association tests show that the majority have an implicit bias against Blacks, Muslims, gays, the obese, and others – and why people in these groups even have biases towards themselves. Why should the will of some have such a strong effect on all? If ideology is formed by repetition of experience within a cohesive material logic, then this explains how racism, misogyny, and oppositional sexism become ingrained and how identities formed around gender and sexual expression, cultural norms, the practice of moral systems, and all manner of assumptions arise. It is not just what a ruling class broadcasts Orwellian-style into the brains of the masses, it is also how our daily lives reflect social arrangements. The practice of hypnosis is instructive. If you play along with the hypnotist's game and relax into your chair when he commands, laughing to yourself about how you're fooling him with the illusion of compliance, you'll be surprised to find that, when he commands you to jump to your feet, you will. What matters in the situation isn't what you believe about your agency. What matters is what you do.

But there is something more than this at work here. First, commitments form from the repetition of actions, and those actions are responses to interpretations of material life. Statistics consistently show that the most homophobic people are those who think they have never met a gay or lesbian person. The map of their experiential world is written against the possibility. When they find that there are queer people that they care for, their map is rewritten; it is either slowly rewritten to incorporate queer people or they double down by reinforcing the parameters of their original map. On the picket line, the phenomenon of strike hardening happens in the same way. The union and the bosses do not need to 'brainwash' workers. When a strike vote is called, a worker may be unsure about whether to trust the union, they may not like their co-workers very much, maybe they are only on strike because they morally oppose crossing picket lines, maybe they only show up for picket duty to claim their strike benefits. But after they walk the line, after they repel the scabs, after they chat with fellow workers during the interminable boredom of picket duty, they become hardened. However, strike hardening goes both ways. A worker might like their co-workers very much, they may think the union has a legitimate claim, and maybe they make excuses about why they are in exceptional circumstances, why they need to cross the picket line. Soon their position will become hardened: the bosses start to have a point. Strikers and strikebreakers are making history – though not in circumstances of their own choosing – and, simultaneously, the histories they make make them. The war of position is critical because it involves challenging hegemonic ideological interpretations resulting from the instrumental production of schisms, epistemologies of ignorance, and the repetition of obsessive-compulsive behaviors based in paranoia and magical thinking: in the latter case, that one can prove that one is valuable to the system by showing commitment to it, by directing one's hostility towards excluded populations it assigns as surplus – the elderly, migrants fleeing war and poverty, races and castes produced by the system, those who don't conform to gender expectations, people dehumanized as sexless or hypersexual, slum dwellers, people existing off the informal economy. These populations are not beneath the working class, but fluid with it. 'Working class' is not an identity; it is a position in the system, one that shapes people's minds, bodies, and lives. Most importantly, it is a position with leverage. It is the source of value production under capitalism, and it is its weakest link.

Solidarity and ideologies of sex/gender

What about the ideological development of sex and sexuality? Is sex a biological fact? A social construction? A self-creation? It turns out to be all these things at once. There are facts of biology, law-like interactions. But the facts of biology are not 'men have penises' and 'women have vaginas' or 'men are rational' and 'women are emotional'. The facts of biology are that cells are influenced by chromosomes, not just XY versus XX but XY, XX, XXX, XO, XXY, and XYY. Within any individual, at the cellular level, one might have a set of cells in one sex configuration and a set of cells in another. The composition of our cells will determine the shape and size of genitalia and gonads, how they function in terms of human reproduction, what sort of shape and texture our bodies will take as we reach adulthood – i.e. what kind of secondary sex characteristics we will manifest. Our bodies exist on a continuum with most people falling on one side or the other. But karyotypes that make a human body do not make a human person. Personhood is constructed through our metabolic interaction with the natural world, including other persons – our life on the planet within a universe operating within the laws of physics. Our experience of this metabolic interaction with the natural world (which is experienced in part as resources that sustain us) is conditioned by the social ordering of those resources and the social relations required to maintain that order. Social relations organize human biology according to what is compatible with the needs of the system and what is biologically possible. This is not done just through propaganda campaigns but also through material pressures. During the hunter-gatherer epoch, children were spaced according to the need for group mobility.[6] In settled agriculture, more children were needed and women were tasked with childcare roles. (And the women were sorted into the category according to their assumed reproductive faculties based on a general inductive logic of signs of the roles in reproduction – guesses about future genitalia and secondary sex characteristics.) Even women who did not bear children, like the person at a traffic light in the desert, would be disciplined into understanding their place in the world. The problem with poststructuralist conceptions of discipline is the assumption that social discipline comes from language and power, and therefore personally resisting discipline becomes a socially transformative act. Certainly, we can use Fields to develop a materialist conception of Butler's theory of iterability. But it is one thing to say that gender is disciplinary, it is another to say why, and yet another to know what course of action to take.

On the other hand, psychoanalytic explanations based in object relations theory are circular: girls become women because they look at a woman (their mother) and say, 'I am going to be a woman someday, I must break from my mother but somehow also become one.' This is naturalized through the presence of the phallus (first the biological penis from Freud, then the conceptual phallus from Lacan), which is understood as provoking a response in the child as symbolic of having and lacking.[7] Because the phallus is the dominant signifier of sexual relations, there is what Nina Power called the 'tragic-psychoanalytic model' of Lacanian sexual relations, where there is no genuine possibility of love between the sexes (Power 2009). This view is influenced by the structuralist paradigm, where gender discipline is produced from a matrix generated from the deep structures of presence and absence. The Foucauldian model of discipline operates through the reflection of power throughout the social field, like a spotlight refracted through a house of mirrors; discipline makes you confess, makes you expose yourself. However, another model of discipline, a Marxian model, could be derived from the experience of material *social relations*. In this model, people are shaped by interactions, by the adoption of behaviors they predict will satisfy desires, by their rejection of behaviors that seem to hold no promise of satisfaction, and by the pressure to repeat behaviors, even those they experience as irrational, because they are standard operating procedures within the system in which they exist.

For example, the figure of the loving and gentle mother is an attractive one, particularly in a brutal world. It is attractive for those who need soothing and it is attractive to those who find meaning in life by caring for others. So the idea of 'mother' is ideologically powerful under capitalism in that it is logical and satisfying. It is also logical to the systemic drive for profit: a mother's love means less social spending for childcare, schooling, and eldercare. However, this ideological phenomenon, this reification – hagiography even – of motherhood has its dark underside in that it reinforces the logic of oppositional sexism: a woman *must* be all these things – the system requires it. In a less brutal world, the relation between mother and child would be more contingent, resulting in greater freedom for individual development, and the freedom from enforced drudgery for many of those organized into the 'woman camp'. It is not likely that the mythology of Holy Motherhood will wither away under capitalism – and especially not among the working classes and the poor. In a sense, it has already withered away for the ruling classes who are not raised by their mothers but by their nannies and maids. Here, caretaking is not just something women do: it is something that *poor* women do. Motherhood is not only a gendered configuration, it is understood through class dynamics: the feminization of care is dialectically related to the feminization of poverty.

People are sorted by assumptions of gender in order to satisfy a system of social relations by satisfying themselves. Here, we are still clearly in the terrain of social constructivism, even though it is a materialist constructivism. So, what accounts for gender *variance*? What accounts for the fact that some assigned to the 'woman camp' feel relatively at home in their bodies but wish to integrate the behaviors and expectations of men, and others do not feel at home in their bodies at all? Here, the ideology of oppositional sexism no longer makes sense. For those who find gender ideology to be patently irrational or personally unsatisfying, it is only through force that they keep adhering to it: through fear of social alienation, fear of not being able to sell a complexly gendered self on the market,[8] and fear of violence.

While this explains the development of queerness, it does not explain the existence of transness. If gender is ideological, how can some desire to change their *bodies* to match an ideological framework, one that they, perhaps, are also contesting? The foundation of the answer is not so difficult: what is socially constructed is material in motion, and bodies are part of the material shaped. We know that bodies are not born into two ideal categories – XY man with testes and XX woman with ovaries; rather, we are comprised of cells, combinations of which produce different reactions. There is no reason to assume that some configurations do not produce a sense that one's body composition is 'off'. However, when one has the desire to change one's body, one is also, depending on the changes made, expected to change one's social gender. At that point, social gender must be dealt with. Just as those assigned as females at birth might not reject social gendering, there is no reason to assume that those who adjust the composition of their bodies would not also sometimes challenge gender expectations and sometimes not challenge them. Some trans women want to be beautiful flowers because there are aspects of feminine gender expression that they find lovely and edifying – for the same reason that cis women do. Other trans women have no interest in being delicate in any way and do not see how femininity has anything at all to do with being a woman – just like some cis women do. In addition, some trans *men* also want to be beautiful flowers. Some intersex people feel at home with some social gender expectations; others do not feel at home with any at all. Everything that is possible exists. Nothing exists *ex nihilo* sprung from a well-formed or ill-formed Platonic vision. Queer, trans, and intersex people are real. Queer, trans, and intersex people are rational. Queer, trans, and intersex people are part of the everybody.

However, one cannot personally perform one's way out of ideology. We can perform against the prevailing ideology – break from what is generally repeated – but the parameters of that ideology will not change unless the material social relations that support the ideology also change. Social relations – class relations – do not prescriptively determine exactly what *will* be, but they constrain the parameters of what *can* be. A eunuch in Byzantium could not imagine the parameters of liberal pluralism, and a boy in a tenth-century Germanic tribe could not imagine 'anti-Black racism'; in fact, even seventeenth-century Americans didn't know the terms 'Black' and 'white'. Queer politics based on challenging binaries through demonstrating the ideological character of those binaries is not itself a sufficient condition to eradicate gender ideologies brought about by the forces of everyday material life as it is organized through capitalist social relations. Likewise, demonstrating the absurdities of racist ideologies is not a sufficient condition to eradicate racism. Even if every white person in the United States were to recognize the fallacious reasoning in the construction of racial ideology, even if every white person were to become sensitive to the absurdities faced by Black people in the criminal justice system, nothing would change until there were an organized movement to challenge those absurdities.[9] Twelve-year-old Tamir Rice was deemed responsible for failing to prevent his own murder. Acceptance of this absurdity, like the repetition of stopping at a stoplight in an empty desert, enforces its meaning; if you accept that some small children deserve to be mowed down in a matter of seconds for holding a toy gun on an empty sidewalk, then your epistemological map will adopt this as a natural consequence of 'the way things are'. The next atrocity down the line will be that much easier to accept. Many people will not accept that such atrocities are logical, but without organizing with others to solve the problem, they will be left to quietly submit to a map that makes no sense. Change requires awareness and solidarity, but change also requires change.

II. Ten axioms towards a queer Marxist future

1. The politics of the fragment should be replaced by an inclusive politics of everybody

The affirmation of an inclusive politics is simply a counter to the late twentieth-century 'dictatorship of the fragments' (Best 1989: 361).[10] The dictatorship of the fragments was, in part, a response to two very real political problems of the mid-twentieth century: the concept of an ossified totality projected by the leading sects of Soviet Marxism, and, in some ways related, the failure of Marxists to fully incorporate a challenge to traditional and oppositional sexism, which made sexed and raced populations appear as fragments, as sections of the public with issues only tangentially related to political economy. As a response to having their situations bracketed by Marxist politics, feminists assumed that their situations were motivated by another, external vector of oppression. The intellectual product of this engagement developed the ultimately untenable idea of two systems at work: arguing that the problem was, on the one hand, a concrete political economy called capitalism, and, on the other, a generalized 'patriarchy' still lingering as a sort of spiritual holdover from feudalism. The logic of dual-systems theory drove it towards a model where there would have to be an infinite number of systems that could make intersecting cuts through the individual person, but that were not necessarily phenomena generated from the same system. To suggest that such phenomena were generated from the same system was considered reductionist, but, at the same time, no proper explanation was given for how such social phenomena were generated. Two explanations became popular: one based in free will, the other in structure. In the former, phenomena such as racism and sexism came from the individual will to power; the incorporation of groups to consolidate power was the systematization of this power. In this Hobbesian war of all against all, it is up to conscientious individuals in each power group to speak truth to power and make others aware of the injustices they are committing. In the latter configuration of power, individuals have little significant agency, since all are born into language that structures consciousness. The subject in this model, despite structuralist attempts to break from Cartesianism, remains a ghost in the machine. In poststructuralist variants of this model, the best one can do is be aware of how language is operating within you and construct yourself as a challenge to the structures and strictures of discourse: instead of the prefigurative utopian slogan 'be the change you want to see', this model of political consciousness suggests 'be the resistance you wish could exist but cannot exist because we are always already interpellated into language and, by extension, the state'. The dictatorship of the fragments is also promoted by the free-market attitude in its masquerade as anti-totalitarian empiricist skepticism: one can never know if there is a thing called everybody because no one mind can experience the existence of everybody. By extension, there is no such thing as capitalism, just individuals trading freely and equally. No one experiences *all of capitalism*! As the great philosopher Margaret Thatcher once put it: there is no society, only individuals and families. To the free-marketer, strictures are irrelevant so long as the market's invisible hands aren't tied.

Thus, including everybody is not about a feeling of unity or a group's commitment to tolerance or a hatred of the concepts of closure and finitude. An inclusive political understanding of 'everybody' is a simple affirmation that we can logically deduce that the world is a whole – a flickering, pulsating movement of birth and death, of appearance and disappearance, of social relations that are at once real and mutable. Once we accept such a politics, we can either fall on the side that says this universe needs to be purified, segregated, and ordered, or the side that says that beings are equal in their infinite complexity. The only question that remains after that is: 'Which side are you on?'

2. Analyses of political economy should be concrete, dialectical, and gender/sex inclusive

In order for Marxist political economy to be both concrete and dialectical, it cannot separate social phenomena from political analysis. Including analyses of reproduction into analyses of economic production can only further complete our understanding of the political conditions of a given locale. It is not just that, in order to understand the position of women, one needs to understand economics, but if one wants to understand economics, one needs to analyze the position of women. Except for very specific abstract questions about production (for example, is financialization a response to the law of the tendency of the rate of profits to fall?), a *fuller* understanding of the dynamics of gender relations within a society can only help assess the dynamics of capitalist social relations. What this means is that Marxist materialism should not just 'make space' for the analysis of racism and oppositional sexism in an international and transnational context; it should analyze how the development and maintenance of racial and gendered social sections affect the outcome of production processes. To put it bluntly, if the construction and maintenance of bullied population sets do not factor into debates about political economy, then either aspects of economic conditions are not being factored in out of epistemological ignorance, or else the anti-Marxists are correct: Marxism has nothing to say about oppression. The majority of the world's factory work is racialized and gendered for a reason; suffice to say that analyzing those reasons would complement any economic analysis. The study of gender and sexuality is integral to economic analyses, and the inverse is also true: economic analyses are integral to understanding gender and sexuality. Economics is not a subject that should be separated from its social and philosophical context, nor should we allow it to be presented as inscrutable to ordinary people, or treated as the intellectual property of straight, cisgendered men.

3. The intersectional model of oppression should be replaced with a unitary, relational model

Intersectional feminism has been a critical corrective to the feminism of the Universal Womanhood, whether that universality be cultural feminism, radical feminism, or imperialist feminism. All of these have served as a megaphone for white, upper-class women in the developed world who sometimes spoke for their poor brown sisters instead of listening to what they were actually saying about themselves. Intersectional feminism called these feminisms to task for their failure to account for the social discrepancies in the lives of women in terms of race, sexual orientation, gender identity, nationality, or social mobility (the latter often unhelpfully referred to as 'class'). It is for good reason that the maxim *'my feminism will be intersectional, or it will be bullshit'* was adopted.

Intersectional feminism was not the first attempt to develop an understanding of the obstacles faced by those whose gender struggles were conditioned by racism and homophobia. The Black lesbian feminist tradition and the Marxist-feminist traditions of the second wave used terms such as 'double and triple oppression' or being a 'double or triple threat'. It makes sense that, as more immiserations were openly discussed, numerical assignations – being a sextuple threat – would have been unwieldy. *Intersecting oppressions* was a clearer way to discuss collective problems.

But the model of intersecting oppressions is an expansion of dual-systems theory. While intersectionality is an immense improvement on a dysfunctional set theory that naturalizes the experience of 'woman', it is a weak and confusing metaphor. The model of intersecting oppressions assumes that each oppression is a vector with a nebulous origin intersecting with the individual subject: race, gender, class, sexuality, appearance, ability, and so on cut through the subject at various angles. However, this reifies race and strictures on social gender instead of understanding these terms as the outcome of processes called racism and sexism, processes that condition one another. Racism and sexism don't just hit the body out of the blue: racism and sexism are social processes developed within a material matrix. Disconnected from material life, oppression seems as if it were born from ill will and bad ideas.

What's more, a Marxian understanding of class cannot be understood as an *additional vector* of oppression. Material social organization is the matrix of social injustice. In the intersectional model, class is calculated into the sum of an individual's hardships. Class is not understood as a situation, as a position within a regime of production, but as a static identity. From this perspective, in the West, the demand that class be included comes across as a demand for white men to have their 'hardships' recognized and is therefore thought to be an attempt to evade responsibility for the racism and sexism that they perpetuate. From this perspective, it sounds reactionary to insist upon the centrality of class. However, class is not another vector of oppression; it is the mystification of all social relations in service of the production of surplus value. Oppression is oppression because it is felt – the *point* is that it is felt. Exploitation is characterized by the mathematical discrepancy between the value labor adds to a commodity and the surplus value handed over to those who purchase labor power. The *point* of exploitation is that it is easily mystified. Gender relations can be mystified as well (to accelerate exploitation), but there is an additional subtractive element to exploitation. If biological essentialism were true and all women truly loved the roles assigned to them, it could not be considered oppression. But even if all workers were happy as elves, the mathematical core of expropriation – of the flow of value from the producers to the owners – would remain, the boom and bust economy would continue, as would the systemic need for surplus populations and the environmental destruction caused by crises and overproduction. Class is primary – not in the sense of more important, but in the sense of being the limit, the foundation, the point where profit is extracted and the point where it can be challenged. The centrality of class is tactical, not moral.

4. Being queer/trans is neither reactionary nor revolutionary

Much of the debate surrounding queer radicalism involves assessing whether demands are normativizing or radically queer. Life is normativized when one acts like heterosexuals do, wants what heterosexuals want, and participates in capitalist economic relations as a consumer or as a laborer, with capitalism often defined as a network of monolithic, homogeneous, and homogenizing corporations – the small capitalists often get a pass.

The argument that capitalism thrives off normativity ignores the fact that it also thrives off diversity, pluralism, fashion, and market segments. While the heteronormative family is productive for capital, queer urban individualists and drop-out counter-culturalists are also productive for capital – the former as 'creatives' in the labor market, the latter as a surplus population (or, in the US, low-cost service industry labor). Queers without children are also not entirely outside the family matrix in that unmarried and childless family members are often taxed with eldercare. It is romantic to think that you can change the world through diverse sexuality, creative self-expression, and communal bonding. But you can't.

Also, trans and intersexed people should not be used as a flag of radical possibility for a new, postgendered future. First of all, trans and intersexed people are, more often than not, *gendered*. Second, trans bodies have enough pressures without being required to have to intentionally position their bodies as political objects.[11] However, if queerness is not progressive, it is also not reactionary or a product of bourgeois deviation, as it was sometimes caricatured by mid-century Marxist and Third Worldist movements. Nor is it a Eurocentric import external to precolonial peoples. It is also not useful to conflate queerness with class, including the portrayal of queerness as a hedonistic property of the elite.

Thus, those who are gender non-conforming are not necessarily poor; those who are gay and lesbian are not necessarily middle class. Opposing normativity is a politically empty gesture. Queer culture is not anti-capitalist. And so neither is queering culture.

5. The binary is not the problem and non-binary thinking is not the solution

Since the poststructuralist turn, the West has been enamored with the death of the binary. All ills can be attributed to it: us and them, Black and white, straight and gay, man and woman, rich and poor, ones and zeros. Such a world does not account for diversity, let alone poetry. Or so the story goes.

It is true that false dichotomies are fallacious and present us with a rigid and unchanging map of the universe. Between us and them there is all, there are multiple sexualities, ethnicities, religions, and so on. But, paradoxically, struggles against dichotomies present new dichotomies: binary versus multiple, heteronormative versus queer, trans versus cis.[12] Moreover, there are important political dichotomies that this language evades: there is racism and antiracism, there is the picket line and there is crossing it, there is the murder of queer/trans people and there is the absence of those murders, there is welcoming immigrants who land on your shores and there is letting them drown. Of course, these antagonisms need to be understood dialectically – racism and antiracism aren't just abstract conceptual objects but relational processes in a material world. Strikebreakers can be brought into the fold, and strikers can betray solidarity. Moving from violence against queer people to the absence of violence is a process that involves transforming those who would harm queer and trans people into those who won't. However, this procedural complexity does not mean that the antagonisms aren't real.

It should also be remembered that not all 'third ways' are progressive: politicians who triangulate interests destroy movements; intellectuals who deconstruct labor struggles deconstruct labor in favor of the bosses; and fascism touts itself as a 'third position' between capitalism and communism by harmonizing the complaints of labor with the needs of the national bourgeoisie.

6. Marxists must stand against trans-exclusionary radical feminism

While Marxists have little compatible ground with radical feminist views, especially on patriarchy being the origin of all class oppression, sometimes Marxist-feminists have operated from a second-wave framework, turned off by the shortcomings of third-wave feminism's failure to fully deal with issues such as commercial surrogacy in South Asia, the economic contributions of household and reproductive labor, and femicide.

However, the liberation of women is not threatened by the liberation of men who are able to bear children or women who aren't.[13] Trans-exclusionary radical feminism's paranoid vision of trans women as rapists and bathroom predators – reminiscent not only of right-wing conservative opinions, but also of earlier panics about lesbians in bathrooms and locker rooms – has no place in Marxist theory. Neither does the moralistic women-blaming-women hysteria over 'female chauvinist pigs' or 'female collaborators', which always upholds sex workers as sex-selling enemies instead of treating them as *workers*, as subjects operating in an economic system. Historically, along with cisgendered straight women, working-class trans women and femme lesbians have taken the brunt of this misogyny. Marxism is a politics based on solidarity and action within an economic context, not wild accusations and gender panics. Nor should Marxists bow to the claim that trans people are trying to erase the word 'woman' at a time when women are under attack. Capitalism is not simply misogynistic, it is intent on upholding the traditional and oppositional sexism that secures the system. An injury to one is an injury to all.

7. Queer communitarianism should be replaced with queer political demands

The need for queer safe spaces is not an eternal political good: it is evidence of a sad state of affairs. All communitarianism provokes questions of boundaries and exclusions. Why be a community, if there is no outside to it? Queer people, insofar as they are excluded from the general public, isolated, and immiserated, have a right to self-determination; but the goal must not be striving towards a permanent sense of queer nationalism or separatism – particularly because the existential nature of queerness is a cross-border and cross-cultural phenomenon. Could a queer Palestinian group be expected to form a nation of queerness that excluded heterosexual Palestinians? Instead of queer nationalism, the goal should be queering internationalism – not in the sense of a Universal Queerness, but in the sense of creating a section of the queer movement aligned with the working class to expand its solidarities to other oppressed, immiserated, and exploited people, *whether or not they accept queer people.*

What's more, as Lise Vogel's work shows, queer and trans liberation depends on the liberation of heterosexual, cis working women's reproductive rights and health. Oppositional sexism is wedded to traditional sexism, and much traditional sexism comes from the political economy of pregnancy and motherhood under capitalism. For queer people's own liberation, queer people have cause to support demands for straight, cisgendered women, globally, *whether or not they accept queer people.*

8. Queer Marxism is not the analysis of queer consumption habits

Of late, much of the Marxist analysis of queer oppression has been the analysis of queer co-optation into the market economy (see point 4 above). It is curious for Marxists to approach queer politics through criticizing the consumption habits of middle-class and status-conscious queers. Marxist-feminists are not transfixed by the consumer habits of women in households, but by concrete issues such as social reproduction, sexual assault, and reproductive freedom. Marxists examining Black oppression do not focus on how the Black middle class buys into a petit bourgeois vision of itself, but rather on concrete issues such as police violence and housing discrimination. Standing in solidarity with immigrants does not involve contemplating their consumer purchases or criticizing them for being assimilationist when they choose to adopt the customs of their new community.

The only reason I can assume that there is so much hand-wringing about how queers fail to live up to the expectations of radical subjects is that Marxists are buying into the concept that there is something inherently radical about queer existence; that, in itself, it poses some sort of challenge to capitalism because it challenges the family – forgetting that capitalism does not actually care about the family; rather, it cares about the free maintenance of its future workforce and ensuring that the assembly line is not disrupted.

The complaint is generally that queers are ignoring the violence and immiseration of the poorest segments of 'the community'. But a significant number of other oppressed populations also have no interest in violence done to their cohorts: women blame women for rape, middle-class women are too busy 'partying and consuming' to deal with the feminization of poverty. So why would the queer middle class not behave like any other middle class? Why would the queer professional and upper classes take care of poor and working-class queers? Once again, my only guess is that there is some stock taken in the notion that queerness is inherently radical. The other side of the coin is a belief that there is some sinister conservatism inherent to queerness. Not just that queerness is a 'bourgeois deviation' per se, but that queerness as a political identity emerges as a possibility only within capitalism: ergo, it must be a pro-capitalist politics. This reactionary paranoia is as dangerous as it is useless.

Queer Marxists must disengage with queer nationalism. The time spent denouncing upper echelon queers for behaving like upper echelon queers would be better spent fighting the battles it is wrongly assumed they will fight.

9. Queer politics must oppose 'imperialism with a queer face'

In line with Jasbir Puar's notion of homonationalism, American imperialism after Obama's election moved from rampant homophobia to encouraging the integration of queers with the hope of selling liberal progressives on the project of endless war. But this contradiction is merely politicians trying to dominate the entire political field. The neoconservatives who engineered the ostracizing of gays at the turn of the millennium are now the self-same group that is pinkwashing Israel. In fact, the pinkwashing campaigns were *simultaneous* to their anti-gay campaigns in the 'homeland'.

The protection of queers – like the protection of women – can become a modern, progressive cover for domination of the Middle East by establishing a narrative of 'barbarians' against the West. Queer imperialism would be another arm of this campaign. The way out of this impasse is solidarity with queer people of occupied countries. Instead of supporting a 'civilizing' mission in Iraq, we can support IraQueer. Instead of supporting the occupation of Gaza, we can support Aswat and alQaws.

10. Wherever there is solidarity with the goal towards eradicating expropriation, there is queer Marxism

Just as ecosocialism is only something more than socialism insofar as countering ecological devastation isn't seen to be a logical concern of socialists, and just as Black feminism (as Fields notes) is only needed if feminism means ignoring the concerns of Black women, the term 'queer Marxism' is only necessary insofar as Marxism does not automatically include trans, gender non-conforming, and sexually diverse people into its analyses of social relations. However, we can fight for a future in which there is no need for Marxist-feminism or queer Marxism, but only the international movement to expropriate the expropriators, a movement where traditional and oppositional sexism are addressed as a condition and consequence of exploitation. It is the only future worth fighting for.

Notes

Introduction

1 I am, of course, referring here to the arguments in Michael Hardt and Antonio Negri's *Multitude: War and Democracy in the Age of Empire* (Hardt and Negri 2004).

2 The term 'liberal' here refers to economic liberalism, i.e. capitalism.

3 The Canadian psychiatrist Ewen Cameron's early self-help manifesto *Life is for Living* argues that psychological and sexual orthodoxy was the causal root of Nazi Germany. Cameron went on to conduct a number of experiments in the hope of finding ways to solve the problem of orthodoxy. His 'depatternization' project, funded by the CIA, helped people become less orthodox through sensory deprivation, massive doses of psychedelic drugs, and being forced to listen to a repeated sentence for days on end (see Cameron 1948; Klein 2007).

4 This is not a reference to postcolonial theory. I mean postcolonial in the literal sense: the political subjects currently existing within colonized lands and those who struggle to cope with the complications that emerge after campaigns of national liberation.

5 In short, anticolonial campaigns can also empower the national capitalist class.

6 Lean manufacturing is a neoliberal precept that nothing must be wasted. This sounds good on the surface – capitalist processes create a ton of waste. But what is meant by waste reduction here is not the end of planned obsolescence or the banning of toxic processes. Efficiency and waste reduction mean squeezing the most possible labor out of wage workers for the least possible cost, using the ideological discipline of workers to replace management, and outsourcing as much as possible. Examples of

this in action are: having employees do the work of finding their own last-minute replacements when they come down with food poisoning; using the surfeit of PhD holders hoping to make it into the middle class to transform the professoriate into a contingent (adjunct) labor force; timing autoworkers so that they work 58 seconds per minute instead of 45 seconds per minute. For documentation of the latter, see Post and Slaughter (2000).

7   Alain Badiou (Badiou 2012) describes techniques for striking that involve the whole community. One traditional problem of the strike weapon is that workers endure financial hardship along with their bosses – and bosses have deeper pockets. However, if workplaces are occupied by the unemployed members of the community so that workers cannot do their jobs, then surplus value extraction is interrupted while paychecks continue to be issued – paychecks that can provide bail money and sustenance for occupiers.

8   This is not to say that we should embrace victimhood. Precisely the opposite.

1. Terms of the debate

1   Some examples of class-reductionist models of anti-capitalism include variants of syndicalism and other workerist approaches. Marx, however, analyzed systemic subjugation outside the workplace: for example, land seizures, religious alienation, and the objectification of women.

2   Unlike liberal philosophers, Marx is averse to a priori theories of justice. Two clear examples of this are Marx's criticism of the idea of 'fair distribution' (see Marx 1978b; Marx's letter to Engels of 4 November 1864 regarding an address written to the Workingmen's International Association: 'I was, however, obliged to insert two sentences about "duty" and "right", and ditto about "truth, morality and justice" into the preamble to the rules, but these are placed in such a way that they can do no harm' in Marx and Engels 1987b; cf. Rawls 1971).

3   Although poststructuralist theory considers existentialism to be naïve in its attitude towards language and agency, queer theory's privileging of the queer subject as epistemological grounds for confronting 'the system' strongly reflects Sartre's ethical conception of bad faith: in other words, the heteronormative subject lives the unexamined life and has embraced heterosexual herd mentality (see Sartre 1993). For an overview of existentialism, see the section in Chapter 1 of this book 'From Western Marxism to poststructuralism'.

4   Victor Serge's writing models this, particularly *Witness to the German Revolution* (2011) and *From Lenin to Stalin* (1973).

5   The strategy of urban occupation was generalized during the Occupy Movement of 2011. The French tract *The Coming Insurrection* by The Invisible Committee was influential (see The Invisible Committee 2007).

6   A scathing letter to the editor of the *Weekly Worker*, the newspaper of the Communist Party of Great Britain, colorfully describes such out-of-touch revolutionary practice in response to the thirtieth anniversary of the British miners' strike: 'Thankfully, you [the CPGB] have lost some of that excruciating self-opinionated leadership arrogance you displayed at that time, telling battle-hardened, class-conscious coalminers where we were going wrong and how you'd worked this all out for us and here's what we should do' (see David Douglass, 'Fools', *Weekly Worker*: weeklyworker. co.uk/worker/1044/letters).

7   For an analysis of the implications of Drucker's contribution to queer Marxism, see 'The world is a very queer place' in Chapter 3.

8   Sworn virgin status was (and to a lesser extent still is) a practice in rural, patriarchal, and patrilocal Albania in which a girl child is designated to become a man at birth. Because this practice is involuntary, there are debates about the appropriateness of its inclusion in queer politics, since there is an assumption that 'the queer' is defined by free expression of an individual truth. However, sworn virgins can also choose to become men, and some do so, citing reasons similar to transgendered men in other parts of the world (see Magrini 2003; Littlewood and Young 2005). For work on the *muxe* population, see Mirandé (2013). See also Alejandra Islas's 2006 documentary *Muxes: Authentic, Intrepid Seekers of Danger*, distributed by Ethnoscope. For examples of Native American gender diversity, see Williams (1986). For an analysis of Asian/Pacific queer identities including *kathoey*, *tóngzhì* (the word 'comrade' in Chinese, both a pun on the Chinese word for homosexuality and a term implying solidarity between sexual minorities), *mak nyah*, and *fa'afafine*, see Martin et al. (2008). Numerous sources documenting the lives of *hijra* have been published in the past two decades, including autobiographies *The Truth About Me* (Revathi 2010) and *Me Hijra, Me Laxmi* (Laxmi et al. 2015).

9   See http://alqaws.org/siteEn/index.

10 For analyses of American butch/femme working-class culture, see the ethnography *Boots of Leather, Slippers of Gold* (Kennedy and Davis 1993); the memoir *Stone Butch Blues* (Feinberg 1993); and Joan Nestle's classic anthology *The Persistent Desire* (Nestle 1992). Hollibaugh and Moraga (1981; reprinted in Snitow et al. 1983: 440–59) give an autobiographical perspective on the anti-gender hegemony of second-wave feminism. For

a classic sociological study of butch/femme patterns among mid-century American female-identity assigned youth, see Giallombardo (1974).

11 *The Material Queer* is subtitled 'A LesBiGay reader' (Morton 1996).

12 There is a long history of debates among trans people over the words 'transgender' and 'transsexual'. For this reason, I will generally use the term 'trans' in place of these words.

13 Carol Queen describes the lesbian-feminist 'uniform' not as ungendered, but as 'Butch Lite' (Queen 1997: 154). Judith Butler would famously demystify genderlessness as an impossibility on the grounds that one is always interpellated into the structure of language, one is always called to account for one's body, one is always 'read' through discursive conditions. The very point of the denunciation of gender creates an essentialist gender/sex split (see Butler 1990; on the materiality of the body, see Butler 1993).

14 Janice Raymond's *The Transsexual Empire* (1979) is the classic text for anti-trans feminism. In paranoid fashion, Raymond imagines a socially powerful 'empire' of transsexual women. Postmodern writer and media inventor Sandy Stone called her witty response to Raymond (Raymond's work was a long personal attack on Stone) 'The "Empire" Strikes Back' (in Stryker and Whittle 2006).

15 Making sure that trans women have nowhere to pee has been the life work of lawyer Cathy Brennan. See Cathy Brennan and Elizabeth Hungerford, '2011 Letter to the UN on "Gender Identity" Legislation' at http://sexnotgender.com/gender-identity-legislation-and-the-erosion-of-sex-based-legal-protections-for-females/.

16 There is now evidence that trans subjects are neurologically distinct from cis subjects and that aspects of trans brain patterning diverge from cis brain patterning: even without hormone replacement, the patterns of trans people are closer to the patterns of their cis counterparts on a spectrum (Kranz et al. 2014).

17 For an example of a re-emergence of criticism of butch/femme identity, see Erin Tatum 'Who's the Man: Heteronormativity and Queer Relationships' at http://everydayfeminism.com/2014/04/whos-the-man/. Paradoxically, in challenging queer people to accept all forms of desire, Tatum warns: 'You don't need rigidly enforced gender roles to build a real connection ... Internalizing the expectation for a gender dichotomy within your partnerships might also be subconsciously limiting your own sexual expression.' The writer explains that they originally sought only masculine lovers because of their own inability to break away from heterosexual norms, which implies that, unlike other gendered desires, the butch/femme dyad could be a mere heteronormative gesture. However, this personal narrative

misses the larger phenomenon of actually heterosexual 'bicurious' women who almost exclusively seek out sexual relations with feminine women, often adding 'no butches!' to their personal ads. Oddly enough, we are back in the terrain of second-wave anxiety over butch/femme relations, but with a third-wave requirement for absolute gender fluidity instead of absolute refutation of gender as a concept. The femme position is particularly difficult to reconcile with the idea of challenging 'normativity' because many femmes are indistinguishable from heterosexual women. Since queer culture is by definition inclusive of anyone who wants 'in' (i.e. anyone committed to the project of subverting gender), there has been a consensus in defense of cisgendered femmes, an explanation that femmes *queer* femininity in ways that heterosexual, non-queer women do not. But this is based on a very restrictive definition of heterosexual women's gender. In reality, femmes are not truly distinguishable by gender markers, but by their relation to others within the queer world and the role they play in the overall sexual and emotional affirmation of other queer women.

18 There has also been a debate between those who think the term intersex is preferable to the term disorders of sexual development (DSD). Others have argued that DSD is more accurate or more pragmatic because it will reduce stigma and encourage parents to obtain treatment for their children. Of course, many of those who embrace the term 'intersex' maintain that their bodies are not disordered. The term behind the initials DSD has recently shifted to *differences* in sexual development to remove the sense of pathology.

19 This is a symbol of the Human Rights Campaign, a mainstream American lobbying group notorious for its poor record on trans inclusivity.

20 The majority of humans, that is. There has been no emotional census of other life forms; however, pampered pets aside, animal life has not fared well since capitalism commodified it.

21 For Rosa Luxemburg's critique of Bernstein's reformism see 'Reform or Revolution' in Luxembourg (2007).

22 As Henning notes, the difficulty here for Marxists becomes avoiding a turn towards normative ethics which would render economic understanding a pedantic excursus to political action. Henning criticizes Lenin for accelerating this normative move in his argument that imperialism and monopoly capitalism are distinct from earlier capitalism. Henning is not convinced that imperialism and monopolization weren't already features of capitalism as described by Marx (see Henning 2014: Chapter 2.2; Lenin 2010). For other readings of capitalism's trajectory in early twentieth-century Europe, see Hilferding (2006). While I am sympa-

thetic to the critique of normative politics, it seems like too much is laid at Lenin's feet here: anyone striving towards social change along Marxist lines will likely push politics to the forefront because it is political force that decides political questions for Marx ('between equal rights, force decides'), not economic mechanisms.

23 Debates over the origin of capitalism are hotly contested among Marxist (and anti-Marxist) historians and theorists. Even those who agree that capitalism's origins are internal to Europe disagree as to why the change occurred. Robert Brenner and Ellen Meiksins Wood locate capitalism's origins in the oddities of the development of the English feudal economy and in the fact that political unrest led to the disruption of feudalism and the consequent development of capitalism. For Brenner's arguments in this historical context, see Aston and Philpin (1987). Other internalists argue that the development of capitalism emerged out of objective material conditions, particularly the development of trade during the Renaissance (see Sweezy 1978: 33–56; Wallerstein 1974). However, there are also 'externalist' scholars who oppose 'internalist' positions as Eurocentric. The externalists accept the general framework of the rise of capitalism in the West; however, they wish to decenter Europe and refocus on the role of the East in the development of the West (see Hobson 2004: 313–16). Alexander Anievas and Kerem Nisancioglu put forward a Marxist critique of Eurocentrism, arguing for an internationalist understanding of the development of capitalism rooted in an interpretation of Trotsky's theory of uneven and combined development (U&CD). Trotsky's theory of the role of unevenness in development distinguished him as the one theorist who was able to predict that workers' revolution would happen in Russia and not industrialized Germany. Anievas and Nisancioglu use U&CD to analyze the role of the Mongol invasions, the expansion of the Ottoman empire, and colonial developments in the Americas. Anievas and Nisancioglu defend charges against U&CD as 'stagist, Eurocentric, and linear' by pointing out that Trotsky, in trying to understand Russian development, uses the concepts of stages in order to subvert them through a more complex and multilinear model (see Anievas and Nisancioglu 2013). For further argument of U&CD's internationalism – including the role of the agrarian history of Byzantine Egypt, late medieval Islam, the Sung dynasty in China, and slavery in capitalism – see Banaji (2010). For Marx's original text, see Marx (1978a: Volumes I–III).

24 'Whilst the cotton industry introduced child-slavery in England, it gave in the United States a stimulus to the transformation of the earlier, more or less patriarchal slavery, into a system of commercial exploitation. *In fact, the veiled slavery of the wage workers in Europe needed, for its pedestal,*

slavery pure and simple in the new world' (Marx 1978a: Volume I, Chapter 31, italics mine).

25 For arguments debating the influence of the (intercontinental) Black Plague on the development of capitalism, compare Ladurie (1981: 28–83) with Davidson (2012: 407).

26 Although, as Jairus Banaji (2010) notes, modes of domination and control do not necessarily predict or define the mode of production in a given age (cf. Chibber 2013, discussed at length in the section on Marxist critique of postcolonialism in Chapter 3).

27 Originally a Roman term, the proletariat were a category of people with no property whose only function was to produce offspring. Although Marx's use of the term implied the class of people who had lost access to their land for self-reproduction and were later forced to produce industrial commodities to survive, the idea of the proletarian as having nothing to give but 'offspring' (be it human goods for an empire or commodities for industrial capitalists) has interesting implications for Marxist-feminist social reproduction theory.

28 This is a truism of classical political economy (see Smith 1986).

29 For an introduction to the irreconcilable foundations of neoclassical and Marxian models of economics, see Wolff and Resnick (1987).

30 See Jean Baudrillard's *The Mirror of Production* (Baudrillard 1975), in which Marx is critiqued as 'productivist' (confusing the alienation emanating from capitalism, the object of Marx's study, with Marx himself) and as 'fetishizing' labor (conflating perhaps Soviet imagery of the worker with Marx's rational breakdown of labor within an economic model).

31 As summarized by Christoph Henning, 'Whether the basic assumptions of neoclassical theory were *straightforwardly* retained (as in Okishio, Steedman, and Roemer) or whether they were only retained ex negative – because monopoly capital was considered the index of a new era – Marxian essentials such as the labour theory of value, exploitation and the falling rate of profit were abandoned by Marxists' (Henning 2014: 156, italics in the original). For a defense of value as well as a defense of the law of the tendency of the rate of profit to fall, see especially Chapters 2.1.5 and 2.1.6, pp. 50–78 (ibid.).

32 This does not mean that all workers will always be paid at subsistence level at all times. There can be a number of counterbalancing factors, including the level of class struggle and the number of skilled workers in the labor force.

33 This is different to saying that uncompensated labor directly produces profit for capital.

34 For an excellent model of how the law of the tendency of the rate of profit to fall works, see Henning (2014: 50–77); for its role in recent economic crises, see Kliman (2011). For an overview of the debate, see Harvey (forthcoming) and the discussion between Kliman and Harvey on Kliman's blog *New Left Project*: 'Harvey Versus Marx on Capitalism's Crisis Part 1: Getting Marx Wrong' (10 March 2015); 'Harvey Versus Marx on Capitalism's Crisis Part 2: Getting Profitability Wrong' (12 March 2015); 'Harvey Versus Marx on Capitalism's Crisis Part 3: A Rejoinder' (13 May 2015).

35 See the organic composition of capital (Marx 1978a: Volume I and Volume III) and the law of the tendency of the rate of profit to fall (ibid.: Volume III, Part III).

36 My analysis limits itself to industrial capital because of its clear and immediate impact on social gender. For Marx's views on finance capital, see Marx (1978a: Volume III, Chapter 25).

37 Marx's doctoral dissertation was entitled 'The Difference Between the Democritean and Epicurean Philosophy of Nature'.

38 For a debate about the relationship (or non-relationship) of Eastern and Western culture to dialectics, see Peng and Nisbett (1999). A response to Peng and Nisbett can be found in a later volume of the same journal (Ho 2000).

39 Plato's work reconciled the two, with an eternal ideal world being discovered through dialectical thought.

40 In a letter to Engels dated 14 January 1858, Marx noted that it would take no more than 'two or three printers sheets' to explain dialectics. Unfortunately, he never got around to writing this simple explanation.

41 Some queer theorists place Friedrich Nietzsche as the originator of perspectival thinking (see Hall 2003). Nietzsche's 'On Truth and Falsity in the Extramoral Sense' poetically compares human epistemological arrogance with a mosquito 'feeling within itself the flying center of the world', but Marx was publishing while Nietzsche was still a young child.

42 By unemployed people, I mean people who need employment but cannot find it – not the children of industrial and financial capitalists who do not need to work.

43 These terms are put forward by trans theorist Julia Serano to clarify what is typically called sexism and homophobia or transphobia. Traditional sexism is the ideology that women are inferior to men. Oppositional sexism is the ideology that women and men are distinct, opposite creatures whose very distinct gender essences belong in opposite but complementary bodies (see Serano 2013).

44 Marx himself never used the term 'false consciousness', and Engels used the term only once in a discussion with Franz Mehring a decade after

Marx's death. In his letter, Engels mentioned that perhaps false consciousness was something that he and Marx should not have ignored ('Engels to Franz Mehring', London, 14 July 1893, in Marx and Engels 1942).

45 For a particularly wooden woman-blaming analysis of how the cosmetics industry oppresses women (not as workers but as consumers), see Hansen and Reed (1986). The book reprints the internal party debates on women's make-up held by the American Socialist Workers Party in the 1950s. For a blunt socialist-feminist critique of the book, see 'Make-up Moralism and Misogyny', an undated editorial from the Freedom Socialist Party (www. socialism.com). The uncritical absorption of second-wave feminism is by no means marginal among contemporary Marxists. Beyond the point that many of the documents provided by Hansen and Reed trivialize women's lives and reduce them to bodies – hard to imagine internal party documents about men's toupees – I would venture to say that wearing cosmetics is as common, if not more common, with working-class American women (masculine women excepted) than with those in the middle classes. While social workers and scientists are relatively free from such expectations, waitresses and cash register operators are not. When middle-class feminists reproach working-class women for wearing cosmetics, the result is an understandable class rage. You don't get much more politically out of touch than when approaching someone making minimum wage with lectures about her eyeliner.

46 This is where essentialism arising from some variants of psychoanalytic feminism becomes quite toxic. Theories that celebrate women as reducible to anatomical logic are mystical, reactionary, and irreconcilable with a trans-inclusive feminism (see Irigaray 1985).

47 I am using the term 'woman's' as a response to cultural feminists, the most vocal critics of medical science. Queer people, trans people, and intersex people have also been historically mistreated and ignored by medical professionals, along with indigenous peoples, immigrants, Black people, poor people, those suffering caste discrimination, and other marginalized groups.

48 See Christoph Henning's Kantian affirmation of Marx, G. A. Cohen's analytic Marxism – or, as he called it, 'No Bullshit Marxism' – and Louis Althusser's attempt at critiquing Hegelian Marxism – while keeping the complex understanding of causality in Marx – by using the psychoanalytic concept of over-determination and the structuralist concept of the epistemological break to rework dialectics.

49 Some Marx-inspired Hegelian or Hegelian-inspired Marxist works of note include: Kojève (1980), Hook (1994), Smith (1990), Sartre (1991) and Žižek (2012).

50 'Since, according to their fantasy, the relationships of men, all their doings, their chains and their limitations are products of their consciousness, the Young Hegelians logically put to men the moral postulate of exchanging their present consciousness for human, critical or egoistic consciousness, and thus of removing their limitations. This demand to change consciousness amounts to a demand to interpret reality in another way, i.e. to recognize it by means of another interpretation. The Young Hegelian ideologists, in spite of their allegedly world-shattering statements, are the staunchest conservatives. The most recent of them have found the correct expression for their activity when they declare they are only fighting against phrases. They forget, however, that to these phrases they themselves are only opposing other phrases, and that they are in no way combating the real existing world when they are merely combating the phrases of this world' (Marx 1978c).

51 Judith Butler examines Austin's idea in terms of gendered language in *Excitable Speech* (Butler 1997).

52 For example, Trotskyist political circles emphasize that the working class becomes 'fit to rule' through the experience of struggle (see Draper 1966; Hallas 1986). This position is based on Marx's statements in *The Poverty of Philosophy* (Marx 1973: Chapter 2).

53 This is generally the approach used by labor struggles. To provide a counterexample, the opposite tactic would be the way in which solidarity is approached in middle-class circles, where experts facilitate anti-oppression training sessions for colleagues and activists (see McIntosh 1989).

54 I am referring here, in part, to politicized versions of 'safe spaces' where marginalized individuals of like identities come together to share experiences and therefore where individuals without those identities are considered hostile and disruptive. This is distinct from expelling political antagonists from organizing meetings (i.e. expelling protestors from economic forums or expelling bosses and their agents from a strike committee meeting). In the therapeutic meeting, the interaction of subjects themselves is the political act. In organizing meetings, there is nothing identitarian about such expulsion; the goal of the latter is to preserve secrets in the heat of class struggle, not to provide a space for personal and community development.

55 Proponents of Lacanian psychoanalysis, for example, are critical of the idea of 'the subject'; Gilles Deleuze critiques both psychoanalysis and the idea that there is such a thing as a subject (see Deleuze and Guattari 1983). Deleuze opposes the idea of the world as a container filled with interactive individuals and communities and replaces this with the conception that existence is a horizontal network of flows and desires.

56 For a critique of Fourier, see Luxemburg (2007).

57 A notable instance here is the publication of Herbert Marcuse's *Heideggerian Marxism* (Marcuse 2005), written simultaneous to the publication of Marx's *Economic and Philosophic Manuscripts of 1844* (Marx and Engels 1975a: 229–347). Marcuse was searching for a way to 'reinvent Marx' away from Stalinist orthodoxy when the publication of Marx's own work on alienation reinvented Marxism itself.

58 In this debate a third antiwar camp emerged, the Zimmerwald Left, consisting of Luxemburg, Lenin, and Trotsky. The Zimmerwald Left opposed both pacifism and chauvinism; however, this small group did not manage to gain hegemony (see Nation 2009).

59 For a classic analysis of how gay identity emerged after feudalism, see D'Emilio and Freedman (1998) and Weeks (2012).

60 For example, David Harvey argues that capital still operates through primitive accumulation – the seizure of assets. If capitalism largely operates through accumulation, the labor theory of value becomes contingent (see the debate between Harvey and Kliman cited in note 34).

61 Telos is an Aristotelian concept that an object's purposiveness unfolds, that it blossoms into being. A teleological understanding of history means that history matures, that it unfolds into what it is 'destined' to be.

62 For an analysis of totalitarianism as a liberal democratic invention, see Žižek (2001).

63 Heidegger famously argued that Sartre's work was a failure because giving primacy to existence over essence did not cause existentialism to transcend metaphysics, it only changed the metaphysical schema (see Heidegger 1978: 208).

64 Classical Marxists are distinct from 'orthodox Marxists' of the Kautskyian variety.

65 'The owl of Minerva takes its flight only when the shades of night are gathering' (Hegel 1967: Preface, p. 13).

66 The practico-inert has also been described not as a refutation of Stalinism but as a resignation to bureaucracy. For a complex analysis of the ways in which Sartre's work both capitulates to and challenges Stalinism, see Badiou (2007).

67 Alain Badiou has taken up this question in interesting ways; being a subject to political truth is having *fidelity* to an event while working to create something new. Fidelity to an event implies being able to embody and transmit something of what is important from the earlier event, not just a collection of historical facts but a contribution that has real political weight (see Badiou 2006; 2001).

68 It could be argued that phallogocentrism, as a concept, is transmisogy-nistic in that it identifies the phallus as a sign of masculinity. It could also be argued that Derrida intends to expose such assumptions by creating the concept.

69 The term originates in Patrick Hamilton's play *Gas Light*, which was adapted into a Hollywood film by George Cukor in 1944. In the story, a man causes gaslights to flicker to make his wife believe that she is insane so that he can remove her from their home and search for a secret stash of jewels.

70 See ongoing debates about Foucault's relationship to neoliberalism, with some scholars finding his work clearly open to neoliberal readings and with a strong libertarian bent to his later work (see Zamora 2014a; 2014b), whereas others remark that Foucault's relation to neoliberalism exists without making claims of libertarianism (see Lemke 2009).

71 Corporatism means a political system in which labor and capital work together as the body of the nation against international pollutants, i.e. fascism. But in American populist politics it is a term that means something like the domination of society by multinational corporations as opposed to the primacy of small family businesses that care about their community. In other words, the popular meaning of corporatism is the exact opposite of the word's actual meaning.

72 Hardt and Negri's reworking of Marx in *Empire* (2001) and *Multitude* (2004) by inventing the terms 'immaterial labor' and 'affective labor' only re-mystifies global production. However, the crux of their project makes sense from the experience of the neoliberal, de-industrialized West. According to their thesis, post-Fordist and Toyotist methods of non-linear, networked just-in-time production have transformed capital's relation to labor. Labor is now a matter of analytic labor (the manip-ulation of symbols and numbers) and the affective labor of the service economy. In fact, the whole of capitalist production for Hardt and Negri has been transformed into intellectual and affective labor. They solve the riddle of how material manufacture fits into their scheme by arguing that it, too, is a service economy. An analysis of post-Fordist production is beyond the scope of this book; however, for a critique of the idea that the new post-industrial age marks a decline of traditional factory discipline and a lighter, airier sense of work, see Caffentzis (1999).

73 Subsumption in Marxian economics is when household or community production is absorbed by the market: for example, women were once responsible for making candles and clothing for the family, but those processes have been subsumed by mass manufacturing.

74 'In order to understand the continuation of U.S. hegemony, then, it is not sufficient to cite the relations of force that U.S. capitalism wielded

over the capitalists in other countries. U.S. hegemony was actually sustained by the antagonistic power of the U.S. proletariat' (Hardt and Negri 2001: 269). For other explanations of US hegemony, see McNally (2010).

2. Marxism and gender

1 Second-wave feminism still continues to identify other women as 'collaborators' with patriarchy. The most recent example is *Female Chauvinist Pigs* (Levy 2005), which, after long sections of hand-wringing angst about the victims of sex trafficking, goes on to entitle a chapter about sex workers 'Pigs in Training'. Of course, the term 'pig' is supposed to refer to the phrase 'male chauvinist pig', but when women are called pigs for their sexual behavior, the term clearly connotes the use of the term to signify a filthy, promiscuous woman. There is also a highly symptomatic chapter titled 'From Womyn to Bois', which uses a few journalistic interviews as evidence to paint trans men, butches, femmes, and gender queer people as shallow, hyper-sexual misogynists.

2 The exchange of women as a structural feature of human existence is a main argument in structuralism's foundational text, *The Elementary Structures of Kinship* by Claude Lévi-Strauss, especially Part One, Chapter V: 'The Principle of Reciprocity' (Lévi-Strauss 1969). Lévi-Strauss's work informed Lacanian psychoanalytic perspectives on sex and gender. Gayle Rubin criticizes Lévi-Strauss on a number of grounds, including that his theory does not account for the trafficking of men and boys, and that incest is not the only sex- or gender-related taboo (see 'The Traffic of Women' and 'The Trouble with Trafficking' in Rubin 2011). For materialist refutations of the universal trafficking of women, see Leacock (2008).

3 The classic text on the 'male' gaze is Laura Mulvey's essay 'Visual Pleasure and Narrative Cinema' (in Mulvey 2009).

4 The character Rabeya is a fierce, burqa-wearing pro-LGBT feminist riot grrrl who uses religious prohibitions to dominate space in the punk house where she lives with other Muslim punks (see Knight 2009).

5 Trans-exclusionary radical feminist Julie Bindel has written op-eds about the scourge of the niqab. Bindel doesn't wish to see the niqab banned because she argues that it isn't the state's job to dictate what women wear; the political purpose of her writing is to criticize *other feminists* who fail to criticize the niqab. She rejects the idea that wearing the niqab can be a 'choice', saying that it is not a *genuine* choice. This argument paints Muslim women as victims too stupefied by their culture to make their

own sartorial choices – victims who must be uplifted, not by the state but by white European feminism.

6   A prime example of this is Robert Jensen's *Getting Off: Pornography and the End of Masculinity* (2007).

7   The story goes that by advocating for the rights of sex workers, third-wave feminism cannot advocate for victims of trafficking. But the real story is much more complicated. Anti-trafficking campaigns must be coordinated with the military-industrial complex. Victims of trafficking do not have their lack of agency stamped on their foreheads, so when they come forward, they are often prosecuted as illegal sex *workers* and not sex *slaves*.

8   This is a contentious statement as many classical revolutionary Marxists disagree with the idea that infrastructural elements persist after the transformation of the base. However, I think it is dangerously mechanical to imagine that the social arrangements of the old system spontaneously combust after a revolution. Even Lenin wrote that the transformation of many attitudes would take at least a generation (see Lenin 2014). On the other hand, the anti-Marxist, anti-materialist notion that modern life still retains patriarchal gender relations left over from feudalism seems implausible.

9   For a brief overview of the ethical problems associated with genital surgery on infants and children, see Creighton et al. (2014). For a longer analysis, see Kessler (1998).

10 See Marx, *The German Ideology* (in Marx and Engels 1975c: especially 21–37).

11 The idea of the Anthropocene (that environmental crisis is caused by the existence of humans), for example, does not explain why our humanity has only become a real problem in the past 2,000 years, when homo sapiens have been in existence more along the lines of 200,000 years.

12 For an excellent analysis of the logic of capitalist development and its role in organizing environmental crises, see Angus and Butler (2011).

13 Antonio Gramsci's terms 'war of position' and 'war of maneuver' refer to his assessment of the openings for anti-capitalist struggle in democratic civil societies. Wars of maneuver occur when a class engages the state by force. Wars of position are the disruption of hegemony (popular consent) through cultural or non-physical means. Gramsci argued that the material conditions of civil societies generally produce extended periods in wars of position. However, intellectuals have expanded the concept to imply that any criticism of any normative aspect of modern democracy is tantamount to a war of position, including, for example, queer critiques of heteronormativity in video games, making sure women are appointed presidents of universities, buying local and eating organic. I would argue

that a war of position does not include every small change in the status quo. A war of position means something more akin to popularizing explanations of capitalist economics and their relation to everyday life, using media to build global solidarity with an eye towards wars of maneuver. It is a quality-to-quantity dynamic (see Gramsci 2003).

14 Heather Brown shows that, for Marx, natural means 'spontaneously emerging' and 'as a consequence' more often than it means something biologically or teleologically given (see Brown 2013: 39).

15 Marx, *Economic and Philosophical Manuscripts. Third Manuscript: Private Property and Labor* in Marx and Engels 1975a: 290–3.

16 Marx's analysis of Fleur de Marie and Louise Sorel can be found in *The Holy Family* (Marx and Engels 1975b: especially 166–96).

17 For Brown on Marx's analysis of Fleur de Marie and Louise Sorel, see Brown (2013: 38–9).

18 In response to the argument that communism will entail a 'community of women', Marx and Engels famously remark in *The Communist Manifesto* that the bourgeois class's assumption that communism implies that women will be freely exchanged objects points to the fact that bourgeois men already treat women as privately exchanged objects.

19 Quoted from the English translation of the article in Plaut and Anderson (1999).

20 Of course, one could argue that this means women should follow a politics of respectability and rail against sex workers because they 'cheapen' women. But there is a distinction between the abstract 'worth' of sets of women as objects within a *libidinal economy* and the wages they can demand as workers in the labor market. Case in point: men also engage in sex work and appear in porn but this does not affect the ability of all men to command a wage on the market.

21 I write 'the disabled' and 'disabled people' rather than 'persons with disabilities' because I find the argument persuasive that disability is a product of social organization rather than a quality a person possesses. A person in a wheelchair does not possess a disability because they cannot climb a flight of stairs; they have been disabled because no one cared enough to build a ramp.

22 For a historical explanation of the relationship of urban development to same-sex desire, see D'Emilio and Freedman (1998).

23 For differing views on Marx's position on the family wage, see the debate between Harold Benenson and Kevin B. Anderson (see Benenson 1984).

24 For a critical reading of Weeks' argument, see Wolf (2009: especially 82–3).

25 For an analysis of low birthrates among non-sedentarized people, see Seccombe (1995).

26 For a further discussion, see Brinton (1970). However, the work of Eleanor Burke Leacock is foundational to a full analysis of Engels' ideas as applied to anthropology.

27 Personally, I am not as dismissive of Engels as Lukács, but not as celebratory as George Novack. I agree with Etienne Abrahamovici's criticism of Novack's comment: 'Materialism maintains that the objective (in nature or in society) has an existence prior to and independent of the subject.' Novack takes it too far when he argues that society exists 'independent' of the subject. Subject–object relations are dialectical. Abrahamovici's comment on the third thesis in Marx's 'Theses on Feuerbach' is clarifying: '[T]he Materialist doctrine that men are products of circumstances and upbringing, and that therefore changed men are products of other circumstances and changed upbringing, forgets that circumstances are changed precisely by men and that the educator himself must be educated.' However, I would argue that people's ability to change social circumstances is further complicated by the requirements of political organization (the actions of isolated individuals do not change circumstances) and that this organizing is also conditioned by material circumstances. The debate between Novack and Abrahamovici is reprinted in Novack (2009: 133–64). For Marx's 'Theses on Feuerbach', see Marx and Engels (1975c: 3).

28 The former corresponds with Trotsky's idea of combined and uneven development; the latter is predictive of the material situation of the Russian Revolution.

29 The sexual abuse of men by other men or women provokes different social responses than the sexual assault of women by men: either the boy/man does not come forward because he is worried that the fact of the assault will feminize him, or it is assumed that he is trying to deny homosexual desire or that assault is impossible because males are in a constant state of conscious sexual arousal. The point here is that there is no secret self that unconsciously seduces or is seduced regardless of sex or gender presentation.

30 It is possible to hold both opinions at once. One can believe that formal essences predict behavior while still believing that violating the behavior associated with one's form has the power to change it. In fact, it would logically correspond that engaging in 'unnatural practices' has material consequences.

31 Fausto-Sterling analyzes the now refuted work of French researcher Alfred Jost, who, between 1947 and 1969, developed and popularized the biological theory that female infants are formed from a lack of activity. Given the time and location of Lacan's seminars, I think it is reasonable

to imagine that Lacan's idea of woman as 'lack' might echo Jost's outdated assumptions.

32 Anti-trans crusader Cathy Brennan often refers to trans people as 'special snowflakes': 'Transgender is a collection of special snowflake individuals clinging to the same life preserver, not a class of human with defining characteristics' (see http://bugbrennan.com/2012/10/30/lets-be-honest/ (accessed 2 February 2015)).

33 Deep Green Resistance expelled transsexual persons based on a logic that connected trans bodies to anti-feminism and pro-imperialist policy. The Anglophone blogosphere lit up, with sharp debates among environmental activists (see www.decolonizingyoga.com/how-derrick-jensens-deep-green-resistance-supports-transphobia/; http://deepgreen resistance.org/en; http:/earthfirstjournal.org/newswire/2013/05/15/deep-green-transphobia/).

34 The notion that men cannot be penetrated by women, of course, requires strong cognitive dissonance. Women are not spherical beings who lack appendages.

35 This is not to say that Native American society was without gender structuring and that there were no prohibitions or limitations on gendered possibilities. I simply raise the example to show that there are other ways to envision the concept of 'choice'.

36 Additional data is taken from Haines (2008).

37 For example, Fourier responded to the incarceration of a man who raped elderly women by remarking that, in Harmony, the man's tastes would be catered to, thereby making elder rape unnecessary (Goldstein 1982: 106).

38 The New Left mantra of 'liberating desire' has been rightly criticized by psychoanalytic thought as politically ambivalent if not conceptually meaningless. The liberation of desire *qua* desire is the language of the circulation of goods under capitalism, where 'desire' as lack is displaced onto a potentially interminable series of objects. In many ways, the goal of desire is dissatisfaction. For psychoanalytic perspectives on politics and desire, see Žižek (2008); for an overview of psychoanalysis and desire, see Lacan (2007: 671–726).

39 *Batrachkas* are rural, female agricultural workers. For an analysis of relations between the Soviet government and *batrachkas*, see Farnsworth (2002).

40 Taken from Engels, 'Origin of the Family, Private Property, and the State' in Marx and Engels (1990: 129–275; italics added).

41 The book (Vogel 2014) was published at the onset of decades of neoliberal reaction. For the reception of Vogel's work, see Ferguson and McNally (2014: XVII–XL).

42 Of course, this is a tendency and not a rule. When there is not enough skilled labor – when the reserve army of skilled labor is depopulated – capitalists might make concessions to their workforce. Capitals might also give carrots to some workers to justify using sticks on others. In the US, capitalists sometimes get workers to concede benefits by marketing the job to the workers themselves: appealing to their desire for belonging, flattering them, exchanging benefits for flexibility, making the job seem fashionable or glamorous – in short, managing costs through ideological appeals to pleasure and freedom.

43 Working laborers to death can be understood here as wages being reduced to 0 percent and surplus value being 100 percent.

44 A variety of economic analyses refute that the USSR, China, and Cuba were socialist societies in the Marxist sense. These analyses characterize them in a number of competing ways: as deformed workers' states, degenerated workers' states, or as state capitalism.

45 The gendered, racist underpinnings of neighborhood safety networks are outlined in Maria Lowe's forthcoming sociological study (Lowe et al. forthcoming).

46 Of course, the complex relationship of Black queerness to Black nationalism is not the only historical difficulty here: Black queer subjects must also navigate white supremacy within queer culture. For an examination of Black queerness in relation to both Black nationalism and non-Black queer culture, see Dunning (2009).

47 For a dissection of the fallacies of neo-Malthusian populationism, see Angus and Butler (2011) and Mukherjee (2014).

48 The line of reasoning that sterilization was a way to keep social spending on poor pregnant women down is fallacious. During the age of forced sterilization, more white women in the US were impoverished than Black women (see Bureau of the Census 1976).

49 Lesbian women and trans people earn significantly less than white, cisgendered men (see Wolf 2009: 147, 155).

50 The term 'rich' here is not just a synonym for a citizen of a rich nation or someone who is rich in comparison to the surrogate they use. The cost of a surrogate in America is two to three times the average yearly US salary, or roughly equal to paying the average listing price for two houses in some small towns. In comparison, a South Asian surrogate costs merely one year's average salary. It should be remembered, however, that wealthy heterosexual couples are the standard target market for surrogates.

51 As stated above (n.11), the Anthropocene is the idea that human life itself is the cause of the planet's decline. Whereas the radical feminist Mary Daly pronounced that men were necrophiles, lovers of death and destruction

(see Daly 1990), proponents of the Anthropocene treat human existence as innately destructive and selfish. However, the Anthropocene model has no reasonable explanation for why, in the hundreds of thousands of years of human existence, ecological destruction has largely taken place in the past few hundred years.

52 By reproductive labor, I specifically mean labor that sustains the lives of workers, not just pregnancy and childbirth.

53 When a transgender man becomes pregnant, the social recognition of his manhood depends on his level of self-sufficiency. If he is self-sustaining and can support his pregnancy, pregnancy can be merged into the 'self-made man' narrative. However, if he is poor and needs assistance, this economic vulnerability inserts him into the cultural narrative of 'the weaker sex' regardless of his actual gender identity.

54 In the United States, anti-Black racism was an excuse to pay lower wages. The demonization of Black men led to Black women predominating in the workforce. As a result, Black familial relations did not grant Black men the status of patriarch in the home. For this reason, Black feminism had to chart a separate course from white feminism. Clearly, Black women would not want to argue that Black men should be integrated into the specific brand of white hetero-patriarchy developed under capitalism. However, the consequences of Black women being part of a distinct political sequence also meant that they could not simply modify the demands of other (especially white) feminisms.

55 Some examples are enlisting cis women in anti-trans papers-to-pee laws, recruiting women to slut-shame and gaslight rape survivors, and getting cis heterosexual women to refer to equality movements as 'special rights for gays' by pointing to their own economic disadvantages as mothers.

56 An economic analysis makes the dreadful sex wars of second-wave feminism unnecessary. Pornographic images of women are not what lowers women's status. Low-income women are already seen as sexually immoral and therefore always sexually available to wealthy men. Pornography is not the invention of women's position; it is the reflection of it.

3. From queer nationalism to queer Marxism

1 'If we may take an example from outside the sphere of production of material objects, a schoolmaster is a productive labourer when, in addition to belaboring the heads of his scholars, he works like a horse to enrich the school proprietor. That the latter has laid out his capital in a teaching factory, instead of in a sausage factory, does not alter the relation'

(Marx 2007: 558). Of course, globally speaking, the capitalist state is the employer of many modern schoolmasters; however, even state universities in the United States are trending towards privatization of services.

2 What Slavoj Žižek would call the 'Big Other' – that valorizing entity for whom we are all always performing and who also does not exist.

3 This rejection of the overt war of maneuver is emblematic of much post-Marxist, social-democratic thought. For the classic text, see Mouffe and Laclau (2014).

4 For a complete treatment of Barbara J. Fields' argument that race is produced through racism, and the implications of this analysis on the notion of the post-racial society, see Fields and Fields (2014).

5 For a discussion of the categorical mixing of 'female masculine' inverts and prostitutes, see Halberstam (1998: 51).

6 This desire to 'reimagine' Marx's concept of capital as something poetic and ineffable always makes for a false equivalence. If one has the money commodity, then purchases other commodities to increase one's money commodity, one is a capitalist. The idea of 'cultural capital' makes no sense in comparison to the original term. You cannot go to a stockbroker with a college diploma and exchange it for shares in silver in the hope that, when you return to the broker, he will give you three college diplomas, or triple your return. What 'cultural capital' means is 'cultural advantage': that is, those with cultural advantages can get favors done for them, can get a better salary, etc. The things that Bourdieu and others note as 'cultural capital' tend to be forms of knowledge that have the potential to make individuals more marketable to capitalists: a degree from an Ivy League institution, understanding which fork to use, and so on. It is not meaningless to investigate the mores and cultural expectations of the privileged. But that doesn't transform knowledge and material benefits into 'capital'.

7 For a broad overview of global queer diversity in the context of various historical points in capitalist development, see Drucker (2015).

8 In Frank Ripploh's 1980 German experimental autobiographical film *Taxi zum Klo*, the protagonist is excited to go to the bathhouse and then realizes in dejection that he is supposed to go to a Chile Solidarity meeting.

9 This is not only because of the militant gay movements failing to lend support to Black liberation, but also because of the newness of the concept of gay liberation to Panthers. For a first-person account of how Huey P. Newton led the charge, see Dixon and Jeffries (2012). To read Huey P. Newton's 1970 speech on the women's and gay liberation movements, see Newton and Hilliard (2002: 157–9).

10 This is the positivist, non-dialectical Comtean view of history as naturally maturing towards order and progress without the need for struggle. The

'next generation' will always solve current injustices by nature of their next-ness.

11 As a result of the group Lesbians and Gays Support the Miners being among the staunchest supporters of the UK strike, the miners later pushed the British Labour Party towards a gay rights platform. The solidarity was not built by heterosexuals proving their solidarity with queers, but by queers showing solidarity without expectation of reciprocity.

12 I say this from personal experience. In late 1995 I joined a radical queer group in Philadelphia called Grassroots Queers. At the founding meeting there was a sense of pride and relief at the decision to make a commitment *against* coalition building and towards the development of queer nationalism.

13 The chapter that is most symptomatic (in the Lacanian sense) involves Andrew Parker's scathing review of Marx and Engels' work and personal lives that begins: 'Dramatizing links between core elements of Marxist theory, moments from nineteenth-century political history, and scenes from Marx's and Engels's "private" lives, this essay suggests that Western Marxism's constitutive dependence on the category of production derives in part from an antitheatricalism, an aversion to certain forms of parody that prevents sexuality from attaining the political significance that class has long monopolized.' The essay goes on to hit all the usual anti-Marxist notes. The deductions made are often not links but leaps. For example, Parker accuses D'Emilio and Weeks of 'proceeding from what they assume to be a known and invariant category (production) in order to illuminate what is, from this perspective ... contingent (sexuality)'. Production is *exactly* what Marxists argue to be historically *variable*. And is not the very premise of queer theory that sexuality is contingent and constructed? The chapter tries to undermine Marxism as a theory and a method using ad hominem attacks on two Victorian men who failed to embrace queerness. In addition to ad hominems, Parker's case is undermined by special pleading. That queer theory's philosophical origins are Nietzsche (a misogynist), Heidegger (a Nazi), and Foucault (also accused of misogyny by prominent feminists) is never similarly 'problematized'. See Parker (1993: 19–41); see also Néron (1996).

14 The collection's opposition to theorizing gender diversity, along with queer theory's reduction of trans existence to performance and play, cemented the exclusion of trans people from the text. Both queer theory and the materialist response tended to reduce trans issues to eroticized cross-dressing.

15 Morton quotes Warner as saying: 'If you lick my nipple the world suddenly seems comparatively insignificant' (Morton 1996: 35). (Rhetorical request politely declined.)

16 It is important to note that Judith Butler, roundly criticized in the volume, would not put herself in the 'postmodern' camp alongside, for example, Jean-François Lyotard and Jean Baudrillard. Nor is Butler apolitical. Her anti-identitarian stance has been particularly fruitful in her critique of Zionism (see Butler 2012).

17 I would agree with some of Ebert's criticisms, particularly the 'ludic' character of third-wave feminist currents; however, I do not see queer theory as an unequivocal retreat in the history of social movements. Understanding 'iterability' not as play but as repetition in the sense used by Barbara Fields can put it squarely in the materialist camp.

18 For my argument on how issues of social reproduction can be taken up by queer and trans people, as well as my position on the difference between the normative/posited, classed social categories called 'woman' and the actual empirical people who can be lumped into the category, see the end of Chapter 2.

19 On the other hand, this is just one aspect of poststructuralism's Heideggerian influence, where 'By thinging, things carry out world' (Heidegger 2001: 197).

20 For the push to elevate Deleuze above Butler and Foucault as the theoretical basis for queer theory, see Hickey-Moody and Rasmussen (2009).

21 This is the subject of Gavin Brown's article 'Homonormativity: A Metropolitan Concept that Denigrates Ordinary Lives' (Brown 2012).

22 Transnormativity is a much clearer concept than homonormativity and approaches class in ways that are solidly materialist. Transnormativity is pressure to look identical to a cis person. This involves body-shaming people who do not want to or are unable to rid their bodies of secondary sex characteristics that socially identify them as the sex they were assigned at birth. In materialist terms, this means pressuring people into surgeries they do not want or could not possibly afford. The pressure to pass as cisgendered is especially difficult for non-binary trans people and for women who did not have the opportunity to go on hormone blockers before puberty. Without health insurance or state-sponsored healthcare, hormone blockers are cost prohibitive. If not covered by healthcare, the costs of trans-related surgeries for adults can range from cost prohibitive to outright impossible for someone without extraordinary wealth. At other times, transnormativity can be the social pressure to adopt stereotyped gender behaviors: for example, the suggestion that trans women should not be tomboys or that trans men should not be feminine or soft and that they should be sure to reject sartorial choices common to butch lesbians. Homonormativity, in contrast, is not pressure to pass as heterosexual; it signifies a pressure to behave in ways that are acceptable to a mythical

consensus of what white professionals expect gay people to be. Homonormative refers to professionals and business owners who live in suburban enclaves, especially those who are monogamous, have a child, and support imperialism. Alternatively, sometimes homonormative is used to describe queer couples where one partner is on the masculine side of the spectrum and the other is feminine: in other words, couples who embrace a butch/ femme dynamic.

23 Jo Freeman's 'The Tyranny of Structurelessness' is the go-to essay for understanding how structurelessness in political organizing reaffirms the hierarchies it intends to challenge (Freeman 1973).

24 Scott Lively and his book of absurdist pseudo-scholarship *The Pink Swastika* have directly influenced the global anti-gay movement. Lively is now on trial for crimes against humanity in the United States for his role in the persecution of Ugandan LGBTI people (Lively and Abrams 1995).

25 Radical queer academia may be aware of these issues on a theoretical plane. But when it comes to practical organization, an economic and political understanding of class is abandoned for a sociological one. For an excellent overview of radical queer left perspectives in the second decade of the millennium, see DeFilippis et al. (2011–12).

26 Wendy Brown argues that the problem of grounding identity in victimhood and then seeking out the state as a protector is that one puts oneself in a position of not sharing power, but being governed by a great protective other. I would argue that appealing to the charitable spirit of rich gays and lesbians follows the same destructive dynamic (Brown 1995).

27 Okay, I am equivocating using the materiality of the original trickle-down metaphor here to make a rhetorical point. Spade is not, of course, suggesting that the poor should have their meager earnings trickle up to the rich. It is true that if social conditions improved for the marginalized poor, they would certainly improve for the marginalized rich. But the very reasons that people are marginalized are the same reasons why people are rich in the first place.

28 Only 32 percent of white male same-sex couples are raising children as opposed to Black and Latino male same-sex couples, 52 and 66 percent of whom, respectively, are raising children. While 23.1 percent of white female same-sex couples are raising children, 36 and 50 percent of Black and Latino female same-sex couples, respectively, are raising children. The percentage of transgender Americans raising children are as follows: 45 percent of trans Native Americans, 40 percent of trans Latino/as and whites, and 36 percent of Black trans people. The dynamic is clear: it isn't just white middle-class gays and lesbians pushing strollers (Movement Advancement Project et al. 2011).

29 Around a quarter of children in many American southern states live in poverty.

30 Case in point: from 2009 to 2014, Under the Hood Café, a few blocks from the entrance of the Fort Hood army base in Killeen, Texas, was one of two antiwar coffee houses in the United States. Some queer people were engaged in the coffee-house movement – not as emissaries from the LGBT community, but because they were involved in socialist organizations or organizations promoting religious pacifism. One of the most decisive moments of internal dissent within the military arose when twenty-four-year-old army specialist Victor Agosto decided to protest against the war while living on base by refusing to deploy to Afghanistan, not as a conscientious objector opposed to war in general but as a political militant opposed to imperialism. While others had resisted deployment to Iraq on grounds of political injustice, such as Camilo Mejia, no one had yet mounted a campaign against going to war in Afghanistan, which was a war effort that still had a fair amount of public support. Agosto's logic was that, if he went AWOL, his protest would not be visible to other soldiers, but by refusing to deploy in front of his platoon, he might encourage the antiwar spirit. Engaging radical queer support for war resistance in the liberal city of Austin, Texas turned out to be a fairly useless endeavor. Few understood the rationale behind a potential queer movement to support a heterosexual who chose to enlist and changed his mind on political grounds, especially when they were skeptical about the value of even supporting 'their own kind' in the military. Once again, the antiwar rhetoric of radical queer politics was just that. As someone formerly involved in Agosto's campaign, I am citing my own 'lived experience' here. (And, as a side note, even Agosto's militant and public defiance of the commanding officers did not even warrant a dishonorable discharge.)

31 See note 30.

32 This statistic is from a talk given by Gopal at the 2009 Socialism Conference in Chicago.

33 The Hegel-inspired orientalist comments of Marx's early work tend to be used to write off the whole of Marx's political thought. A number of scholars have done work that counters the argument that Marx was a Eurocentric thinker (see Anderson 2010; Ahmad 2008).

34 Ahmad accuses Said of specifically setting himself up to be the agent of change. He argues that when Said makes Ranajit Guha an example of the new sort of postcolonial political agent specifically because of his move from the anticolonial upper classes to the university, he is actually referring to himself (see Ahmad 2008: 200–1).

35 'When the words of the master become the site of hybridity ... then we may not only read between the lines, but even seek to change the often coercive reality that they so lucidly contain' (quoted in Larsen 1995: 6).

36 Many criticisms of Chibber argue from shaky ground. Chris Taylor's scathing blog review of Chibber's work, 'Not even Marxist: On Vivek Chibber's Polemic Against Postcolonial Theory', is a case in point. Taylor writes: 'Chibber then defines physical well-being as freedom from "dangerous working conditions, poverty-level wages, high mortality, ill health, environmental hazards, and so on ..." ([Chibber 2013:] 203). One wonders what the "so on" covers. I'm willing to bet, though, that if we drew a portrait of this universal body of the worker, he might look a lot like me: a white male with the "normal" bodily capacities ascribed to human beings.' Paul Heideman's response on his Verso blog is apposite: 'Here, we have Taylor, quite literally, attacking Vivek *not* for what he wrote, but for *what Taylor imagines he might write* ... We have descended into the realm of the absurd here.' What I find fascinating, however – even symptomatic here – is that Taylor imagines Chibber imagining his own (Taylor's own) white body as the universal worker. That Chibber himself is not white and that he is writing about India and Indian workers, not white academics, does not seem to factor into the equation for Taylor. See 'Not Even Marxist? Paul M. Heideman examines Chris Taylor's critique of Vivek Chibber' at www.versobooks.com/blogs/1297-not-even-marx-ist-paul-m-heideman-examines-chris-taylor-s-critique-of-vivek-chibber (accessed 10 June 2015).

37 The fact that China is scrambling for resources in Africa alongside American and European interests seems to undermine the theory that colonialism and imperialism are purely Western rationalist enterprises. Nineteenth-century Japanese imperialism also troubles the model.

4. Conclusions

1 Essential nationalisms would be the opposite of the strategic, 'existential' nationalisms of anticolonial struggle.

2 I am sticking to international instead of transnational for the simple reason that the fact that nations exist is still relevant within global capitalism. Transnational describes the crossing of or transcending of borders – a real activity. Transnational*ism* is ambivalent in that it implies the political movement to transcend or 'move beyond' the nation-state, which could be either communist or capitalist. In other words, I use international in a non-prescriptive sense.

3 An idea developed throughout his work, especially in *Saint Paul: The Foundation of Universalism* (Badiou 2003).

4 For an explanation of the analogy between racism and witch trials, see 'Witchcraft and Racecraft: Invisible Ontology in its Sensible Manifestations' in Fields and Fields (2014: 193–224).

5 The turn towards analyzing epistemologies of ignorance is valuable to political development, especially within the dialectic of political organizing – where the political collective confronts its own inability to build critical mass due to cultivated ignorance. Critical race theory's criticisms of Marxist blind spots might be valuable in this one respect. While it is material social relations that set ideological forces in motion, discussions of consciousness are inevitable in political organizing. Reductive standpoint epistemologies that treat positions as essences or that see a direct causal link between location and knowledge are unhelpful for political organizing. In other words, a particular standpoint might make knowledge possible, but such knowledge is rarely inevitable (see Mills 1997).

6 'Birth spacing in gathering and hunting bands averages three or four years, as prolonged and vigorous nursing suppresses ovulation, thus permitting mothers to remain mobile as food-gatherers throughout their childbearing years ... only under sedentary conditions do birth intervals shorten' (Seccombe 1995: 17).

7 Lacan's work is solidly opposed to biological determinism and goes to great lengths to acknowledge that the phallus/lack paradigm is not representative of genitals. However, I would argue that this break is not complete, but a social abstraction of existing assumptions (including biological assumptions) within the bourgeois nuclear family. The sticky problem with divorcing the conceptual from the anatomical is that when real people undergo psychoanalysis or when it is used to analyze a social whole, the pure logic of phallus/lack is used to explain the lives of people whose secondary sex characteristics have already caused them to be sorted into social genders.

8 We sell gendered bodies on the market, and the labor we do has physical effects on bodily processes, so, in this sense, social gender shapes sexed bodies. One iconic example of labor gendering the body is when the protagonist, Jess, a self-identified butch unloading trucks on the docks, worries about how laboring on the docks in the winter injures and hardens the exposed parts of the bodies of the other workers (Feinberg 1993: 75).

9 Michelle Alexander notes that the maintenance of racism does not require racial hatred; it only requires that the injustices continue to be ignored.

10 This is also discussed at length in Floyd (2009).

11 The rate of sexual assault, suicide, and murder of LGBTQ people is astronomical, with gender non-conforming people bearing the brunt of violence from the general population and from law enforcement. This violence is not abating with legal progress: in the United States, statistics show that it may even be increasing (see National Coalition of Anti-Violence Programs 2014).

12 The difficulty with labeling the binary as automatically a problem is featured in Serano (2007; 2013).

13 See 'Trans Women: There's No Conundrum About It' in Serano (2013: 43–7).

Bibliography

Abu-Lughod, Janet (1989) *Before European Hegemony: The World System A.D. 1250–1350*. New York NY: Oxford University Press.

Ahmad, Aijaz (2008) *In Theory: Nations, Classes, Literatures*. London: Verso.

Ainsworth, Claire (2015) 'Sex Redefined', *Nature* 518: 288–91.

Aldrich, Robert (2003) *Homosexuality and Colonization*. New York NY: Routledge.

Alexander, Michelle (2012) *The New Jim Crow: Mass Incarceration in an Age of Colorblindness*. New York NY: The New Press.

Althusser, Louis (2006) *For Marx*. London: Verso.

Anderson, Kevin (1999) 'Marx on Suicide in the Context of His Other Writings on Alienation and Gender' in Eric Plaut and Kevin Anderson (eds) *Marx on Suicide*. Evanston IL: Northwestern University Press.

— (2010) *Marx at the Margins: On Nationalism, Ethnicity, and Non-Western Societies*. Chicago IL: University of Chicago Press.

Angus, Ian and Simon Butler (2011) *Too Many People? Population, Immigration, and the Environmental Crisis*. Chicago IL: Haymarket Books.

Anievas, Alexander and Kerem Nisancioglu (2013) 'What's at Stake in the Transition Debate? Rethinking the Origins of Capitalism and the "Rise of the West"', *Millennium: Journal of International Studies* 41(1): 78–102.

Aston, T. H. and C. H. E. Philpin (1987) *The Brenner Debate: Agrarian Class Structure and Economic Development in Pre-industrial Europe*. Cambridge: Cambridge University Press.

Aucoin, Michael William and Richard Wassersug (2006) 'The Sexuality and Social Performance of Androgen Deprived (Castrated) Men Throughout History: Implications to Modern Day Cancer Patients', *Social Science & Medicine* 63(12): 3162–73.

Austin, J. L. (1975) *How to Do Things With Words*. Oxford: Oxford University Press.

Badiou, Alain (2001) *Ethics: An Essay on the Understanding of Evil.* London: Verso.

— (2003) *Saint Paul: The Foundation of Universalism*. Redwood City CA: Stanford University Press.

— (2006) *Polemics*. London: Verso.

— (2007) *The Century*. Cambridge: Polity Press.

— (2012) *The Rebirth of History: Times of Riots and Uprisings*. London: Verso.

Banaji, Jairus (2010) *Theory as History: Essays on Modes of Production and Exploitation*. Leiden: Brill.

Baudrillard, Jean (1975) *The Mirror of Production*. St Louis MO: Telos Press.

— (1994) *The Illusion of the End*. Cambridge: Polity Press.

Bell, Daniel (1996) *The Cultural Contradictions of Capitalism: Twentieth Anniversary Edition*. New York NY: Basic Books.

Benenson, Harold (1984) 'A Reply', *International Labor and Working-Class History* 26 (Fall): 45–51.

Benston, Margaret (1989) 'The Political Economy of Women's Liberation: A Reprint', *Monthly Review* 41(7): 31–43.

Bernstein, Eduard (1961) *Evolutionary Socialism: The Classic Statement of Democratic Socialism*. 2nd edition. New York NY: Schocken Books.

Bérubé, Allan (2011) *My Desire for History: Essays in Gay Community and Labor History*. Chapel Hill NC: University of North Carolina Press.

Best, Steven (1989) 'Jameson, Totality, and the Poststructuralist Critique' in Douglas Kellner (ed.) *Postmodernism/Jameson/Critique*, Washington DC: Maisonneuve Press.

Bhabha, Homi (1994) *The Location of Culture*. New York NY: Routledge.

Bozorgnia, S. M. H. (1998) *The Role of Precious Metals in European Economic Development: From Roman Times to the Eve of the Industrial Revolution*. Westport CT: Greenwood Press.

Brinton, Maurice (1970) 'The Irrational in Politics', *Solidarity Pamphlet* 33, June; 2nd edition, August 1975.

Brown, Gavin (2012) 'Homonormativity: A Metropolitan Concept that Denigrates Ordinary Lives', *Journal of Homosexuality* 59: 1065–72.

Brown, Heather (2013) *Marx on Gender and the Family: A Critical Study*. Chicago IL: Haymarket Books.

Brown, Wendy (1995) *States of Injury: Power and Freedom in Late Modernity*. Princeton NJ: Princeton University Press.

Bureau of the Census (1976) *A Statistical Portrait of Women in the United States*. Current Population Reports, Special Studies Series P-32, No. 58. Washington DC: Bureau of the Census (Department of Commerce).

Burkett, Paul (2014) *Marx and Nature: A Red and Green Perspective*. Chicago IL: Haymarket Books.

Bustelo, Jack (1954) 'Sagging Cosmetic Lines Try a Face Lift', *The Militant*.

Butler, Judith (1990) *Gender Trouble: Feminism and the Subversion of Identity*. New York NY: Routledge.

— (1993) *Bodies That Matter: On the Discursive Limits of Sex*. Abingdon and New York NY: Routledge.

— (1997) *Excitable Speech: A Politics of the Performative*. New York NY: Routledge.

— (2012) *Parting Ways: Jewishness and the Critique of Zionism*. New York NY: Columbia University Press.

Caffentzis, George (1999) 'The End of Work or the Renaissance of Slavery? A Critique of Rifkin and Negri', *Common Sense: Journal of the Edinburgh Conference of Socialist Economists* 24: 20–38.

Cahnman, Werner J. and Rudolf Heberle (eds) (1971) *Ferdinand Tönnies on Sociology: Pure, Applied, and Empirical. Selected Writings*. Chicago IL: Chicago University Press.

Cameron, D. Ewen (1948) *Life is for Living*. New York NY: Macmillan.

Campbell, Kirsten (2004) *Jacques Lacan and Feminist Epistemology*. London: Routledge.

Carter, David (2004) *Stonewall: The Riots That Sparked the Gay Revolution*. New York NY: St Martin's Press.

Casey, Edward S. and Mary Watkins (2014) 'Juan Crow: The American Ethnoracial Caste System and the Criminalization of Mexican Migrants' in *Up Against the Wall: Re-imagining the U.S.–Mexico Border*. Austin TX: University of Texas Press.

Chakrabarty, Dipesh (2000) *Provincializing Europe: Postcolonial Thought and Historical Difference*. Princeton NJ: Princeton University Press.

Chatterjee, Partha (1993) *The Nation and its Fragments: Colonial and Postcolonial Histories*. Princeton NJ: Princeton University Press.

Chibber, Vivek (2013) *Postcolonial Theory and the Specter of Capital*. London: Verso.

Creighton, Sarah M., Lina Michala, Imran Mushtaq and Michal Yaron (2014) 'Childhood Surgery for Ambiguous Genitalia: Glimpses of Practice Changes or More of the Same?', *Psychology & Sexuality* 5(1): 34–43.

Croom, J. Halliday (1898–99) 'Two Cases of Mistaken Sex in Adult Life', *Transactions of the Edinburgh Obstetrical Society* 24: 102–4.

D'Emilio, John (1983) *Sexual Politics, Sexual Communities: The Making of a Homosexual Minority in the United States, 1940–1970*. Chicago IL: University of Chicago Press.

— (1998) *Sexual Politics, Sexual Communities: The Making of a Homosexual Minority in the United States, 1940–1970*. 2nd edition with a new preface and afterword. Chicago IL: University of Chicago Press.

— and Estelle B. Freedman (1998) *Intimate Matters: A History of Sexuality in America*. 2nd edition. Chicago IL: University of Chicago Press.

Dalla Costa, Mariarosa and Selma James (1972) *The Power of Women and the Subversion of the Community*. Bristol: Falling Wall Press.

Daly, Mary (1990) *Gyn/Ecology: The Metaethics of Radical Feminism*. Boston MA: Beacon Press.

Davidson, Neil (2012) *How Revolutionary Were the Bourgeois Revolutions?* Chicago IL: Haymarket Books.

Davis, Angela Y. (1983) *Women, Race, and Class*. New York NY: Random House.

DeFilippis, Joseph N., Lisa Duggan, Kenyon Farrow and Richard Kim (guest eds) (2011–12) *A New Queer Agenda: The Scholar & Feminist Online*, issue 10.1–10.2 (Fall 2011/Spring 2012). Available at http://sfonline.barnard.edu/a-new-queer-agenda/.

Deleuze, Gilles and Félix Guattari (1983) *Anti-Oedipus: Capitalism and Schizophrenia*. Minneapolis MN: University of Minnesota Press.

— — (1987) *A Thousand Plateaus: Capitalism and Schizophrenia*. Minneapolis MN: University of Minnesota Press.

Dixon, Aaron and Judson L. Jeffries (2012) *My People Are Rising: Memoir of a Black Panther Party Captain*. Chicago IL: Haymarket Books.

Draper, Hal (1966) 'The Two Souls of Socialism', *New Politics* 5(1): 57–84.

Drucker, Peter (2015) *Warped: Gay Normality and Queer Anti-Capitalism*. Leiden: Brill.

Duggan, Lisa (2002) 'The New Homonormativity: The Sexual Politics of Neoliberalism' in Russ Castronovo and Dana D. Nelson (eds)

Materializing Democracy: Towards a Revitalized Cultural Politics. Durham NC: Duke University Press.

Dunning, Stephanie K. (2009) *Queer in Black and White: Interraciality, Same Sex Desire, and Contemporary African American Culture.* Bloomington IN: Indiana University Press.

Ebert, Teresa (1995) '(Untimely) Critiques for a Red Feminism', *Transformation* 1 (Spring).

Eklof, Ben (2008) 'Russian Literacy Campaigns 1861–1939' in Robert F. Arnove and Harvey J. Graff (eds) *National Literacy Campaigns and Movements: Historical and Comparative Perspectives.* New Brunswick NJ: Transaction Publishers.

Engels, Frederick (1973) 'Origins of the Family, Private Property, and the State' in *Marx-Engels Selected Works.* Volume 3. Moscow: Progress Publishers.

Fanon, Frantz (1963a) *The Wretched of the Earth.* New York NY: Grove Press.

— (1963b) 'The Trials and Tribulations of National Consciousness' in *The Wretched of the Earth.* New York NY: Grove Press.

Farnsworth, Beatrice (2002) 'The Rural Batrachka (Hired Agricultural Laborer) and the Soviet Campaign to Unionize Her', *Journal of Women's History* 14(1): 64–83.

Fausto-Sterling, Anne (2000) *Sexing the Body: Gender Politics and the Construction of Sexuality.* New York NY: Basic Books.

Federici, Silvia (2003) *Caliban and the Witch: Women, the Body and Primitive Accumulation.* New York NY: Autonomedia.

— (2012) *Revolution at Point Zero: Housework, Reproduction, and Feminist Struggle.* Oakland CA: PM Press.

Feinberg, Leslie (1993) *Stone Butch Blues: A Novel.* New York NY: Alyson Books.

Ferguson, Ann and Nancy Folbre (1981) 'The Unhappy Marriage of Patriarchy and Capitalism' in Lydia Sargent (ed.) *Women and Revolution: A Discussion of the Unhappy Marriage of Marxism and Feminism.* Boston MA: South End Press.

Ferguson, Susan and David McNally (2014) 'Capital, Labour-Power, and Gender-Relations: Introduction to the Historical Materialism Edition of *Marxism and the Oppression of Women*' in Lise Vogel, *Marxism and the Oppression of Women: Towards a Unity Theory.* Chicago IL: Haymarket Books.

Fields, Barbara J. (1990) 'Slavery, Race, and Ideology in the United States of America', *New Left Review* 181 (May–June): 95–118.

Fields, Karen E. and Barbara J. Fields (2014) *Racecraft: The Soul of Inequality in American Life*. London: Verso.

Firestone, Shulamith (2003) *Dialectic of Sex: The Case for Feminist Revolution*. New York NY: Farrar, Straus, and Giroux.

Floyd, Kevin (2009) *Reification of Desire: Towards a Queer Marxism*. Minneapolis MN: University of Minnesota Press.

Foster, John Bellamy (2000) *Marx's Ecology, Materialism and Nature*. New York NY: Monthly Review Press.

Fourier, Charles (1996) *Fourier: The Theory of the Four Movements*. Cambridge: Cambridge University Press.

Freeman, Jo (1973) 'The Tyranny of Structurelessness' in Anne Koedt, Ellen Levine and Anita Rapone (eds) *Radical Feminism*. New York NY: Quadrangle.

Friedan, Betty (2001) *The Feminine Mystique*. New York NY: W. W. Norton & Company.

Fukuyama, Francis (1992) *The End of History and the Last Man*. London: Penguin Books.

Giallombardo, Rose (1974) *The Social World of Imprisoned Girls: A Comparative Study of Institutions for Juvenile Delinquents*. New York NY: John Wiley and Sons.

Gimenez, Martha E. (2005) 'Capitalism and the Oppression of Women: Marx Revisited', *Science & Society* 69(1) 'Marxist-Feminist Thought Today': 11–32.

Goldstein, Leslie F. (1982) 'Early Feminist Themes in French Utopian Socialism: The St.-Simonians and Fourier', *Journal of the History of Ideas* 43(1): 91–108.

Gramsci, Antonio (2003) *Selections from the Prison Notebooks*. Edited by Q. Hoare and G. Nowell Smith. New York NY: International Publishers.

Grant, Jaime M., Lisa A. Mottet, Justin Tanis, Jack Harrison, Jody L. Herman and Mara Keisling (2011) *Injustice at Every Turn: A Report of the National Transgender Discrimination Survey*. Washington DC: National Center for Transgender Equality and National Gay and Lesbian Task Force.

Guha, Ranajit (1998) *Dominance Without Hegemony: History and Power in Colonial India*. Cambridge MA: Harvard University Press.

Haines, Michael (2008) 'Fertility and Mortality in the United States', EH.Net, edited by Robert Whaples. Available at http://eh.net/encyclopedia/fertility-and-mortality-in-the-united-states/.

Halberstam, Judith (1998) *Female Masculinity*. Durham NC: Duke University Press.

Hall, Donald A. (2003) *Queer Theories*. Basingstoke: Palgrave Macmillan.

Hallas, Duncan (1986) 'Marx and Politics', *Socialist Review* 83: 17–19.

Hansen, Joseph and Evelyn Reed (1986) *Cosmetics, Fashions, and the Exploitation of Women*. New York NY: Pathfinder Press.

Hardt, Michael and Antonio Negri (2001) *Empire*. Cambridge MA: Harvard University Press.

—— (2004) *Multitude: War and Democracy in the Age of Empire*. London: Hamish Hamilton.

Hartmann, Heidi (1979) 'The Unhappy Marriage of Marxism to Feminism: Towards a More Progressive Union', *Capital & Class* 3(2): 1–33.

Harvey, David (forthcoming) 'Crisis Theory and the Falling Rate of Profit' in Turan Subasat and John Weeks (eds) *The Great Meltdown of 2008: Systemic, Conjunctural or Policy-created?* Cheltenham: Edward Elgar. Available at davidharvey.org.

Hegel, Georg Wilhelm Friedrich (1967) *Hegel's Philosophy of Right*. Oxford: Oxford University Press.

Heidegger, Martin (1971) 'Language' in *Poetry, Language, Thought*. New York NY: Harper & Row.

— (1978) 'Letter on Humanism' in *Basic Writings: Nine Key Essays, Plus the Introduction to* Being and Time. Translated by David Farrell Krell. London: Routledge.

— (2001) *Poetry, Language, Thought*. New York NY: HarperCollins.

Henning, Christoph (2014) *Philosophy After Marx: 100 Years of Misreadings and the Normative Turn in Political Philosophy*. Leiden: Brill.

Hickey-Moody, Anna and Mary Lou Rasmussen (2009) 'The Sexed Subject In-between Deleuze and Butler' in Chrysanthi Nigianni and Merl Storr (eds) *Deleuze and Queer Theory*. Edinburgh: Edinburgh University Press.

Hilferding, Rudolph (2006) *Finance Capital: A Study in the Latest Phase of Capitalist Development*. London: Routledge.

Ho, David Y. F. (2000) 'Dialectical Thinking: Neither Eastern nor Western', *American Psychologist* 55(9): 1064–5.

Hobson, John M. (2004) *The Eastern Origins of Western Civilization*. Cambridge: Cambridge University Press.

Hollibaugh, Amber and Cherrie Moraga (1981) 'What We're Rollin' Around in Bed With: Sexual Silences in Feminism', *Heresies* 12.

Hook, Sidney (1994) *From Hegel to Marx*. New York NY: Columbia University Press.

Institute of Demography at the National Research University Higher School of Economics (2015) 'The First National Census of the Russian Empire in 1897: Distribution of the Population by Religion and Region', Демоскоп *Weekly* 655–6 (21 September–4 October). Available at http://demoscope.ru/weekly/ssp/rus_rel_97.php.

Irigaray, Luce (1985) *This Sex Which Is Not One*. Ithaca NY: Cornell University Press.

Jensen, Robert (2007) *Getting Off: Pornography and the End of Masculinity*. Boston MA: South End Press.

Kampwirth, Karen (2004) *Feminism and the Legacy of Revolution: Nicaragua, El Salvador, Chiapas*. Athens OH: Ohio University Press.

Kautsky, Karl (1910) *The Class Struggle: Erfurt Program*. Chicago IL: C. H. Kerr & Company.

Kennedy, Elizabeth Lapovsky and Madeline D. Davis (1993) *Boots of Leather, Slippers of Gold: The History of a Lesbian Community*. New York NY: Routledge.

Kennedy, Hubert (2005) *Karl Heinrich Ulrichs: Pioneer of the Modern Gay Movement*. 2nd edition. Concord CA: Peremptory Publications.

Kessler, Suzanne J. (1998) *Lessons from the Intersexed*. New Brunswick NJ: Rutgers University Press.

Kirsch, Max H. (2000) *Queer Theory and Social Change*. London: Routledge.

Klein, Naomi (2007) *The Shock Doctrine: The Rise of Disaster Capitalism*. New York NY: Picador.

Kliman, Andrew (2011) *The Failure of Capitalist Production: Underlying Causes of the Great Recession*. London: Pluto Press.

Knight, Michael Muhammad (2009) *The Taqwacores*. New York NY: Soft Skull Press.

Kojève, Alexandre (1980) *Introduction to the Reading of Hegel*. Ithaca NY: Cornell University Press.

Kon, Igor (1995) *The Sexual Revolution in Russia: From the Age of Czars to Today*. New York NY: The Free Press/Simon & Schuster.

Kranz G. S., A. Hahn, U. Kaufmann, M. Küblböck, A. Hummer, S. Ganger, R. Seiger, D. Winkler, D. F. Swaab, C. Windischberger, S. Kasper and R. Lanzenberger (2014) 'White Matter Microstructure in Transsexuals and Controls Investigated by Diffusion Tensor Imaging', *Journal of Neuroscience* 34(46): 15466–75.

Krivickas, Kristy M. and Daphne Lofquist (2011) 'Demographics of Same-Sex Couple Households With Children'. Presented at the Annual Meeting of the Population Association of America, Washington DC, 31 March–2 April. Available at www.census.gov/hhes/samesex/data/acs.html.

Lacan, Jacques (2007) *Ecrits: The First Complete Edition in English*. Translated by Bruce Fink. New York NY: W. W. Norton & Co.

Ladurie, Emmanuel Le Roy (1981) 'A Concept: The Unification of the Globe by Disease (Fourteenth to Seventeenth Centuries)' in *The Mind and Method of the Historian*, Chicago IL: University of Chicago Press.

Laqueur, Thomas (1992) *Making Sex: Body and Gender from the Greeks to Freud*. Cambridge MA: Harvard University Press.

Larsen, Neil (1995) 'Determination: Postcolonialism, Poststructuralism, and the Problem of Ideology', *Dispositio/n* XX(47): 1–16.

Lasch, Christopher (1976) 'The Family as a Haven in a Heartless World', *Salmagundi* 35 (Fall): 42–55.

Laxmi, R. Raj Rao and P. G. Joshi (2015) *Me Hijra, Me Laxmi*. New Delhi: Oxford University Press India.

Leacock, Eleanor Burke (2008) *Myths of Male Dominance: Collected Articles on Women Cross-culturally*. Chicago IL: Haymarket Books.

Leeb, Claudia (2007) 'Marx and the Gendered Structure of Capitalism', *Philosophy and Social Criticism* 33(7): 833–59.

Lemke, Thomas (2009) *Foucault, Governmentality, and Critique*. Boulder CO: Paradigm.

Lenin, Vladimir (1933) 'The Emancipation of Women' in *Writings of V. I. Lenin*. New York NY: International Publishers.

— (1992) *The State and Revolution*. London: Penguin Books.

— (2010) *Imperialism: The Highest Stage of Capitalism*. London: Penguin Books.

— (2014) *State and Revolution*. Chicago IL: Haymarket Books.

Lévi-Strauss, Claude (1969) *The Elementary Structures of Kinship*. Boston MA: Beacon Press.

Levinas, Emmanuel (2011) 'Ethics and the Face' in *Totality and Infinity: An Essay on Exteriority*. 4th edition. New York NY: Springer.

Levy, Ariel (2005) *Female Chauvinist Pigs: Women and the Rise of Raunch Culture*. New York NY: Free Press.

Littlewood, Roland and Antonia Young (2005) 'The Third Sex in Albania: An Ethnographic Note' in Alison Shaw and Shirley Ardener (eds) *Changing Sex and Bending Gender*. New York NY and Oxford: Berghahn Books.

Lively, Scott and Kevin Abrams (1995) *The Pink Swastika: Homosexuality in the Nazi Party*. Sacramento CA: Veritas Aeternas Press.

Lopes, Ann and Gary Roth (2000) *Men's Feminism: August Bebel and the German Socialist Movement*. Amherst NY: Humanity Books.

Lowe, Lisa (1996) *Immigrant Acts: On Asian American Cultural Politics*. Durham NC: Duke University Press.

Lowe, Maria R., Angela Stroud and Alice Nguyen (forthcoming) 'Suspicious Person or Neighbor? Heightened Surveillance of Black Men on a Predominantly White Neighborhood Listserv'. Paper submitted to *Social Currents* and presented at the 2014 American Sociological Association meeting in San Francisco.

Lukács, Georg (1972) *History and Class Consciousness: Studies in Marxist Dialectics*. Cambridge MA: MIT Press.

Luxemburg, Rosa (2007) 'Reform or Revolution' in Helen Scott (ed.) *The Essential Rosa Luxemburg: Reform or Revolution and the Mass Strike*. Chicago IL: Haymarket Books.

Magrini, Tullia (2003) *Music and Gender: Perspectives from the Mediterranean*. Chicago IL: University of Chicago Press.

Marcuse, Herbert (1964) *One-Dimensional Man*. London: Routledge & Kegan Paul.

— (2005) *Heideggerian Marxism*. Lincoln NE: University of Nebraska Press.

Martin, Fran, Peter Jackson, Mark McLelland and Audrey Yue (eds) (2008) *AsiaPacifiQueer: Rethinking Genders and Sexualities*. Champaign IL: University of Illinois Press.

Martin, Wednesday (2015) *Primates of Park Avenue: A Memoir*. New York NY: Simon & Schuster.

Marx, Karl (1913) *The Eighteenth Brumaire of Louis Bonaparte*. Chicago IL: C. H. Kerr & Company.

— (1973) *The Poverty of Philosophy*. New York NY: International Publishers.

— (1978a) *Capital: A Critique of Political Economy*. Moscow: Progress Publishers.

— (1978b) 'Critique of the Gotha Program' in *The Marx-Engels Reader*. 2nd edition. New York NY: W. W. Norton & Company, pp. 528–32.

— (1978c) 'The German Ideology' in Robert Tucker (ed.) *The Marx-Engels Reader*. New York NY: W. W. Norton & Company.

— (1978d) 'Theses on Feuerbach' in Robert Tucker (ed.) *The Marx-Engels Reader*. New York NY: W. W. Norton & Company.

— (1982) *Critique of Hegel's 'Philosophy of Right'*. Cambridge: Cambridge University Press.

— (1993) *Grundrisse: Foundations of the Critic of Political Economy*. New York NY: Penguin Books.

— (2007) *Capital: A Critique of Political Economy: Volume 1, Part II*. New York NY: Cosimo Classics.

— and Frederick Engels (1942) *The Selected Correspondence of Karl Marx and Frederick Engels: 1846–1895*. New York NY: International Publishers.

— — (1975a) *Marx Engels Collected Works. Volume 3*. London: Lawrence & Wishart.

— — (1975b) *Marx Engels Collected Works. Volume 4*. London: Lawrence & Wishart.

— — (1975c) *Marx Engels Collected Works. Volume 5*. London: Lawrence & Wishart.

— — (1976) *Marx Engels Collected Works. Volume 6*. London: Lawrence & Wishart.

— — (1979) *Marx Engels Collected Works. Volume 11*. London: Lawrence & Wishart.

— — (1985) *Marx Engels Collected Works. Volume 20*. London: Lawrence & Wishart.

— — (1987a) *Marx Engels Collected Works. Volume 25*. London: Lawrence & Wishart.

— — (1987b) *Marx Engels Collected Works. Volume 42*. London: Lawrence & Wishart.

— — (1989) *Marx Engels Collected Works. Volume 24*. London: Lawrence & Wishart.

— — (1990) *Marx Engels Collected Works. Volume 26*. London: Lawrence & Wishart.

—— (1996) *Marx Engels Collected Works. Volume 35.* London: Lawrence & Wishart.

—— (1997) *Marx Engels Collected Works. Volume 36.* London: Lawrence & Wishart.

McIntosh, Peggy (1989) 'White Privilege: Unpacking the Invisible Knapsack', *Peace and Freedom Magazine*, July/August: 10–12. Available at http://nationalseedproject.org/white-privilege-unpacking-the-invisible-knapsack.

McNally, David (2010) *Global Slump: The Economics and Politics of Crisis and Resistance.* Oakland CA: PM Press.

Millett, Kate (2000) *Sexual Politics.* Champaign IL: University of Illinois Press.

Mills, Charles W. (1997) *The Racial Contract.* Ithaca NY: Cornell University Press.

Mirandé, Alfredo (2013) 'Transgender Identity and Acceptance in a Global Era: The Muxes of Juchitán' in Joseph Gelfer (ed.) *Masculinities in a Global Era.* New York NY: Springer.

Mitchell, Juliet (1984) *Women: The Longest Revolution.* New York NY: Random House.

Morton, Donald (ed.) (1996) *The Material Queer: A LesBiGay Reader.* Boulder CO: Westview Press.

Mouffe, Chantal and Ernesto Laclau (2014) *Hegemony and Socialist Strategy: Towards a Radical Democratic Politics.* London: Verso.

Movement Advancement Project, Family Equality Council and Center for American Progress (2011) *All Children Matter: How Legal and Social Inequalities Hurt LGBT Families.* Denver CO: Movement Advancement Project. Available at www.lgbtmap.org/file/all-children-matter-full-report.pdf.

Mukherjee, Krittivas (2014) 'Death by Sterilization in India: Chhattisgarh Is Just One Horror', *Hindustan Times*, 12 November.

Mulvey, Laura (2009) *Visual and Other Pleasures.* New York NY: Palgrave Macmillan.

Murray, Stephen O. and Will Roscoe (1998) *Boy-Wives and Female Husbands: Studies in African Homosexualities.* New York NY: Palgrave Macmillan.

Nation, R. Craig (2009) *War on War: Lenin, the Zimmerwald Left, and the Origins of the Communist International.* Chicago IL: Haymarket Books.

National Coalition of Anti-Violence Programs (2014) *Lesbian, Gay, Bisexual, Transgender, Queer, and HIV-Affected Hate Violence in 2013*. New York NY: National Coalition of Anti-Violence Programs.

Néron, Josée (1996) 'Momies et Mommies: Misogynie de Foucault et Politique Maternelle', *Nouvelles Questions Féministes* 17(4): 45–95.

Nestle, Joan (1992) *The Persistent Desire: A Femme-Butch Reader*. New York NY: Alyson Books.

Newton, Huey P. and David Hilliard (2002) *The Huey P. Newton Reader*. New York NY: Seven Stories Press.

Norton, Michael I. and Samuel R. Sommers (2011) 'Whites See Racism as a Zero-Sum Game That They Are Now Losing', *Perspectives on Psychological Science* 6: 215–18.

Novack, George (2009) *Polemics in Marxist Philosophy*. Atlanta GA: Pathfinder Press.

Pallares, Amalia (2015) *Family Activism: Immigrant Struggles and the Politics of Noncitizenship*. New Brunswick NJ: Rutgers University Press.

Parker, Andrew (1993) 'Unthinking Sex: Marx, Engels, and the Scene of Writing' in Michael Warner (ed.) *Fear of a Queer Planet*. Minneapolis MN: University of Minnesota Press.

Peng, Kaiping and Richard E. Nisbett (1999) 'Culture, Dialectics, and Reasoning about Contradiction', *American Psychologist* 54(9): 741–54.

Penney, James (2013) *After Queer Theory: The Limits of Sexual Politics*. London: Pluto Press.

Plaut, Eric and Kevin Anderson (eds) (1999) *Marx on Suicide*. Evanston IL: Northwestern University Press.

Poniatowska, Elena (1995) *Nobody, Nothing: The Voices of the Mexico City Earthquake*. Philadelphia PA: Temple University Press.

Post, Charlie and Jane Slaughter (2000) 'Lean Production: Why Work is Worse Than Ever, and What's the Alternative? A Solidarity Working Paper', Detroit MI: Solidarity.

Power, Nina (2009) *One-Dimensional Woman*. Ropley, UK: Zero Books.

Puar, Jasbir (2007) *Terrorist Assemblages: Homonationalism in Queer Times*. Durham NC: Duke University Press.

— (2013) 'Rethinking Homonationalism', *International Journal of Middle Eastern Studies* 45: 336–9.

Queen, Carol (1997) *Real Live Nude Girl: Chronicles of Sex-positive Culture*. Pittsburgh PA: Cleis Press.

Rawls, John (1971) *A Theory of Justice*. Cambridge MA: The Belknap Press.

Raymond, Janice (1979) *The Transsexual Empire: The Making of the She-male*. Boston MA: Beacon Press.

Revathi, A (2010) *The Truth About Me: A Hijra Life Story*. Gurgaon: Penguin Books India.

Riasanovsky, Nicholas Valentine (1969) *The Teaching of Charles Fourier*. Berkeley CA: University of California Press.

Rorty, Richard (1989) *Contingency, Irony, Solidarity*. Cambridge: Cambridge University Press.

Rubin, Gayle (2011) *Deviations: A Gayle Rubin Reader*. Durham NC: Duke University Press.

Sargent, Lydia (ed.) (1981) *Women and Revolution: A Discussion of the Unhappy Marriage of Feminism and Marxism*. Boston MA: South End Press.

Sartre, Jean-Paul (1957) *Being and Nothingness*. New York NY: Methuen.

— (1991) *Critique of Dialectical Reason*. London: Verso.

— (1993 [1965]) *Essays in Existentialism*, Part II. New York NY: Citadel Press.

Scott, Helen (ed.) (2007) *The Essential Rosa Luxemburg: Reform or Revolution and The Mass Strike*. Chicago IL: Haymarket Books.

Seccombe, Wally (1995) *A Millennium of Family Change: Feudalism to Capitalism in Northwestern Europe*. London: Verso.

Seidman, Steven (1993) 'Identity and Politics in a "Postmodern" Gay Culture: Some Historical and Conceptual Notes' in Michael Warner (ed.) *Fear of a Queer Planet: Queer Politics and Social Theory*. Minneapolis MN: University of Minnesota Press.

Serano, Julia (2007) *Whipping Girl: A Transsexual Girl on Sexism and the Scapegoating of Femininity*. Emeryville CA: Seal Press.

— (2013) *Excluded: Making Queer and Feminist Movements More Inclusive*. Berkeley CA: Seal Press.

Serge, Victor (1973) *From Lenin to Stalin*. 2nd edition. New York NY: Pathfinder Press.

— (2011) *Witness to the German Revolution*. Chicago IL: Haymarket Books.

Smith, Adam (1986) *The Wealth of Nations*. London: Penguin Classics.

Smith, Tony (1990) *Logic of Marx's 'Capital'*. New York NY: State University of New York Press.

Bibliography

Smith-Rosenberg, Carroll (1985) *Disorderly Conduct: Visions of Gender in Victorian America.* New York NY: Alfred A. Knopf.

Snitow, Ann, Christine Stansell and Sharon Thompson (eds) (1983) *Powers of Desire: The Politics of Sexuality.* New York NY: Monthly Review Press.

Stalsburg, Brittany L. (2010) 'Lesbian, Gay, Bisexual, and Transgender Women in the Military: The Facts'. New York NY: Service Women's Action Network. Available at http://servicewomen.org/wp-content/uploads/2012/10/Final-DADT-Fact-Sheet-10.4.12.pdf.

Stryker, Susan (2008a) *Transgender History.* Berkeley CA: Seal Press.

— (2008b) 'An Introduction to Transgender Terms and Concepts' in *Transgender History.* Berkeley CA: Seal Press.

— and Stephen Whittle (eds) (2006) *The Transgender Studies Reader.* New York NY: Routledge.

Sweezy, Paul (1978) 'A Critique' in Rodney Hilton (ed.) *The Transition from Feudalism to Capitalism.* London: Verso.

The Invisible Committee (2007) *The Coming Insurrection.* Los Angeles CA: Semiotext(e).

Tönnies, Ferdinand and Charles P. Loomis (ed.) (1957) *Community and Society (Gemeinschaft und Gesellschaft).* East Lansing MI: Michigan State University Press.

Vaughan, Alden T. (1989) 'The Origins Debate: Slavery and Racism in Seventeenth-Century Virginia', *Virginia Magazine of History and Biography.*

Vogel, Lise (2014) *Marxism and the Oppression of Women: Towards a Unity Theory.* Chicago IL: Haymarket Books.

Wallerstein, Immanuel (1974) *The Modern World-System: I. Capitalist Agriculture and the Origins of the European World Economy in the Sixteenth Century.* London: Academic Press.

Weeks, Jeffrey (1975) 'Where Engels Feared to Tread', *Gay Left: A Socialist Journal Produced by Gay Men* 1 (Autumn). Available at gayleft1970s.org.

— (2012) *Sex, Politics, and Society: The Regulation of Sexuality Since 1800.* 3rd edition. New York NY: Routledge.

Williams, Walter (1986) *Spirit and the Flesh: Sexual Diversity in American Indian Culture.* Boston MA: Beacon Press.

Wittig, Monique (1992) 'The Straight Mind' in *The Straight Mind and Other Essays.* Boston MA: Beacon Press.

Wolf, Sherry (2009) *Sexuality and Socialism: History, Politics, and Theory of LGBT Liberation.* Chicago IL: Haymarket Books.

Wolff, Bernard and Dunbar Roy (eds) (1899) 'A Menstruating Man', *Atlanta Journal-record of Medicine*, Volume 1.

Wolff, Richard and Stephen Resnick (1987) *Economics: Marxian versus Neoclassical*. Baltimore MD: Johns Hopkins University Press.

Zamora, Daniel (2014a) *Critiquer Foucault: Les années 1980 et la tentation néolibérale*. Brussels: Les Editions Aden.

— (2014b) 'Can we criticize Foucault?', *Jacobin Magazine*, 10 December.

Zavarzadeh, Mas'ud, Teresa Ebert and Donald Morton (eds) (1995) *Post-Ality, Marxism and Postmodernism*. Washington DC: Maisonneuve Press.

Zetkin, Clara (1984) *Selected Writings*. Edited by Philip Foner and translated by Kai Schoenhals. New York NY: International Publishers.

Žižek, Slavoj (2001) *Did Somebody Say Totalitarianism?: Five Interventions in the (Mis)Use of a Notion*. London: Verso.

— (2008) *For They Know Not What They Do: Enjoyment as Political Factor*. London: Verso.

— (2012) *Less Than Nothing: Hegel and the Shadow of Dialectical Materialism*. London: Verso.

Index

abortion rights, 146

absolute surplus value, 119; limits to, 146

abstract labor, 44, 153, 253

academic world, cultural turn, 167; Marxism dismissed, 6, 61, 105

ACT-UP, (AIDS Coalition to Unleash Power), 207, 219

Adorno, T., 81

'affective labor' theories of, 153

Afghanistan, 240; invasion progressive cover , 238; US troops in, 243

African-Americans, USA troops desegregation, 238

Africans, enslaved, 198

Against Equality organization, 224, 233

agency, 107

Agosto, Victor, 242

Ahmad, Aijaz, 249-50, 255

AIDS, 207; ACT-UP, *see above*; activism, 29; crisis lessons learned, 218; moral panic, 208; NGOized activism, 211; politics of decline, 30

Alexander, Michelle, 150, 262

Algeria, 249

AlQaws for Sexual and Gender Diversity in Palestinian Society, 26, 280

Althusser, Louis, 72, 84, 188

American queer movement, whites defining, 29

American Revolution, 69

American Socialist Workers' Party, 95

analytic philosophy, USA turn to, 188

'anthropocene', ahistorical theories of, 165

anti-capitalism, 7, 11, 232, 252

anti-gay legislation, California, 237

anti-Humanism, philosophical, 188

anti-Muslim politics, gays and lesbians used, 238

anti-rape organizing, India, 52

apartheid, Black male labor, 155-6

aporia, 76

Apple, gay rights branding, 225

Aquinas, Thomas, 167

Aswat, 280

Austin Gay and Lesbian Pride Foundation, 220

Austin, J.L., 58

authority, ambiguity undermining notion, 77

awareness politics, limits of, 3, 7, 58, 109, 269

Badiou, Alain, 73, 257
Bakan, Abigail, 174
balance of forces, assessment of, 243
Baltimore, USA protest, 158
Barthes, Roland, 99
Baudrillard, Jean, 73
Bebel, August, 135, 137, 139, 169, 185, 204; gay rights championing, 136
Benston, Margaret, 170
Bentham, Jeremy, 240
Bernstein, Eduard, 61-2, 70, 90
binary(ies), 74-5; challenging, 269; death of, 276; privileged term, 76
birthrates, dramatic fertility shifts, 130-1
Black men; Black Lives Matter slogan, 166; contradictory de-gendered, 159; USA criminalization and incarceration, 160, 210;
Black Panther Party, 205-6; decline of, 105
Black people: and Latina queer couples, 237; Blacklivesmatter hashtag, 256, 259; civil rights, 207; communities HIV infection rates, 209; gay and trans youth resistance, 246; men, *see above*; systemic dehumanization USA, 164; USA criminalized, 150; USA slavery, 174, 236
Black women: lesbian feminist tradition, 273; motherhood denigration, 242; oppression of, 157, 160; sterilized, 163; trans women murder rate, 27; violence against, 161

Blake, William, 48
body, the social meanings shifts, 126
Bolsheviks, 140; rural women attitude, 141
Bourdieu, Pierre, *habitus*, 200
Briggs Initiative, fight against, 207
Britain, liberty hypocrisy, 113
Brown, Heather, 107, 110-12, 117, 119, 124-5
Brown, Michael, 80
'burden on the system' moralizing, 179
Burkett, Paul, 109
Bush, George W., 241
butch/femme culture, 28, 30
Butler, Judith, 198-200, 254; iterability theory, 266
'buying local', liberal humanist solution, 89

capitalism/capitalist mode of production, 94; financial, 2; Fordist, 245; household labor in, 152; optimal functioning, 36; surplus population moralizing, 163, 179; state costs avoidance, 181
caretaking, poor women, 267
Cartesian dualism, binaries, 46
Carver, T., 124
Castro, Fidel, persecution of gays, 67
cause-and-effect, 56; simplistic claims, 66
change, 49, 269; demand for, 20
Chatterjee, Partha, 254
Chiapas, 91
Chibber, Vivek, 251-5
Chicago, undocumented immigrants, 156
Chick-fil-A, 225
childcare (and elder care) unwaged, 44, 148; African American women, 225

China, 152; Cultural Revolution, 105; economic liberalization, 176; foot-binding banned, 168; labor camps, 156; Mongol invasion gutted, 37; strike activity, 176
Christian ideology, USA militant, 208
chromosomes, 265, 268; mixture, 129
'cisgendered', 34, 268; cissexism, 221
class, 201-2; academic secondary consideration, 191; American academic models, 201; centrality of, 275; conflict, 235; consciousness, 212; Marxian understanding of, 274; normativity reclassing, 229; politics of, 203; relations possibility paramaters, 269; struggle, 234
classical economics, 46, 91
'coercive reality', colonization's, 250
Cold War cinema, American, 86
colonialism, 18, 67; capitalism integral, 41; 'coercive reality', 250; European, 36; Marxist approaches to, 247; material legacy of, 5; reactionary sexual politics of, 205
Columbus, Christopher, India goal, 37
'coming out' narrative, 222, 224
commercial surrogacy, South Asia, 277
commodity fetishism, 89
communalism, Anglocentric, 26
communitarianism, 278; conservative, 9
Compton's Cafeteria, San Francisco confrontation, 205, 244, 246
conformity, fascist goal, 4
consciousness: development of, 261; imputed, 71; limited politics of, 7, 58, 109, 269

constructivism, materialist, 267
consumerism: anti-moralism, 94, 97, 232; deceptive notion of, 3, 10; 'ethical' consumption, 193
Cooper's Donuts Los Angeles, 246
Cooper, Dennis, 213
Copernican Revolution, 2
counterbalancing forces, Marx accounting of, 62
counterculture, dominant queer, 164
Cuba, 152; homosexuality imprisoned, 168; revolution, 67
cultural politics: 'cultural capital', 200; 'culture wars', Western, 8-9; Venn diagram, 210
Cultural Revolution China, violence against gays, 168

D'Emilio, John, 245
DADT, 238, 239-40; repeal campaign, 239, 241, 243
Dalla Costa, Mariarosa, 153-4
Darwin, Charles, 125
Davis, Angela, 155, 157, 159-60, 163-4
de Beauvoir, Simone, 67, 73, 198; Second Sex, 94
De Rouvroy, Claude (Henri Saint-Simon), 133
de-industrialization, Western, 175
'deadbeat' dad, fantasy, 177
declarations, 58
decolonial activists, 5
deconstruction, 75-7, 79-80, 188; unrestrained, 78; maxims, 190
deep ecology, 165
defense of women, paternalistic, 215
Defoe, Daniel, Robinson Crusoe, 40
deregulation, 209
Derrida, J., 74-80; deconstructive method, 188

Descartes, R., 65
determinism, linguistic and cultural, 190
Dewey's Lunch Counter, 246
dialectics, 70
'dicatorship of the proletariat', idea of, 71
'dictatorship of the fragments', 21, 270-1
difference: *différance*, 75; multicultural politics of, 217; non-antagonistic ideology of, 9
discipline: Foucault model, 266; labor, 162; social, 38, 266
dishonourable discharge, consequences, 240
division of labor, gendered, 157
domestic labor debates, 151, 153, 170-1; double working day, 185; unwaged, 143
dormitories, labor, 156
dress code laws, 227
Drucker, Peter, 107, 246-7
dual-systems theory, 136, 142, 172-3, 177, 270, 273
Duggan, Lisa, 30, 142, 224, 226
Dunayeskaya, Raya, 124

Ebert, Teresa, 214, 216, 219-20, 222
eclecticism, countercultural, 164; ludic, 219
ecologists, Marxist, 109
economics: fetishized, 272; Marxist, 17
economism, 94
egalitarianism, 90; liberal, 137
elderly people: eldercare, 148; 'unnecessary surplus population', 149
emasculation, men's fear of, 97

employed/unemployed split creation, 163, 209
Engels, Friedrich, 47, 70, 113-17, 126, 137, 143-6, 169, 171, 234; critique of, 123-4; *Dialectics of Nature*, 63; heterosexism, 120; teleological tendency, 122; *The Origin of the Family*, 121, 135, 162, 184, 225, 233
England: enclosure movement, 37; Poor (anti-vagrancy) Laws, 39
Enlightenment, the: failures of, 187; feminist critique, 49; philosophy of, 40, 60
environmental damage, individual consumer moralizing, 2
epistemologies: Marxist, 19; situated knowledge-based, 18; standpoint, 49-50, 65, 71
equal pay, -equal work demand, 117
Erfurt Program, 61, 63, 102; failed predictions of, 62
essentialism: Aristotelian, 194; biological, 274
ethics: as horizon of politics, 192; conscience 'invisible hand', 109; liberal ideology, 3
ethnic-cleansing behavior, 225
'eunuch', 126
'everybody', Marxist understanding of, 7
Evolutionary Socialism, 62
exchange-value, dominance of, 40-2, 152
Existentialism, 66-7
exploitation, mathematical discrepancy, 274

Fairness Doctrine USA, 1987 repeal, 209

'false consciousness', 51; spurious
   notion, 52-3
family(ies), 121, 279; Black, 159;
   challenges to nuclear, 236;
   dismantling insufficiency, 163;
   Engels's false universalization, 123;
   female-headed, 119; ideological
   image of, 162; patrilineal, 122;
   role of, 142 ; romanticized peasant,
   139; 'wage', 118-20, 180; working
   class, 236
fascist politics, imaginary of, 4-5, 7
'female chauvinist pig', image, 52
femininity: disdain for, 167;
   historically and socially specific,
   159
feminism/feminists, 198; collective
   action, 52; cultural, 52; Lacanian
   psychoanalytic, 98; Latin
   American, 169; *ludic*, 214-15;
   radical, 171 second-wave, *see
   below*; socialist movement hostility,
   173; theory failings, 157; third-
   wave, *see below*; trans-exclusionary,
   129; Western middle-class, 95
femme lesbians, 277
Ferguson, USA, protest, 158
feudal society, 37
Feuerbach, Ludwig, 47
Fields, Barbara, 196-7, 199-200,
   227, 260, 266
FIERCE, 235
finance capitalists, fictions of, 2
Firestone, Shulamith, 171
First International, 135
Floyd, Kevin, 107, 245
Foster, John Bellamy, 109
Foucault, Michel, 74, 85, 87, 192,
   254; genealogical method, 84
Fourier, Charles, 110, 132-6
France, Muslim hatred, 223

Frankfurt School, 69
Frederici, Silvia, 154
French Revolution, 69; sodomy laws
   overturned, 204
Friedan, Betty, 151
Fukuyama, Francis, 69

Garner, Eric, 260
'gaslighting', 80, 112
gay: and trans liberation movements,
   205; consumerism critiques,
   221; culture commodified, 225;
   liberationists -striking miners UK
   merger, 207; male identity, 107;
   Pride corporate sponsorship, 220;
   rights 204, 231
'Gay Inc', 219
Gay Liberation Front, 205-6; demise
   of, 105
Gay Men's Health Crisis, 207
gemeinschaft, reactionary impulse,
   214
gaze, the, 97-8
gender, 13; constructionist position,
   129; dimorphism myth, 25;
   diversity, 129; expectations, 218;
   'heat theory', 128; interpersonal
   violence, 165; negative equality,
   158; non-binary categorizations,
   128-30; performance, 199-200;
   queering, 185; social gendering,
   268; social norms, 126; studies,
   215; gender relations: dynamics,
   272; India/Italy/Ireland, 124
genetic assumptions, ideological
   frippery, 129
German Romanticism, failures of,
   187
German Social Democratic Party
   (SPD), 61, 135
GI Bill, USA, 240-2

Gimenez, Martha, 174
global warming digital satellites, 2
Gopal, Anand, 243
Gramsci, Antonio, 56, 261; war of position distortion, 194,264
grand narratives, 82, attack on, 81-3, 202
Greece, Bangladeshi strawberry pickers, 156; Golden Dawn, 77
Guesde, Jules, 117

Haitian Revolution, 69
Hapsburg Empire, 37
Hardt, Michael, 90-1
Harman, Chris, 174
Hartmann, Heidi, 171-2
hassas, Morocco, 246
Hegel, G.W.F., 56-8, 63, 68, 81-2; dialectics, 47-8, 68; Marx critique of, 55; master-servant dialectic, 75-6
Heidegger, Martin, 188
Henning, 48, 62, 64, 67
Henning, Christoph, 46, 48, 61-2, 64, 67, 232; *Philosophy After Marx,* 218
Heraclitus, 47, 48
heteronormativity, 227; historical shifts, 204
heterosexual couples,
heterosexuality mythologies, 203; Saint-Simonian couples norm, 133
'heterotheory', 211
hierarchy, 105
'high femme', 99
hijab, as choice, 100
hijra, India and Pakistan, 25, 126, 238-9, 246; India, 25
Hirschfeld, C.L., 204
historical materialism, 72, 188
history, notion of, 188

Hitler, A., 77
Holocaust, the, 79
homonationalism, 26, 226
homonormativity, concept of, 30, 34, 221, 224, 226, 228
homophobic people, 263
homosexuality: 'homosexual', 14; nineteenth-century political-medical concept, 204
Horkheimer, Max, 81
Human Rights Campaign, 228
human condition, unchanging truth ideology, 40
humility, intellectual, 258
hunter-gatherer epoch, 265
hybridity, 250
hyper-exploitation, sewing machines, 115

idealism, philosophical, 24; linguistic, 26; Marxist criticism of, 251
identity, as disciplinary apparatus, 19; gay male, 107
'identity politics', 24, 190-1, 221-2; as slur, 17-18
ideology, 197; as repetition, 227, 263; Marxist explanations, 84
'immaterial labor', 90
indentured servants, decline, 197
independent journalism, Marxist legacy, 20
India: capitalist class, 251; commercial surrogacy, 216; *hijra, see above*; patrilocal communities, 174; sterilization campaign, 160; workers, 252
individualism, 192: Cartesian emphasis, 65; Enlightenment, 60; epistemological, 61; ideological, 1, 182; paranoid, 8; political, 58

infant mortality, 131
infanticide, American slaves, 116
inheritance: lines of, 130; paternity knowledge, 38
intensity of labor, 44; gendered, 45
internationalism, queer, 232, 255, 278
interpersonal objectivity, 53; failure of, 54
intersectional model, 273-4
intersex people, 13, 34, 126, 104, 268; children, 102; conservatives, 29; infants surgical 'correction', 12
intertextuality, 74
'invisibilized' categories, 85
Iran, gays oppressed, 221; revolution conservative co-optation, 249
Iraq, 240; civil society, 244; IraQueer, 280; progressive cover for invasion of, 238
Iroquois society, 124
Islamophobia, 244
Israel: pinkwashing of, 223, 233, 280
Israeli Pride, 26

James, Selma, 153-4
jathoeys, Thailand, 246
Jenner, Caitlyn, 185
'Juan Crow' laws, labor supply, 210

Kant, Immanuel, 56-8, 62
Karyotypes, 265
Kautsky, Karl, 61-2, 70
Keynes, J.M., 116
khanith, Oman, 246
Kierkegaard, S., 66
kinaidi, Ancient Greece, 246
Kirsch, Max, 216-17
knowledge, change, 57
Kollontai, Alexandra, 139-40
Kon, Igor, 140, 167-8

Khrushchev, N., secret speech, 67
kyriarchy, 105

labor, 6; cheap women, 117; cost lowering drive, 44; de-gendering, 133; disciplining of, 162; feminized force, 106; generational replacement unpaid, 182; global factory work, 272; individual reproduction of, 144; -LGBT rights relationship, 206; productive-unproductive, 91, 109, 151-2; segregated camps, 156, 236 sexual division of, 103, 171, 177; social reproduction processes, 23, 150; special commodity, 43, 114; surplus racialization, 164
Lafargue, Paul, 117
land, non-commodified period, 38
language: linguistic constructivism, 35; linguistic disruption insufficiency, 23; linguistic turn, 218; policing politics, 21, 30; unequivocal, 77-80
Laquer, Thomas, Making Sex, 127
Larsen, Neil, 250-1, 255
Lasch, Christopher, 214
Latin America, left nationalist movements, 168
Le Pen, Marine, 223
Leibniz, 167
Lenin, V.I., 64, 71, 77, 169; women's liberation approach, 140
lesbian women; lesbian baiting, 239; wealthy, 185
'lesbigay', 28-9
Levinas, Emmanuel, 89
LGBT people, 34, 106; LGBTQI, 29; of colour, 237
liberal democracy: debate fetishizing, 3; notions, 69; pluralism, 234

liberation, 94; 'liberation-by-tank' post-Stalinist, 190
libidinal economy, modern, 99
Lukács, G., 64, 70-1, 124
Luxemburg, Rosa, 22-3; reform and revolution dialectic, 142
Lyotard, Jean-Francois, 74, 82, 80; fatalism of, 83
Lytton, Edward Bulwer, 112
Lytton, Lady Rosina Bulwer, 112-13

Majidi, Majid, 130
mancession, 114
Maoists, 166
Maquila Solidarity Network, 52
Marcuse, Herbert, 64, 72, 81, 166
marriage, 224; as patriarchal tool, 233
marriage equality, 224; debate, 227, 237, 242; focus on, 226; movement, 217, 233, 236; opponents of, 162, 234-5
Marx, Karl, 17, 41, 43, 46-8, 50, 54, 59-60, 64, 70-1, 76, 93-5, 113-15, 125, 132-3, 135, 140, 143, 145, 169, 189, 194, 211; academic dismissal of, 6, 61, 105; alienation work, 81; anti-Proudhonist argument, 117; Capital, 119, 121, 146, 177, 189; early writing, 72; economic terms, 152; epistemological realist, 49; Ethnological Notebooks, 107, 124, 144; general tendencies, 62; Hegel critic, 55; 'leads to Stalin' smear, 83; 'linear' thinking criticism, 66; materialism of, 91; neoliberal wall of noise treatment, 5; non-teleological, 254; political activities, 61, 113; politics of suicide essay, 112; Robinsinades ridiculing, 40; sexual violence

analysis, 110-11; teleology accusation, 108; 'The Programme of the Parti Ouvrier', 117; wage system analysis, 39; women's oppression analysis, 118
Marx and Engels: Communist Manifesto, 107, 114; The German Ideology, 120-1
Marxism/Marxists, 65, 106; classical, 222; current thought, 18; debates within, 88; economics, see below; epistemological commitment, 51; feminists, 104, 142-3, 145, 169-70, 273, 277, 279, 281; 'grand narrative' accusation, 249; historical materialism of, 188, 272; intersectionality embrace, 195; political economy critique, 35, 272; practice, 14, 23; queer and trans, 222; system clarity, 22; teleological accusation, 63, 252 'vulgar', 93; will-based, 64
Marxist economics, 150, 173, 248; academically rejected, 176; New Left's critique of, 166
masculinity, physical, 185
Mattachine Society, 206
'Matterism', 214
May 1968 events, 105, 205
McCarthyism, impact of, 206-7
media women's alliance, Uganda, 52
medical establishment, gender opinions, 126
Mexico: City earthquake 1985, 115; corn market, 209; ejidos privatization, 210; femicide, 216; May 1968 massacre, 211; war of independence, 82
Michaloliakos, Nikos, 77
middle-class: academics nation over class move, 166; feminism, 27, 169

military service, gays and lesbians demand, 225; dishnoroubale discharge consequences, 240

military-industrial-prison complex, 236, 243; USA universities, 241

Milk, Harvey, Coors boycott, 207

Millett, Kate, 171

misogyny, 100, 183, 261, 277

Mitchell, Juliet, 169, 170

Möser, Justus, 95

money, commodity, 41-4

'monopoly capitalism', theories of, 43, 64,

Monsanto, 209

moralizing: capitalist, 149; political, 95

Morgan, Lewis H., 121-5, 137

Morton, Donald, *The Material Queer*, 212-16, 219-20, 222

Mothers of the Plaza de Mayo, 52

mother(s): Black motherhood, 164; financial support as moral requirement, 177; powerful idea of, 267

muxues, Mexico, 25

NAFTA, 209

naïve realism, critique of, 49

Namibia, 160

Napoleonic Code, 117

National Gay and Lesbian Task Force, 228

National Liberation Front, Algeria, 67

National Union of Marine Cooks and Stewards, 206, 210

nationalism, queer, 210-12

Nazi regime, sterilizations, 160

necessary labor, concept of, 151

negative equality, gender, 157

Negri, Antonio, 90-1

neoclassical economists, 42

neoliberal political thought, 10

New Economic Policy, USSR, 141

New Left, 190, 207, 241; social movements, 205; project of, 88

New Soviet Family, Stalinist campaign, 141

'New World', the 36

New York police, 260

New York Tribune, 112

news, as wall of noise, 3

Nieztsche, F.W., 66, 81

noble lie, Platonic, 81

'normativity', opposition insufficiency, 229-30, 276

nostalgia, 87, 95

Obama, Barack, 241, 280

object relations theory, 266

objective reality, Marx emphasis, 67

objectivity, 57, feminist scepticism, 53

Occupy Movement, 176, 246

opportunism, 242

oppositional sexism, Engels, 123

oppression(s): individual expression of, 193; intersecting vectors, 194; systematically reproduced, 262

organic intellectuals, 56

Orientalism, 248; postcolonial, 255

outsourcing, strategic, 209

Ottoman Empire, 37

Pakistan, factory fires, 115

Palestine, queers, 26

palimpsest, Freudian notion, 76

Pallares, Amalia, 156

Panopticon, 85

Paris Commune, 117

Parmenides, 47

patriarchy, 19, 31, 118, 125, 136; ahistorical ideology, 51, 173; assumptions, 99; family property, 113; 'laws' of nation, 172; problematic term, 174; sedentarization link, 12, theory, 144 theory incoherence, 176

patrilocal communities, India, 174

Penney, James, *After Queer Theory*, 217

personal responsibility, language internalizing, 163

personhood, constructed, 265

Peru, 160

phallus, 266; phallogocentrism, 74

phenomenology, 65; Heidegger version, 25, 75

picket line, 264

Plato, 48, 65, 132, 167; Socratic dialogue, 47

pointless suffering, 11

police, Black, 260; young Black men killings, 242

politics: consciousness, 70; important dichotomies, 276; -ethical/moral confused, 102; of respectability, 99; parties women's caucus question, 141; 'primacy' of, 232; queer, 231; 'subject' category, 59

poor women's sexuality, immoral label, 184

Pope, Alexander, 77

populationism, neo-Malthusianism, 164

post-Marxist queer theory, anti-realism, 214

postcolonialism: academic, 190; immigrant professionals'; ideology, 249; literary and social theory, 248; Marxist critique of, 247, 251; strategic ambiguity of, 250

postculturalism, 192

postmodernism, 35, 73, 80

poststructuralism, 64, 73, 87, 190, 214, 218, 271; academic turn to, 105, 276; attack on Marxism, 194; 'linguistic turn', 167; queer, 67

poverty: queer, 233; rural, 237

power, 86-7; privileged abstract concept of, 106, 192-3; individualized model, 271

Power, Nina, 266

practico-inert, Sartre concept, 69-71

Pride at Work, 233

'primitive disunity', 250

producer-consumer, ideological divide, 10

productive/unproductive labor, 91, 109, 151; domestic labor issue, 152

profit, rate of, 44

progress, Hegelian notions of, 72

progressive communitarianism, 9

proletariat, 6-7; male household supremacy, 124; 'propertyless people', 38

property realtions, women's chastity link, 122

Proudhon, P-J, 117-18; Proudhonists; anti-women sentiment, 119

psychoanalysis, Lacanian, 217

Puar, Jasbir, 26, 222-6, 238, 280

purified nation-body, notion of

purpose and meaning, motivators, 69

Qatar, Nepaluse and Indian workers, 156

Queer: academics, 230; activism; USA retrenchment, 206; and trans politics, 14, 165; Black, 159; Marxism, 107, 186, 279;

nationalism; cohesiveness of, 244; meanings, 34; radicals family concept, 156; politics, *see below*; radical, 228, 233; sexuality, 117; studies, 204; subculture's potential elitism, 164; term emergence, 28; theory, *see below*; umbrella term, 29

Queer politics, 25, 231; binaries challenging, 269; radical, 243; street decline, 212; theory, 25

Queer theory, 31, 47-8, 203, 213-14, 219; academic, 215-17; Foucault roots, 25; major tenets, 74; Marxist critique, 221; politically radical, 142; poststructuralist, 19-20, 67; rise of, 245; 20th century, 30

QueerBomb, Austin Texas, 220

Queerness, 275; militant cultural, 208; reactionary paranoia towards, 280; Stalin medicalized, 168

Queers for Economic Justice, 233-5

Queer Nation, 210, 234, 244

race, 262; ideology of, 197-9; racism produced, 196

racism, 262; colorblind, 158; reverse racism oppressor rationalization, 202

radicallesbians, 206; movement, 96

rape, 'he said/she said, 127

reactionary ideology, 175

Reagan, Ronald, 233

'redoubled vaccuum', 249

reform-revolution, bogus binary, 23

reformist-voluntarist dialectic, 170

refusal to work, 39

reification, motherhood, 267

relative social value, 114-15

relativism, seedy, 83

reproductive freedom, attacks on poor people's, 165

reserve army of labor, 116, 119, 239; women, 148

respect, 83

revisionism, 62

revolutionary party, 71

Ricardo, David, 46

Rice, Tamir, 269

Robinson Crusoe, ahistorical economics, 41-2

Roma, Eastern Europe, 160

Romania, sworn virgins, 130

Rorty, Richard, 258

ruling class, structure changing, 184

Russia: homophobia restored, 168; patriarchal peasantry, 140

Russian Revolution: decomposition of, 68; legacy of, 85; sodomy laws overturned, 204; women's liberation, 139

Russian Women's Battalion of Death, 238

Rustin, Bayard, 207

safe spaces, 106, 231; militant retreat into, 211, 218; queer need for, 278

Said, Edward, 248, 250

Saint-Simonians, 136

same-sex marriages, *see marriage*

Sargent, Lydia, 172

Sartre, J-P., 64, 66, 69-72; *Critique of Dialectical Reason*, 67-8; practico-inert, 83

Schumpeter, Joseph, 92

Second International, 63, 135

second-wave feminism, 31, 94-6, 103, 143, 145, 155, 169, 203; analysis race deficient, 155; anti-gender thrust, 30; moral tone of, 104; political logic of, 100; politics of respectability, 97

sedentarization, gender landscape shift, 121

self-determination: collective, 98; right to, 35

self-interest, 254

Serano, Julia, 120, 155

serfdom, 37

sex categorization: Greek assumptions, 127; historical perspective, 12

sex work, debates over, 100-1

sexism: ideology, 177; leftist groups, 172; oppositional, 63, 134, 143, 145, 155, 169, 185, 203-4, 216, 261, 267; oppositional-traditional link, 215, 270, 278; traditional, 52

sexual consent, idea of, 53; non-consent assault, 54

sexual difference/diversity, 102; cultural turn, 176; dimorphism critique, 13; ideology of immutable, 12; postcolonial work on, 14

sexual violence, Marx addressed, 110

sexuality, 101; Black women, 208; children reproduction, 183; purifying project, 14

silenced discourse, legitimizing, 84

situated knowledge, 18, 23-4; Marxist, 20

slavery, 157, 198; commodity-children, 161; legacies of, 157, 164; race-based, 197

Slow Food movement, 164

small-scale politics, limitations of, 106

Smith, Adam, 10, 46, 50, 109

Smith, Sharon, 174

social reproduction, 272; capitalist cost avoidance, 179; labor, 23, 146; material process of, 216; problem of, 185; theory, 103, 143, 145, 147, 151; under capitalism, 116

social value, 163

Socialism in One Country, 167

Socrates, 74

Sojourner Truth, 158

solidarity, 11, 59, 92, 115, 230, 257, 261, 277; across borders, 255; assumptions of, 83; building of, 262; confrontational, 259; intellectualized, 24; material reality grounded, 258; obstacles to, 183

Soviet philosophy, idealist turn, 167

Spade, Dean, 226, 233, 235

'speaking truth to power', 250

Stalin, J.V., 67-8, 77; New Soviet Family, 167; Stalinism disaster, 88, 249

sterilization: Black women, 163; forced rationalizations 160-1, 216

Stonewall rebellion, 205, 207, 244-5

Street Transvestite Action Revolutionaries, 206

strikes, hardening, 263-4

structuralism, 72

struggle, history as material legacy, 60

Subaltern Studies project, 251

subject: for-itself, 68; in-itself, 68; -object relations, 56-8, 65

Sue, Eugene, Les Mysteres de Paris, 110-11

suicide, 112; politics of, 112 transgendered people rates, 27

'surplus population(s)', 116; capitalism's, 149; forced sterilization, 160; non-immigrant, 151; racism inherent, 150; sexually moralized, 178;

structural unemployment, 162; systemic need for, 274; working class, 161

sworn virgins, Albania, 25

Syria, civil society, 244

'system', deceptive term, 21-2; 'systemicity', 19

Tahrir Square, 246

Tanzania, women's alliances, 52

techno-liberalism, 212

TERFs, 101, logic, 130

terrorism, queered concept of, 222

Thatcher, Margaret, 271

Third World, nationalist movement, 250

third-wave feminism, 14, 18, 21, 64, 67, 95-6, 99; freedom of choice emphasis, 100

TINA (There Is No Alternative), age of, 175

Tlateclolo massacre, Mexico City, 105

Tönnies, Ferdinand, 214

tokenism, 68

totality, connotations of, 2; idea of, 1; misrepresentation of, 8, 248; Soviet ossified, 270

'trace', 74, 76

trafficking, 101-2

Trans people, 126, 159; activists, 221; and intersexed people politically fetishised, 275; politics, 31; systematic exclusion, 34; transness, 268; violence against, 224

Trans women, 245, 268; Black and Latina, 224; working class, 277

transmisogyny, 53

tribades, Ancient Greece, 246

'trickle-down' propaganda, 233, 235

Trotskyist International Socialists, 174

trust, 23

tuition costs, working class imposed, 175

Uganda, gays extermination, 223

Ulrichs, Karl Heinrich, 28

unbounded multitude, illusion of, 2

unemployment: Black communities, 209; structural, 50

uneven development, states, 7

union membership, USA decline, 208

universal alterity, acknowledgement of, 258

universalism(s), 8, 11; ahistorical, 246; disparaging of, 248; from below, 12; Marxist non-reductionist, 195

university(ies): political activity restricted, 175; queering of, 212

unlimited wealth, capitalist notion of, 39

uranian ('mental hermaphrodites'), 28

USA (United States of America): AFL-CIO, 233; anti-LGBT violence, 27; anti-science movements, 255; antiwar movement, 241-2; birthrates variations, 131; Black women sterilization legacy, 160; Disco Wars; 1970s, 259; free-market Christian organizations, 169; inherent racism, 150; military forces, 240; military, queer enrolment, 239-40; politics of, 187; post-Obama imperialism, 280; social conservative movement,

88; Telecommunications Act 1996, 209; union membership fall, 176
use value, 152
USSR (Union of Soviet Socialist Republics), 152, 208, 249; collapse, 166, 176; cultural feminists, 169; legacy of, 167; People's Commissar for Justice, 168; seamless sexism, 167
utopianism/utopians, 132, 142; feminist arguments, 133; separatist, 96; socialist, 59
Uzbekistan, 160

value, neoclassical models, 43
vector model, 201-2; class suspicious, 201; of oppression, 191, 194; oppressions reifying, 195
Victorian England, exploitation levels, 116
Vietnam, 249
violence, 253; Africa and E. Europe anti-gay, 232; against trans people, 224; bureaucratic disciplinary, 85
Vogel, Lise, 107, 123-4, 136, 145-6, 148, 151, 154-5, 157, 173-5, 177, 200, 204, 215, 236, 278

wage(s): exploitation obscuring, 39; family, 118; for housework, 154;
waged-unwaged split framed, 162
'war of maneuver', 261
'war of position', 261, 264
War on Drugs, 210
Warner, Michael, 212-13; *Fear of a Queer Planet*, 211
welfare state, creation of, 131
Western Marxists, working-class centrality challenged, 166
Western thought, 'linguistic turn', 188-9

witness, the, Marxist situated knowledge, 20
Wittig, Monique, 199
Wolf, Sherry, *Sexuality and Socialism*, 107
womb renting, South Asian women, 165
women, 94; as cheap labor, 117; -blaming-women hysteria, 277; class analysis, 137-8, 174; double day, 145; individualized pregnancy cost, 180; normative ethos, 184; pure/impure paradigm, 96; sexual pleasure valued, 127; trans and cis, 180; unitary exploitation concept, 144; USSR de-gendered, 174; working class sexuality control, 179, 181, 183-4 'womanhood' exchange value, 100
workers: financial demands on men, 181; 'generational replacement', 151, 185;
working class, 264; identities, 51; reproduction of cost burden, 155, 183, tensions among, 184; *see also*, social reproduction
World War I, 63

Yippies, 205
Young Lords, 206
Young, Iris, 173, 177

Zapatistas, 176; uprising 1994, 210; Zapatismo, 91
Zavarzadeh, Mas'ud, 219-20
Zeno, 47, 78
Zetkin, Clara, 123, 135, 137-8, 143, 158, 175, 154, 214, 234; sentimental proletarian conservatism, 139
Zizek, Slavoj, 77